Adopted in Texas

Adopted in Texas

The Story of Homestead

Janice Branch Tracy

ISBN: 1535008962
ISBN 13: 9781535008969

Dedication

This book is dedicated to All Homestead Adoptees, their Birth Mothers, and to the Adoptive Parents who raised them.

"In all of us there is a hunger, marrow deep, to know our heritage, to know who we are, and where we have come from. Without this enriching knowledge, there is a hollow yearning, no matter what our attainments in life, there is a most disquieting loneliness.

-Alex Haley

Acknowledgements

Many thanks go to each individual who contributed in any way, no matter how small, named or unnamed, to the research and development of this book, including staff at the Fort Worth Library; Tarrant County Archives staff, Dr. Dawn Youngblood and Amanda M. Millian; Mary Schwitters Knudsen; Connie Gray of Support Texas Adoptee Rights (STAR); Patty Logsdon Drabing of DNAAdoption; and Teri and John Davidson, former foster parents of dozens of Homestead babies. I especially thank all Birth Mothers, Adoptees, Adoptive Parents, and Siblings of Adoptees who shared their very personal and often emotional Homestead stories with me. To all of you, I am eternally grateful for your involvement and participation in the book project. Without your contributions, the story of Homestead Maternity Home and its child placement agency could not have been told. And finally, I'm extremely grateful to a distant cousin of mine, Kathleen Bradley, whose own Homestead adoption story was the inspiration for this book.

Table of Contents

Preface

Unwed pregnancies have existed since the beginning of time, and society, in general, was unaccepting of young women who became pregnant outside of marriage. For centuries, the widely acceptable resolution to an unwed pregnancy was marriage, and I'm certain you've heard stories from long ago about angry fathers who forced young men to marry their daughters. Although many couples who married in these so-called "shotgun weddings" may have developed relationships that lasted for years, others failed to endure for a lifetime. And as societal values changed over time, families became more accepting of what many referred to as the "seven-month baby," an infant born less than nine months after the marriage occurred.

In addition to religious beliefs, economics and family responsibilities also played significant roles in decisions made in connection with unwed pregnancies. In the twentieth century, society primarily rejected the idea of a young, unmarried woman, regardless of her age, giving birth to a child she was unable to support. In addition, the young woman's parents were less likely to offer help in raising her child, especially if supporting an additional child placed a financial burden on their household. To further complicate the issue, the political and social environment in the United States, before the passage of the Equal Rights Amendment, considered mothers, in general, incapable of adequately caring for their children if they worked outside their homes. Overall, women who worked were paid significantly less than men, so low wages and the likely absence of family support needed to care for a young child, simply made single motherhood an almost impossible situation.

Primary factors contributing to unwed or unwanted pregnancies of women of all ages were inadequate knowledge of birth control options, religious convictions about the use of birth control, and the lack of access by unmarried women to physician-prescribed methods of birth control. These methods included the diaphragm and later, birth control pills. An unwritten rule existed in the medical community that physicians did not prescribe birth control pills and contraceptive devices to unmarried women. As the medical and social communities changed, however, and new methods of contraception became available, physicians gradually became more involved in their patients' family planning efforts. Often, single women were required to "doctor-shop" for physicians and pharmacists who were willing to prescribe birth control pills and contraceptive devices, or to fill prescriptions for the items, without questioning their marital status.

When an underage girl became pregnant, her parents often made the initial decision that she would give up her baby for adoption. Most likely, this decision meant the young woman went away to live with a family friend or relative, or to a maternity home, often referred to as an unwed mothers' home, in another city or state, until she gave birth. Even though the young mother may have wanted to keep her baby, her parents most often were unwilling to face the prevailing community shame frequently placed on them by relatives, friends, and co-workers. Of course, all babies given up for adoption were not born to underage girls or unmarried women. Older women, single, married, separated, or divorced, also chose adoption as the solution to a myriad of issues surrounding their unexpected or inconvenient pregnancies. For decades, maternity homes operated by charitable and religious organizations housed hundreds of thousands of pregnant women who gave birth to babies that many reluctantly surrendered for adoption. One of these many now-closed organizations, Homestead Maternity Home and Child Placement Agency of Fort Worth, Texas, is the subject of this book.

Introduction

In early 2016, I was comparing my father's DNA results with those of other individuals in a large database, when I discovered a distant cousin match with a woman named Kathleen Bradley. At the beginning of our search to determine a common ancestor, Kathleen told me she was the daughter of a young, unwed mother who lived at Homestead Maternity Home in Fort Worth, Texas, and gave birth to her baby at All Saints Hospital. The maternity home in which Kathleen's birth mother and many other pregnant women lived until they gave birth in local hospitals between 1960 and 1972, was located at 1250 W. Rosedale in Fort Worth, Texas. And for a time, Homestead's adoption agency was located just around the corner at 1028 5th Avenue. Although the exact date is unknown, Homestead Maternity Home and its adoption agency closed just before the U.S. Supreme Court decision known as *Roe v. Wade* was handed down in early 1973.

During the course of many emails and phone contacts, Kathleen shared her adoption story and recalled years of searching for the identities of her birth parents and where they lived. The journey to locate and meet her birth parents, Kathleen recalled, involved numerous dead-ends, twists, and turns, and was complicated from the very beginning by the fact that Texas adoptions during the period in which she was born were "closed." I soon learned from Kathleen that all Homestead adoption files are closed, although an adoptee of legal age can petition the Tarrant County courts to open the file. If a judge grants the petition, a court-appointed intermediary, who charges a nominal fee, will review the file and attempt to locate and contact the birth mother identified in documents inside the file. Of course, the opening of an adoption file is solely at the discretion of the judge assigned to hear the petition, and there are no required guidelines the judge must follow.

Since the State of Texas will not release an adoptee's original birth certificate unless the adoptee knows the birth mother's name, the only source of information readily available to Homestead adoptees is often the so-called "non-id information sheet." Homestead staff apparently gave this sheet to adoptive parents when they took their babies home, and although the documents do not include names, they do provide physical descriptions and other details about the adoptees' birth parents and in some situations, grandparents, as well. However, according to adoptees and adoptive parents interviewed for this book, Homestead did not provide these information sheets during the very early 1960s. In many cases, adoptive parents kept the non-id information sheets, along with other Homestead correspondence from social workers and lawyers, in files they maintained for years. In fact, these non-id information sheets and correspondence often are the only items, other than amended birth certificates, incomplete hospital certificates with footprints only, or an occasional adoption decree, that most Homestead adoptees ever saw before initiating searches for their birth parents.

Although there is no tangible proof that Homestead's administrative records were destroyed, the State of Texas currently acknowledges the alleged destruction or burning of the maternity home's records. This longstanding question about the availability of Homestead's records has been addressed in recent letters mailed by the State of Texas to adoptees who contacted the vital records office in Austin for details about their adoptions. Several of these adoptees shared copies of their letters with me during interviews they provided for this book. Included with the letters was a list of maternity homes that operated in Texas for almost a century. Interestingly, Homestead was the only facility on the list for which no records exist.

Throughout the stories shared by adoptees in this book, you will hear numerous accounts of petitions filed with the Tarrant County courts and events that transpired when adoption files were opened and reviewed by court-appointed intermediaries. For most adoptees, going through the process was the ultimate search experience, and for many, it was the only means of learning the identities of their birth mothers and the circumstances surrounding their adoptions. For others, the process was not as rewarding. Although their petitions were granted and their files opened, these adoptees discovered their birth mothers were either deceased or they chose to have no contact with the child they gave up for adoption so many years ago.

Other Homestead adoption search experiences chronicled within the pages of this book offer much insight into the amazing volunteer efforts of Search Angels who assist birth mothers, adoptees, and adoptive siblings at no charge. They are indeed angels; just ask any birth mother, adoptee, or sibling whose reunion with a family member was facilitated by a Search Angel. And last, but certainly not least, you will read stories describing how DNA test results have helped an ever-growing number of Homestead adoptees connect with their birth families.

In early 2016, when Kathleen Bradley and I first met, I was nearing the end of a brief writing hiatus following a series of out-of-state book signings for my most recent book, *Mississippi Moonshine Politics*. But by late January 2016, I still had not made a firm decision about the subject of my next book. Timing is everything, they say, and in my case, the old adage was certainly true. I was both fascinated and intrigued by Kathleen's personal Homestead story, her successful search over many years for her birth parents, and her numerous efforts to help other Homestead adoptees and birth mothers connect. And as I learned more about the Homestead Maternity Home and Child Placement Agency, its staff, and the thousands of women, children, and families impacted by the facility's child placement agency, I knew I wanted to write a book that would tell their stories.

Chapter 1

Fort Worth: Where Homestead Began

Cowtown is the name many Texans use to refer to Fort Worth, the county seat of Tarrant County. And without a doubt, much of the city's history does revolve around cattle drives along the Chisolm Trail and the city's huge stockyards and railroads that transported animals to distant markets. The city's fabled history also includes a tale or two about some of the area's better known cowboys and some cowgirls, as well. Today, however, Fort Worth is an eclectic blend of western culture within a cosmopolitan city of tall buildings, restaurants, museums, and urban living, a place that regularly attracts visitors from all over the world. Throughout the twentieth century, military bases, oil exploration and production, aviation, and industries related to each, played major roles in the development of Fort Worth's economy, population, and the lifestyles of its residents. During a period of slightly less than three decades, beginning in 1940 and ending in the late 1960's, Fort Worth's population grew by leaps and bounds as the city experienced numerous economic changes and challenges. Thousands of military men and women rotated through nearby Carswell Air Force Base, and businesses related to the oil industry changed the industrial landscape of the city and its suburbs. Aided by the presence of large military bases in close proximity to the city, and with help from the state's elected officials, military aircraft manufacturing found its place in Fort Worth. Gradually, downtown Fort Worth became the center of much retail and business activity, and new hospitals, schools, and housing developments were built to accommodate an increase in the city's population. And as the business community boomed, families grew and prospered, too.

According to the city directory published in 1960, Fort Worth was a *"metropolitan area with more than half a million people with downtown skyscrapers, huge suburban shopping centers, modern freeways, large industrial plants and important military establishments."* Additionally, the directory touted *"The median [annual] income of all families in the metropolitan Fort Worth area in 1959 was $5985.* And as a result of a recent completion of a $55 million dollar water supply extension program, Fort Worth promoted its location by saying *"Welcome, New Industries, There's Plenty of Water Here!"* During that same period, also according to the directory, the aircraft industry in Dallas-Fort Worth generated more than $200 million a year in payroll, and thanks to the Convair-Fort Worth Division of General Dynamics Corporation, Fort Worth claimed to be the *"second largest aircraft production center in America."* In addition, the city's business directory proclaimed Fort Worth, Texas, to be *"the second most active oil region in the world,"* only surpassed by Libya.

All seemed well in Cowtown, at least from an economic standpoint. But another enterprise was flourishing in the city - the adoption market - and some believed Fort Worth was fast becoming the country's "Adoption Mecca."

Chapter 2

Homestead: The Beginning

The exact dates that Homestead Maternity Home at 3600 Crescent and the Homestead Hospital and Child Placement Agency, located at 3600 Camp Bowie, officially began providing shelter and care to pregnant mothers, married and unmarried, and placing babies for adoption, is unclear. According to a letter mailed to an adoptee and signed by Patricia Molina, now retired from the State of Texas, the facility was first licensed in 1956, but newspaper advertisements stating the maternity home was open for business prior to 1958 were not located. The first newspaper advertisement discovered during research for the book appeared in the *Paris (TX) News* on Sunday, November 9, 1958, and included two phone numbers, one for the maternity home and another for the child placement agency. In addition, the words *"non-profit organizations"* appeared in all capital letters directly above a photo of the two-story colonial designed building on Crescent.

Details gathered during research for this book indicate a number of pregnant women may have received temporary housing and adoption assistance prior to 1958 from the organization's founder, Mrs. W. W. Slaughter, a Fort Worth hotel owner better known as Clora Pearl Slaughter. A search of old Fort Worth city directories revealed listings for Slaughter's two business entities in the 1952 and 1955 publications. In 1952, the 3600 Crescent location was listed in the directory as *"Homestead Hotel and Apts,"* but in 1955, a variation of the name, *"Homestead Apartment Hotel,"* was shown at the same street address. According to the 1952 city directory entry, *"Gloria P. Slaughter,"* was identified as the hotel's owner, but it seems likely the name should have been "Clora P. Slaughter," since Gloria, Pearl's adopted daughter, was under eighteen years old when the directory was published. The 1952 city directory also included a business listing for the *"Colonial Hotel and Café,"* located at 3600 Camp Bowie, the same address shown for Homestead Hospital and Child Placement Agency in the 1958 newspaper advertisement.

Very few first person descriptions exist of Homestead Maternity Home's facility at 3600 Crescent in Fort Worth. However, a Texas woman who lived at the facility during the last few months of her pregnancy, and who was interviewed for this book, described the building as a *"large white, wooden 2-story house with twenty-two bedrooms and eleven bathrooms that was located on an estate-size lot."* She recalled taking walks around the estate's grounds and remembers the residential facility was far enough away from her obstetrician's office that a staff member drove her there for prenatal checkups. She also said a high fence separated the estate from a new area of houses under construction near the maternity home. In 1964, an advertisement for Homestead Child Placement Agency and Homestead Maternity Home, located at 714 Dan Waggoner Building, appeared in the January 24th edition of the *Texas State Journal of Medicine.* A physical location of the maternity home, however, was not listed. The text of the ad read:

> *"Licensed Adoption Service and Private, Confidential maternity care provided unwed expectant mothers. Obstetrical services by a Diplomat of THE AMERICAN BOARD. Also pediatric care furnished by a licentiate of THE AMERICAN BOARD."*

When the Fort Worth City Directory was published in 1968, there were no businesses or homes listed on Crescent, but a note appearing next to the street name indicated Crescent ran from 4434 Fletcher to W. Vickery, and Valentine and Sherrill Streets ended at Crescent. Although the street named "Crescent" does not appear on current Fort Worth city maps, a visit to the former location, high above W. Vickery and Fort Worth's massive railyards, established the early street was located in an area known later as "Sunset Hills." Presently, TCU stadium is visible from the crest of the hill where the old structure once was located. According to unverified accounts, the building at 3600 Crescent accidentally burned before 1960, an event that may have triggered Homestead's move to its final location at 1250 West Rosedale in Fort Worth.

The reddish-brown, three story brick building, located at the corner of 5th Avenue and West Rosedale, was built in 1903 by Dr. Charles Houston Harris, a 34-year old physician who grew up in Johnson County, south of Fort Worth. Prior to opening the facility on W. Rosedale, Dr. Harris practiced medicine in Moran, a small town located in rural Shackelford County, about one hundred miles west of Fort Worth. According to the *Fort Worth City Directory* published in 1932, Harris Clinic-Hospital operated at 1028 5th Street in Fort Worth. In 1940, Dr. Harris was enumerated in the *U.S. Census* as a seventy-year-old *"surgeon"* in a *"private hospital."* In addition to Dr. Harris, by then a widower, and his sister, who served in 1940 as the nursing school's matron or housemother, the census listed over one hundred individuals who were associated in various ways with the hospital and its nursing school. At least fifty of the individuals specifically were identified as nursing students who resided at the facility. Later, after Dr. Harris allegedly deeded the building and the property on which it was located to the Methodist Church, the Methodist Conference built a new medical facility known as Harris Methodist Hospital several blocks west of the old facility. Unverified information indicates the former sanitarium, hospital, and nursing school also served as a dormitory for other local nursing students before Homestead Maternity Home and Child Placement Agency moved into the building around 1958.

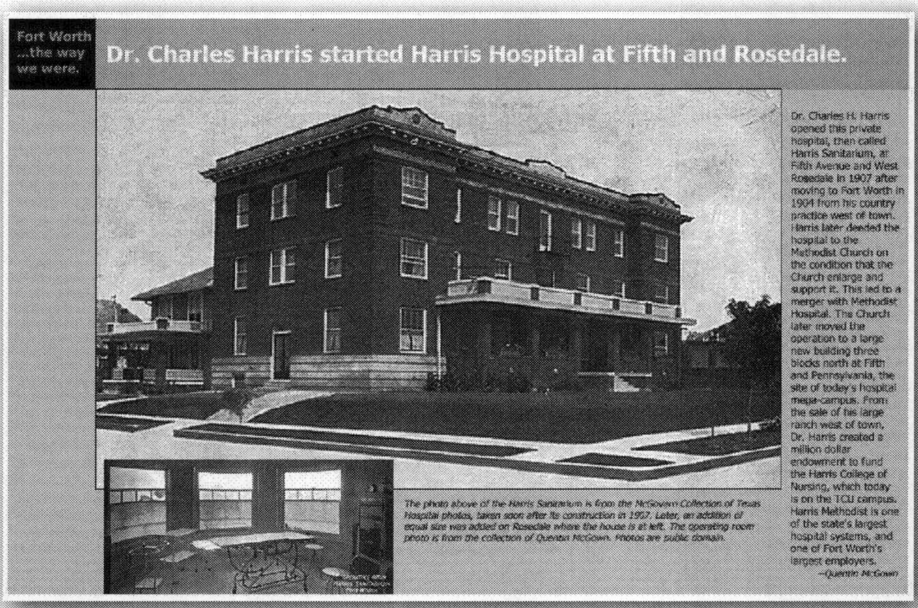
Fort Worth ...the way we were.

Dr. Charles Harris started Harris Hospital at Fifth and Rosedale.

Dr. Charles H. Harris opened this private hospital, then called Harris Sanitarium, at Fifth Avenue and West Rosedale in 1907 after moving to Fort Worth in 1904 from his country practice west of town. Harris later deeded the hospital to the Methodist Church on the condition that the Church enlarge and support it. This led to a merger with Methodist Hospital. The Church later moved the operation to a large new building three blocks north at Fifth and Pennsylvania, the site of today's hospital mega-campus. From the sale of his large ranch west of town, Dr. Harris created a million dollar endowment to fund the Harris College of Nursing, which today is on the TCU campus. Harris Methodist is one of the state's largest hospital systems, and one of Fort Worth's largest employers.

—Quentin McGown

The photo above of the Harris Sanitarium is from the McGovern Collection of Texas Hospital photos, taken soon after its construction in 1907. Later, an addition of equal size was added on Rosedale where the house is at left. The operating room photo is from the collection of Quentin McGown. Photos are public domain.

Harris Sanitarium, corner of West Rosedale and 5th Avenue, Fort Worth, Texas, circa 1907. *McGovern Collection of Texas Hospital photos.*

According to a 1966 report entitled *"Revalidation of Child Placing License"* prepared for Homestead Child Placement Agency, and signed by Mary Elizabeth Power, the agency was *"....a non-profit corporation governed by a Board of Directors which consists of fifteen members. A permanent record of policies and administrative decisions made by this Board is kept. Ten meetings of the Board are held annually. The building was formerly occupied by Harris Hospital, later by Harris Nursing Home. Prior to Homestead occupying it in February, 1963, it was completely remodeled in compliance with all local ordinances related to safety, fire, health, sanitation, etc. The four story, fireproof brick structure consists of an ample number of rooms to comfortably house fifty unwed mothers in single rooms in one wing of the building at the street address, 1250 West Rosedale. The front wing of the building with the street address of 1028 Fifth Avenue, accommodates the offices of the total staff of the Child Placement and the Chapel."*

Throughout the 1960s, Homestead Maternity Home placed advertisements in dozens of newspapers throughout Texas and in other states, soliciting unwed mothers who needed a private place to live until their babies were born and placed for adoption. These ads usually appeared in the "personals" column in the classified section of each newspaper. Services offered in the newspaper ads included *"private, confidential,* [and the] *best professional obstetrical care"* along with a *"licensed adoption service"* for *"unwed mothers."* Two Fort Worth telephone numbers, where collect calls were accepted, and a local post office box address, appeared in the ads as contact points for Homestead's potential clients. Among the cities where advertisements appeared in local newspapers were Abilene, Amarillo, Corpus Christi, Childress, El Paso, Grand Prairie, Irving, Longview, Lubbock, Odessa, Paris, San Antonio, Vernon, and Waco. Ads also ran in newspapers published in a number of other states, including Albuquerque, New Mexico; Greenville, South Carolina; Jackson, Mississippi; Lawton, Oklahoma; Long Beach, California; Los Angeles, California; Orlando, Florida; Shreveport, Louisiana; and St. Louis, Missouri. Interestingly, the top three U.S. cities where Homestead placed newspaper ads were not located in Texas, but instead were in Los Angeles, Shreveport, and St. Louis.

According to at least one Homestead brochure, provided by a birth mother during her interview for the book, Homestead Maternity Home already was in business in 1958. Information contained in the brochure identified Mrs. W. W. Slaughter, also known as Mrs. Clora Pearl Slaughter, as the non-profit organization's Executive Director. A list of the facility's Board of Directors included in the brochure established that prominent and influential members of the city's business and social society governed Homestead's business operations. Board members identified in the brochure were Judge Frank Massey, Chief Justice, Court of Civil Appeals, President; Milton Capers, C.P.A., Secretary; Dr. T. E. Durham, Pastor, Arlington Heights Baptist Church, Treasurer; Mike E. Powell, General Counsel; Dr. Harry Womack, Pediatrician; Mrs. W. A. Schmid; Mrs. Donald Hutt; J. V. Hampton, Hampton Lumber Co; Dr. A. I. Goldberg, M.D.; Mrs. Sue Gaines; C. H. White, Night Manager, Convair; A. I. Endres, General Contractor; Lucien Wright; Major Glenn F. Peska, Chaplain, Carswell AFB; Mrs. Jerry Parker, Denton, Texas; and Richard

Owens, Attorney. It was interesting to note a Baptist minister served as treasurer of the Homestead organization, although a certified public accountant also was listed among the board members. From a social and legal perspective, it is more interesting, however, to see that a woman served as Homestead's Executive Director in 1958. And even more noteworthy, at least from a historical standpoint, is that only four women served on the sixteen-member board of directors. The fact that women made up only twenty-five percent of the Board was a rather significant finding, especially when one considers the group of people directly impacted by Homestead's operation was entirely female.

Newspaper advertisement for Homestead Hospital and Child Placement Center, published November 9, 1958. *Homestead Birth Mother's Private Collection.*

Chapter 3

Wyatt W. Slaughter and Clora Pearl Webb Slaughter

When the U. S. Census of 1900 was recorded in Township 4 of the Chickasaw Nation, Clora Pearl Webb was one year old. The daughter of John Calvin Webb, a farmer, and Maggie, his wife, Clora Pearl was listed on the census record as the youngest of seven children enumerated in the Webb household. Details included on the census record establish that young Pearl, as she would later be known, was born in Indian Territory in 1899. Census information, coupled with a review of Arkansas marriage records, show Pearl's father and her mother, Maggie Stone Webb, were born in Arkansas and were married in 1884 in Hempstead County, Arkansas. There is no way to know how John and Maggie Webb chose their daughter's name, but "Clora Pearl" is quite unique. Interestingly, a rather infamous nineteenth century British-born courtesan who lived in Paris was known by the same name.

U. S. Census information recorded in 1910 listed Pearl, then eleven years old, as a member of her father's household located in the Chickasaw Nation. It seems likely that Pearl's mother, Maggie Webb, may have died after the birth of George, two years younger than Pearl, since John's wife was listed as *"Media"* instead of Maggie. Census details show Media and John Webb had been married for six years, and she had given birth to three children, all under six years old. A subsequent review of Arkansas public records established that

Metie White and John Webb were married in Arkansas County, Arkansas, on October 13, 1903, confirming that Metie was John's second wife and young Pearl's stepmother. In 1920, census data listed John Webb and his large family as residents of Hopkins County, Texas, but it remains unclear as to when or why the family left the Chickasaw Nation and relocated to northeast Texas. Other details included on this census document indicate John and his wife, *"Meda,"* lived on mortgaged farmland near the town of Sulphur Springs, not too distant from the Oklahoma and Arkansas boundaries. In addition to John and his wife, five children whose ages ranged from eighteen months to fifteen years, also lived in the Webb household. Based on the children's ages, it seems likely each child enumerated on the 1920 census was born during John's marriage to his second wife, Metie White. This census also indicates Clora Pearl and her older siblings no longer lived in their father's household.

A subsequent search of 1920 census records found Clora Pearl Webb was enumerated in a residence on Main Street in Sulphur Springs, the county seat of Hopkins County, Texas, not many miles away from her father's farm. Clora Pearl was listed in the record as *"Pearl,"* a 16-year old *"boarder,"* whose occupation was shown as *"none."* Additional census details revealed young Pearl lived in a residence owned by Mattie Mahaffey, a 35-year old widow who worked as a stenographer in a local real estate office. In addition to Pearl, Mrs. Mahaffey's nine-year old son, David, also lived in the residence, where his mother rented rooms to two other women, Hazel Bohman, a 19-year old stenographer at the Chamber of Commerce, and Hazel Guest, 22, a telephone operator. It seems particularly peculiar that Pearl's age recorded on the 1920 census was sixteen, when her age on two previous *U.S. Census* records indicate she was born in 1899. If her stated age on the two previous census records was correct, Pearl would have been twenty-one years old when she was enumerated in Mrs. Mahaffey's household. Also, it appears rather odd that Pearl was listed as an unemployed boarder on that census, with no indication that she attended school, especially since she allegedly told those around her in later years that she had completed two years of college. Further research failed to determine Pearl's possible kinship to Mahaffey or to either of the other two women living in the household. A later review of various documents that included Pearl's date of birth revealed inconsistencies in her birth year, including the September 29,

1907 date of birth she provided on a 1950s application for a number submitted to the Social Security Administration. The earliest and best information regarding Pearl's year of birth, was the date provided by her natural mother in 1900, when one year old Pearl was enumerated on the *U.S. Census* recorded that year.

Very little information exists about Pearl's life between 1920 and 1930, but the *U.S. Census* recorded for Fort Worth, Texas, in 1930 shows she had already married Wyatt W. Slaughter, a partner in a Fort Worth radio business. Although details are sketchy about how Pearl and Wyatt first met, Juliet George, a Fort Worth historian, described the couple's chance encounter in an article she wrote for the *Fort Worth Weekly* magazine. In her article, published on July 10, 2010, George explained that Slaughter, a successful Fort Worth businessman, advertised for a wife on a local radio show and chose Pearl as his bride after she responded to his proposal. Although the couple's marriage record was not located during research for this book, other available information indicates the bride and groom were in their late twenties when they became husband and wife.

Wyatt W. Slaughter and Clora Pearl Webb Slaughter, outside the front entrance to their Arlington Heights home at 908 Dorothy Lane, Fort Worth, Texas. 1930s.
Wyatt and Shelia Webb Collection, Reprinted with permission from Juliet George.

Wyatt W. Slaughter was born in Fort Smith on December 6, 1900, to Lee Slaughter, a shoe salesman, and his wife Caroline Maddux. At some point in time after his father's death, Slaughter moved to Dallas, Texas. Initially, he worked as a clerk at Butler Brothers and lived with his mother in a rooming house she operated at 805 N. Harwood, near the downtown area. On September 12, 1918, when 18-year old Slaughter registered for the World War I draft, he was employed as a clerk for Western Electric, located at the corner of Pacific Avenue and Ervay Street in Dallas. On that document, the young man provided his home address as his mother's residence on N. Harwood. In 1920, Slaughter was enumerated on the *U.S. Census* recorded for Dallas as a member of the household headed by his 40-year old widowed mother, Carrie Slaughter. Other census details listed 20-year old Wyatt's occupation as a *"dry goods salesman,"* and the occupation of his 22-year old sister, Cleopatra Slaughter, as "artist" and "painter." According to her household listing, Mrs. Slaughter also rented rooms to nine other individuals, including two married couples. A Dallas city directory published that same year listed Wyatt as a partner in *"Slaughter-Riter,"* likely the dry goods business identified on the *U.S. Census* record. Apparently the business venture was a successful one, since a Dallas city directory published a few years later indicated Wyatt had moved to 2011 Euclid, a single family dwelling located in northeast Dallas.

The exact date Wyatt Slaughter moved to Fort Worth is unclear, but a 1930 photo showing the former Dallasite standing beside a boxcar of Crosley radios in Fort Worth indicates he was a large volume dealer of the popular new household device. The *Fort Worth City Directory,* also published in 1930, identified Slaughter as the Secretary-Treasurer of *"The Shield Co,"* and a decade later, an updated directory showed the same business sold *"wholesale radios and refrigerators and complete home furnishings"* in its location at 1008-14 Macon.

A Lavish Lifestyle and an Entrepreneur's Spirit

By most standards, Pearl Webb's marriage to Wyatt Slaughter had the makings of an early 1900s movie plot – prosperous Fort Worth businessman woos small-town girl during what Fort Worth historian and author, Juliet George, described as a *"romantic radio promotion."* In her book entitled *Fort Worth's*

Arlington Heights, George explained, *"....Wyatt Slaughter owned the local Crosley radio franchise at The Shield Company, a furniture and appliance store downtown."* Soon after they wed, Pearl and Wyatt Slaughter moved into their newly-built yellow brick, English-inspired bungalow, not too far removed from Camp Bowie Boulevard and its well-heeled Arlington Heights neighborhood. George also wrote, the house's *"design and construction have been attributed to Meredith Carb. A full basement, solarium, recessed shelving, decorative trim, and hideaway storage areas were among distinctive extras."* Located at 908 Dorothy Lane, in Tipton Place, the value of the house and land, according to 1930 census data, was $4,250. Allegedly, the couple often entertained in the basement of their lavishly decorated residence, where they hosted friends and served liquor purchased from a local bootlegger.

The Dorothy Lane Apartments

With steady income, money in the bank, and grand ideas in their plans, Pearl and Wyatt Slaughter decided to construct an apartment building on the rear portion of their property, near what is now Hi-Mount Elementary School. The exact date construction began on the apartment building is unknown, but details captured on the 1930 *U.S. Census* indicate the process may have been ongoing when the enumeration took place. In addition to Pearl and Wyatt Slaughter, an Illinois-born brick mason, Joe Chandler, and his wife, also lived at 908 Dorothy Lane, where they paid rent of thirty-five dollars per month to the owners. Although the information has not been verified, it seems likely that Chandler was a brick mason employed by the couple to work on the apartments under construction behind their Dorothy Lane residence. In 1940, Blanch Ryburn, a 35-year old widow from Dallas, was enumerated as a *"lodger"* in the Slaughter residence on Dorothy Lane. The Arkansas-born woman provided details required on that particular census record indicating she had lived in Dallas in 1935. In addition, the census included a separate household listing at 908 Dorothy Lane, headed by Pennsylvania-born J. C. McFarland, an independent oil producer, whose wife and two children also lived with him. Other census details showed McFarland paid rent of sixty dollars per month for the apartment he and his family apparently rented from Pearl and her husband.

The yellow-brick apartments later known in Fort Worth as "The Dorothy Lane," were Colonial in design, with two stories and third floor dormer windows. In later years, a lavish courtyard and pool, as well as a wishing well and an herb garden, created a spa-like setting in a treed environment, just steps away from each apartment's front door. When the Dorothy Lane apartments were complete and ready for occupancy, Pearl rented them as move-in ready with the newest furniture and most up-to-date appliances from her husband's Fort Worth furniture and appliance store. Slaughter's Dorothy Lane Apartments remain part of the unique history of Arlington Heights. According to an article written by Juliet George and published in the *Fort Worth Weekly* magazine, better known, as well as lesser known, musicians and artists who visited Fort Worth and perhaps lived in the city for brief periods of time, often stayed at The Dorothy Lane. The apartments still exist today, although some of the glitz and glamour once associated with the vintage apartments no longer exists. Some say the apartments are haunted, albeit by friendly ghosts, while others simply wonder what would be said if the walls could talk.

The Dorothy Lane Apartments, built by Pearl and Wyatt Slaughter, Fort Worth, Texas. *Author's private collection.*

The apartment community's current website says this about Pearl Slaughter's first real estate venture:

> *"Each of our units is unique, and no two floor plans are exactly the same. Sizes range from efficiencies to two bedroom duplex units. Our complex is comprised of approximately 30 apartments, and 5 duplexes. If you are looking for an alternative to the sprawling, cookie-cutter apartment complexes that have become so common, the Dorothy Lane Apartments may be just what you desire. Please see below for descriptions and photos of the various types of units we offer in a peaceful, private, and quiet community setting." From the website www.dorothylaneapts.com*

Another listing describes the Dorothy Lane Apartments as a *"unique apartment community, located in the historic Cultural District of Fort Worth, Texas. The complex has a colorful history, dating back to the Gangster era of the 1920's. The property is a Fort Worth Historical Landmark and we have retained the look and feel of its unique background. Most of our units have wood floors, original tile, and antique fixtures, which give them a truly vintage feel. We have tried to restore and retain as much of the original atmosphere as possible. Our complex is situated around a peaceful courtyard, which contains a swimming pool, ponds, flowers, and tables. It is a perfect area for relaxing with a book, or chatting with your neighbors. Our affordable prices and proximity to the University of North Texas Health Science Center, TCU, and downtown Fort Worth make us a perfect fit for students and singles. We are located at 908 Dorothy Lane, two blocks west of Montgomery Street – just a short walk from UNTHSC. Downtown is just 5 miles to the east, and TCU is 3 miles to the south."*

Today, an intricately designed black wrought-iron gate and sign simply stating "Dorothy Lane," is a present-day reminder of the original splendor of the Dorothy Lane Apartments in Fort Worth.

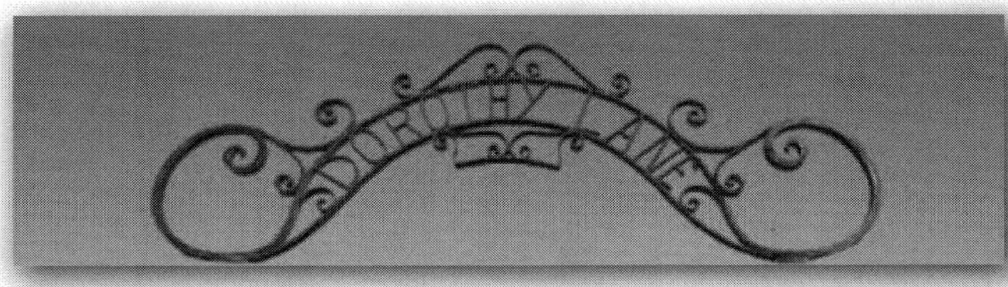

Ornate wrought iron sign over sidewalk entrance to the Dorothy Lane Apartments, Fort Worth, Texas. *Author's private collection*

The Colonial Hotel

The Slaughter's plan to build an income-producing apartment building indicates Pearl may have possessed an entrepreneurial spirit similar to that of her husband, or she had simply paid very close attention to his proven sense of business. But one thing is certain - Wyatt Slaughter participated in his wife's dreams and schemes and willingly shared his financial success with her. The couple's fancy for investing in well-located real estate was not a passing one, it seemed, as they began making plans for another project. Motivated by the popularity and financial success of The Dorothy Lane apartments, Pearl and Wyatt Slaughter chose to create something that would surpass their initial real estate venture. The result was a redo of an existing building on Camp Bowie Boulevard, one of Fort Worth's most traveled thoroughfares, with its new owners converting the existing structure into a hotel, colonial in design, with enormous columns and a cupola on the roof. Befitting its architecture, Pearl and Wyatt Slaughter named their new business enterprise the Colonial Hotel. Local historian, teacher, and author, Juliet George included an image of the hotel in her book, *"Camp Bowie Boulevard,"* and captioned the photo saying the hotel was located at the.... *"wagon wheel intersection of Camp Bowie Boulevard, Montgomery Street, Lancaster Avenue, Clarke Avenue, and Tulsa Way"* and started out as *"......a genteel, small, nicely furnished place. Earlier, Web Maddox had operated one of his ice and food markets in the main building, and his word for the establishment 'Icerteria,' made it into an H.L. Mencken book on such oddities. Prior to the Slaughters' makeover, it had also housed a real estate office and served as apartments. The group of buildings was standing as early as 1927."*

In the months and years that followed, the hotel's restaurant, the Colonial Café, became a popular meeting place not only for its guests, but for residents of the Arlington Heights neighborhood that bordered the property on the north and to the west. Since the hotel occupied a prominent location among other businesses and shops along "The Boulevard," the café also attracted employees and customers who frequented the area. Throughout the fifties and sixties, when thousands of servicemen rotated through Fort Worth's Carswell Air Force Base, the hotel's basement bar became a well-known music venue and local watering hole. Although the rumors cannot be substantiated with facts, some people familiar with the business operation believed the hotel's best-known attractions were the ladies of the evening who allegedly lived in some of the rooms upstairs. On Wednesday, April 10, 1968, a news article published in the *Amarillo-Globe Times* described a fire that occurred at the Colonial Hotel during the previous night:

> "A three-alarm fire about midnight Tuesday gutted the second and third floors of the Hotel on Fort Worth's west side. The blaze caused $25,000 damage at a minimum, fire Chief H. E. Owens said. There were no injuries. Franklin Owens, manager of the hotel, blamed the fire on faulty wiring. Fire officials said, however, that the exact cause had not been determined. Mrs. Owens said four tenants occupied the third floor and she was in the coffee shop on the first floor about midnight when a guest ran in saying, "The hotel is burning! Come quick!" She rushed outside and spotted a policeman whom she asked to go upstairs and "be sure everybody's out." The owner of the hotel is Mrs. W. W. Slaughter of Fort Worth. Owens said the second and third floor were burned out and water damage was severe on the first floor."

Apparently, the extensive fire and water damage to the structure prevented its reopening, and today, no evidence exists at all of the former Colonial Hotel and Apartments.

Colonial Hotel, 3600 Camp Bowie Blvd., circa 1940. Tarrant County Archives, *Dalton Hoffman Fort Worth Collection*.

Pearl and Wyatt's Children

To their friends and business associates, the couple seemed to have everything they wanted or needed – except children. Although details are not available, Pearl and Wyatt Slaughter adopted two young children, a daughter born in August of 1945, and a son born the next month. The couple named their son Wyatt William Slaughter for his father, and their daughter Gloria Pearl Slaughter, a variation of her adoptive mother's own name. Allegedly, the children were raised as fraternal twins and lived in the Fort Worth area until their deaths in 1996 and in 2002. Wyatt Slaughter's continued business success, along with the couple's income from the Colonial Hotel, its café and apartments, and the Dorothy Lane Apartments, substantially contributed to the couple's increasing wealth and social standing in the Fort Worth community. Early pictures of their lavishly-decorated residence and of the middle-aged couple with their two children, other family members, and friends aboard their cabin cruiser on Eagle Mountain Lake, certainly reflected the glory days that only disposable income made possible. In one particular photo, the family posed for the camera on the stern of the "Pearl," while the vessel's African-American steward, attired in full nautical uniform, stood just steps behind the group, ready to serve Captain Slaughter and his guests food and beverages from the onboard bar.

The Homestead Hotel and Apartments

Pearl's quest to manage yet another income-producing property came to fruition in the form of an apartment hotel located at 3600 Crescent. The location was situated high above West Vickery in a residential area later known as Sunset Hills. A few individuals interviewed for this book believe initial guests and residents at the Homestead Hotel and Apartments were men who worked at railroad yards that parallel West Vickery, just below the hotel's hilltop location. Others believe Pearl intended to use the apartment hotel for the exclusive purpose of housing pregnant women, married and unmarried, who planned to give up their babies for adoption. But one thing is certain – by 1958, the Homestead Hotel & Apartments had been renamed Homestead Maternity Home, and the owner actively was promoting the facility's services in a marketing brochure specifically designed to attract unwed, pregnant mothers. According to a photo included in the brochure, the building known as the Colonial Hotel on Camp Bowie Boulevard had been repurposed as *"Homestead Maternity Hospital."*

Rumors persisted for years that Pearl may have been renting hotel rooms by the hour and providing rooms and apartments at the Colonial Hotel to pregnant women until they delivered, well before the apartment hotel-turned-maternity home at 3600 Crescent was advertised as a home for unwed mothers. Although these rumors cannot be substantiated with facts at this point in history, one particular situation lends credence to unsubstantiated stories that

Pearl allowed pregnant women to stay in upstairs rooms at the Camp Bowie location. One of the birth mothers interviewed for this book recalled traveling from another state to Fort Worth to give birth to a baby she planned to give up for adoption. Although she was married, "Tillie" had become pregnant while she was separated from her husband. According to an interview with the woman, she traveled to Fort Worth on a bus, with her two young sons in tow, where she was picked up at the bus station by a representative of the Edna Gladney Home. The maternity home staff member allegedly drove Tillie and her sons to the Colonial Hotel on Camp Bowie, where they ate dinner in the hotel's café and slept overnight in one of the rooms. After breakfast the next morning, the Edna Gladney staff member returned to the hotel and drove Tillie and her two sons to a local boys' home, where their stay during their mother's confinement had been pre-arranged. After Tillie left her sons at the boys' home, the staff member drove her to the Edna Gladney home where she was admitted.

A short time after she arrived at Edna Gladney, Tillie and another resident got into an argument, and she left the maternity home to join another young mother she had met earlier at the home. The other woman recommended that Tillie move to a private home in Fort Worth sponsored by Volunteers of America (VOA) and that she allow VOA to place her baby for adoption. Shortly after the two women talked, Tillie moved into the Avenue J residence of Lucille and Alton Clinton, and she lived there until she delivered a baby girl that VOA later placed for adoption. Soon after giving birth, Tillie said she was hired by the manager of the Colonial Hotel Café, explaining that she needed to work in order to save enough money for bus tickets home for herself and her two sons. Tillie's job at the Colonial Café, however, did not work out, and she left to take another job at the Seybold Café near Carswell Air Force Base. As soon as she saved enough money to purchase the bus tickets, Tillie picked up her boys and left Fort Worth. Before Tillie returned home, however, she believed that she and her husband might reconcile and filed a lawsuit to have her daughter, who already had been placed in the home of adoptive parents, returned to her. An account of the lawsuit and the judge's ruling appears later in the book in the story of Sharon Weiss, the daughter that Tillie gave up for adoption.

Pearl's Relationship with Homestead Takes a Turn

The history of Homestead Maternity Home's operation at the West Rosedale location in Fort Worth allegedly began between 1958 and 1960, when the organization is said to have applied for licensing to operate. A complete reconstruction of the facility's operation is impossible, however, since the maternity home's administrative files, ledgers, and other accounting records no longer exist. The only present means of determining how the facility managed its business affairs or of gaining insight into the people responsible for the operation are through personal stories told by birth mothers who were residents at Homestead, interviews with adoptive parents, or from news articles, lawsuits filed, and other available public records. A lawsuit filed on July 24, 1964, by Pearl Slaughter against Homestead Hospital and Child Placement Agency's Board of Directors, offers a glimpse into a disagreement over a financial matter dating back several years. According to the lawsuit, Pearl's official position as Homestead's Executive Director likely ended in the summer of 1962.

In requesting relief under our Declaratory Judgment Statutes, Plaintiff would show the Court the following: That heretofore, to-wit about August 1962, certain parties on the Board of Directors of the Defendant, attempted to discharge and dismiss the Plaintiff, an executive officer of such organization. Rules and regulations and by-laws of the Defendant organization required that there be a minimum number of people present at any meeting of such Board of Directors before any valid or legal action could be taken. Such number of people were not present. Such attempt to dismiss or discharge this plaintiff was illegal and nothing more than an abortive attempt of certain officers connected with the Defendant organization to dismiss and discharge the Plaintiff.

Since said time, Defendant has refused to recognize that Plaintiff still is an officer of Defendant organization, notwithstanding such a legal attempt to discharge Plaintiff. It is, therefore, a justifiable controversy between Plaintiff and Defendant as to whether or not Plaintiff has continued to be an officer of the Defendant organization.

Pleading further, Plaintiff would show to the Court that the Defendant is an authorized child-placing agency operating under license and permit of the Texas Department of Public Welfare at all times complained of herein. That before the Department of Public Welfare would issue such permit to the Defendant to place children for adoption, the Department of Public Welfare of the State of Texas required that the Defendant put up a twenty-five thousand dollar ($25,000.00) cash deposit. The Defendant attempted to raise such sum by donations but was only able to raise about five hundred dollars ($500.00). In order to procure the remaining twenty-four thousand dollars five hundred dollars ($24,500.00), the Defendant, its agents, servants, and employees, agreed with Plaintiff that (1) if she would advance such sum to be placed with the Department of Public Welfare in accordance with its requirements for the use and benefit of the Defendant, that the Plaintiff, at that time an officer of the Defendant organization, could and would continue to remain an officer of the Defendant organization and (2) that in the event Plaintiff should be discharged by the Defendant as an officer of such organization, that the Defendant would cause such twenty-four thousand five hundred dollars ($24,500.00) so advanced by Plaintiff for the use and benefit of Defendant to be returned to Plaintiff as her own.

In pursuance of such agreement, Plaintiff did advance twenty-four thousand five hundred dollars ($24,500.00) of her own personal funds to meet the deposit requirements of the Department of Public Welfare of the State of Texas for the use and benefit of the Defendant. Such twenty-four thousand five hundred dollars ($24,500.00) belonging to this Plaintiff has continued, at all times complained of herein, to remain on deposit with the Department of Public Welfare in the name of the Defendant organization. Defendant has refused to return or cause to be returned to Plaintiff such twenty-four thousand five hundred dollars ($24,500.00) since such attempted discharge. In the event it should be determined that the Plaintiff was legally discharged from her position as an officer of the Defendant organization, Plaintiff asks the court for her judgment against Defendant for twenty-four thousand five hundred dollars ($24,500.00) in the nature of a repayment to her of her money so advanced to Defendant and held by the Department of Public Welfare in the name of, in behalf of, and for the use and benefit of the Defendant organization.

Pleading further, if same be necessary, Plaintiff would show the court that she has advanced money, automobiles, materials, services, and property for the use and benefit of the Defendant, that such money, automobiles, materials, services, and property were accepted by the Defendant for its use and benefit. The value of that which has been advanced to the Defendant by the Plaintiff has been at least twenty thousand dollars ($24,500.00). Plaintiff asks for judgment for such sum.

Interestingly, Harold Valderas, Fort Worth's City Attorney, who represented Homestead's Child Placement Agency in later adoption proceedings, represented the defendant in the lawsuit Pearl filed against the organization. Attorney Valderas prepared the original answer on behalf of the Defendant organization and denied Pearl's charges, including the allegation concerning the absence of a quorum of board members present when her dismissal and discharge allegedly took place. His initial answer also questioned the timing of Pearl's lawsuit, since the claims alleged occurred outside the state's two-year statute of limitations. Also through its attorney, the defendant organization denied Pearl's allegation that she had loaned Homestead $25,000.00 to be used as a cash deposit required by the Texas Department of Public Welfare before the organization could apply for a license to operate a child placement agency. The Defendant organization claimed the cash deposit put up by Pearl Slaughter was simply a "*donation,*" not a loan, and that no documentation existed to prove otherwise. The organization further denied Slaughter's claim that her position at the time on Homestead's board of directors would be assured if she provided the cash deposit required by the state. And finally, the Defendant organization claimed "*money, automobiles, materials, services, and property for the use and benefit of the Defendant*" addressed in the lawsuit were anything other than donations to the organization by the Plaintiff, Pearl Slaughter.

On October 16, 1964, Pearl Slaughter's attorney, Elvin E. Tackett, filed a *Request to Clerk to Take Oral Deposition* with the 153rd District Court, stating his desire to take Dr. T. E. Durham's oral deposition. The request also asked the Court's commission to order a *subpoena duces tecum* requesting that Dr. Durham produce various documents pertinent to the lawsuit. Documents requested included *"(1) the original charter under which the Homestead Hospital & Child Placement Agency was licensed to do business (2) all amendments to the original charter or the subsequent charter, if any, under which the Homestead Hospital & Child Placement Agency is now doing business, (3) the ledger and journal of the Agency now doing business, (3) the ledger and journal of the agency showing receipts and disbursements beginning in 1957 through 1962, (4) the license from the state of Texas authorizing Defendant to operate a child placing agency, (5) all correspondence from any officer of the Homestead Hospital & Child Placement Agency to the State and all correspondence from the State Department of Public Welfare to any officer of Defendant concerning the issuance of said license, (6) the bank deposit slip showing Defendant's deposit of a check to the Defendant as payee in excess of Twenty Thousand Dollars ($20,000.00) written by Mrs. W. W. Slaughter or Pearl Slaughter in October, 1958, and (7) a copy of the annual auditor's statement concerning receipts and disbursements submitted to the Executive Director of the State Department of Public Welfare for each year from 1957 through 1962."*

Among the individuals listed in Pearl Slaughter's request to depose members of Homestead's board of directors, employees, or others associated with the organization were J. D. Ballard; Dr. T. E. Durham; Dr. A. I. Goldberg; Miss Maybelle Hudgins; Mrs. Helen R. King; Dr. James Murphy; J. R. Pryor; Dr. Jack L. Turner; Mrs. Anna Urban; Mrs. Joe Wagner; Dr. Harry H. Womack, Jr.; and Lucien Wright. Although the court documents reviewed during research for this book were available from the Tarrant County District Court's library and archives, copies of depositions requested and documents submitted under a subpoena *duces tecum*, if these actions actually occurred, were not found. Apparently neither party settled, and the lawsuit lingered on the court's docket until 1968, when the District Judge finally dismissed the case.

Pearl Slaughter's dismissal and discharge by Homestead Hospital & Child Placement Agency occurred approximately seven years after her husband, Wyatt W. Slaughter, died on October 18, 1955. According to Slaughter's Texas death certificate, his last known address was 908 Dorothy Lane, the residence he had shared with his wife since they were newlyweds. The listed cause of Slaughter's death was liver failure and a history of heart disease existing for a decade. Other *"significant conditions"* present at the time of Slaughter's death and listed on the death certificate showed he was *"overweight"* and suffered from *"passive congestion of liver."* After living in Fort Worth for a large portion of her adult life, Clora Pearl Slaughter died at St. Joseph's Hospital in Fort Worth on November 14, 1974. Her death certificate listed liver and lung cancer, as well as Parkinson's disease, as causes of her death. Pearl's last known address of 908 Dorothy Lane also appeared on the document, and her occupation was shown as *"Manager Apartment."* An article published in the *Fort Worth Star-Telegram* shortly after Pearl's death indicated she had lived in Fort Worth for over 50 years. The newspaper account further stated *"She and her late husband founded and operated the Shield Company Furniture Store in downtown Fort Worth from 1922 to 1962. Mrs. Slaughter founded the Homestead Maternity Home and Child Placement Agency for unwed mothers in 1959 and was associated with the home until 1963. She also was the owner and operator of the Dorothy Lane Apartments."*

A review of Pearl Slaughter's last will and probate documents, including the *Inventory, Appraisement and List of Claims*, submitted by court-appointed appraisers, Donald Dalton and Mary E. Woodfin, revealed her personal property and real estate holdings were valued at slightly less than $450,000, while claims due against the estate totaled approximately $18,000. Pearl's will, witnessed by Betty Shaw and

Lavonne Sparkman, and recorded on July 23, 1971, designated individual bequests of $5,000 each to three of her nieces and nephews. One half of the remainder of Pearl's estate's *"rent, residue, and remainder,"* as stipulated by the will, was left to each of her adopted children, Gloria Slaughter Cox and Wyatt William Slaughter II. Both children are now deceased.

Chapter 4

Dr. Thomas E. Durham and Hassie Whitmire Durham

Although Thomas E. Durham and his wife, Hassie, were Fort Worth residents for most of their adult lives, the two individuals originally were Texas transplants. A review of early *U.S. Census* records and other available documents revealed Thomas E. Durham was born in Gwinnett County, Georgia, and that Durham and his wife previously had lived and worked in South Carolina. In 1910, Thomas Durham was listed on the *U.S. Census* recorded the same year as a "boarder" in a Greenwood, South Carolina household headed by Franklin Hunt, a 22-year old *"loom fixer."* Durham's occupation was shown as a *"weaver"* in a *"cotton mill."* Franklin's 23-year old wife, Amanda, and their two young sons, ages one and three years, also lived in the household. Additional details included on the census record showed Hunt household members lived in a rented house on *"Smythe Street."* In 1910, it appeared Greenwood was a mill town, since a very high percentage of households enumerated in the Hunt family's neighborhood contained at least one family member who worked at a cotton mill. Further research determined Amanda Hunt was Thomas Durham's older sister, and her husband's full name was Franklin Benjamin Hunt. Also in

1910, census information available for Pickens County, South Carolina, revealed Hassie Whitmire, later Durham, lived with her mother, sister, and a boarder. Hassie, too, was employed as a *"spinner"* at a cotton mill. Other research established that Hassie Delia Durham was born in South Carolina on September 8, 1890, to John H. Whitmire, a farmer, and Emma K. Wright Whitmire. Although it seems likely that Thomas Durham and Hassie Whitmire married in South Carolina, a copy of their marriage record was not located. When Thomas E. Durham registered for the World War I draft on June 5, 1917, he was living in Easley, SC. Details contained on Durham's draft registration record show he was born in Gwinnett County, Georgia, on May 18, 1891, was already married, and he had one child. Durham's occupation was listed as *"ministry,"* and other details on the registration record indicated he was employed by *"four Baptist churches"* in Easley and Liberty, South Carolina. The registration also included a physical description of Durham, stating he was of medium height and medium build, with light brown hair and brown eyes. Almost a year later, in April of 1918, Durham was inducted into the U.S. Army in Watkinsville (Oconee County) Georgia. On December 19, 1919, Private Thomas E. Durham was discharged from the Army, having served less than two years. In 1920, the *U.S. Census* enumerated Durham, his wife, and their 8-year old daughter, Helen L. Durham, as residents of University Ridge in Greenville, South Carolina, home of Furman University. His occupation on the census was shown as *"minister."* Other individuals living near the Durham household and identified on the same census appeared to be associated with the college, either as students or as employees.

Dr. Durham's obituary published in the Fort Worth *Star-Telegram* shortly after his death in 1989, stated he had served as pastor of the First Baptist Church in Greenville, South Carolina. Apparently, he was associated with the church for a brief time in the early 1920's, before he came to Fort Worth in 1923 to teach at Southwestern Baptist Theological Seminary. When Rev. Durham arrived in what would become his adopted hometown, he already had earned a Bachelor's Degree from Furman University in Greenville, South Carolina, as well as a Master's Degree and doctorate from the University of Arlington in Arlington, Virginia. According to the *Fort Worth City Directory* published in 1924, Rev. Thomas E. Durham served as pastor of Ellison Memorial Baptist Church and lived at the corner of Sandage Avenue and Gambrell, in the vicinity of Southwestern Baptist Theological Seminary. Two years later, when the next city directory was published in 1926, Dr. Durham was listed as *"Superintendent of Baptist Hospital, 1400 Pennsylvania."* That same directory included the couple's residence address of 1326 Pennsylvania, the address of Baptist Hospital's Nurses Home, where Mrs. Durham also served as the home's matron.

Southwestern Baptist Theological Seminary, circa 1950. Tarrant County Archives, *Dalton Hoffman Fort Worth Collection.*

Additional listings published in Fort Worth city directories, beginning in 1929 and continuing until 1952, consistently identify the Durham family's residence as a rented house located at 3728 Camp Bowie Boulevard. This address was located less than two blocks away from Arlington Heights Baptist Church, where Dr. Durham allegedly began serving as the pastor of a small congregation in 1929. Details about Durham's rental arrangement for the house on Camp Bowie Boulevard are unknown, but perhaps the church provided the residence for its pastor. These early directory listings also place Dr. Durham, his wife, and his daughter, Dorothy, a block away from the Colonial Hotel at 3600 Camp Bowie and several blocks away from the Dorothy Lane residence of Pearl and Wyatt W. Slaughter. A review of the *U.S. Census* of 1930 found Thomas and Hassie Durham, each thirty-eight years old, and their 19-year old daughter, Dorothy, still living at 3728 Camp Bowie Boulevard. According to the census listing, Dr. Durham continued to serve as a Baptist minister, and Dorothy worked as a clerk in a dry goods store. In 1940, the *U.S. Census* enumerated Thomas and Hassie Durham as the only occupants of their long time residence at the Camp Bowie address, indicating that Dorothy Durham, the couple's only child, was no longer living in her parents' household. Other details included on that particular census revealed the Baptist minister received an annual salary of $2,600.00 for his ministerial work. A further review of 1940 census documents and other publicly available information established that 29-year old Dorothy and her husband, Horace Spuhler, also 29, lived in Houston, Texas, where Horace worked as a salesman for an oil well supply company. Census information indicated Dorothy and Horace Spuhler were the parents of a five year old son named Thomas H. Spuhler.

A further review of Fort Worth City Directories published in the late 1950s showed Thomas and Hassie Durham no longer lived at 3728 Camp Bowie Boulevard, but lived instead on Clarke Avenue, just off Camp Bowie Boulevard. According to a news article, Arlington Heights Baptist Church *"gave a home to Dr. Durham and his wife, Hassie, in 1958,"* and *"Dr. Durham was made pastor emeritus of the church when he retired in the early 1960's."* The residence on Clarke Avenue apparently was the house given to Dr. Durham and his wife by the church as a gift for the minister's service that lasted more than thirty years. Newspaper articles published in several cities throughout the State of Texas and reviewed during the course of writing this book, indicate Dr. Durham was a well-respected member of the Fort Worth religious community and of the Baptist General Convention of Texas. On October 23, 1945, *The Eagle* in Bryan, Texas, published a news article on its front page, stating Rev. T. E. Durham, a *"member of the convention committee,"* spoke to one of the newspaper's reporters about the fifteen hundred visitors he expected to convene in Fort Worth later that year for the annual Baptist General Convention.

In an article published in Fort Worth's *Star Telegram* on October 29, 1952, Dr. Durham was identified as the *"new president of the General Minister's Association"* and as the *"originator of the plan for teaching Bible in the city's high schools."* The article also attributed growth of the pastor's church, Arlington Heights Baptist, to his leadership, noting that *"during his tenure....the church membership has grown from 35 to 875 and the value of the church property from $10,000.00 to $200,000.00."* A decade later, according to another article that appeared in the *Denton Record-Chronicle*, the Baptist minister was an active conservative crusader against gambling in Fort Worth. This particular news account described Dr. Durham's association with a local Baptist group when he spoke out at a Fort Worth City council meeting against local gambling and the use of pinball devices. Dr. Durham's concerns, as well as the concerns of others who spoke at the meeting, apparently impacted the council's decision when it passed *"an ordinance outlawing all pinball devices"* and voted to levy a *"$200 fine for each day of the offense"* against anyone who violated the city ordinance. Interestingly, Fort Worth city directory listings show the city's religious community included several hundred pastors of various denominations during the years Homestead Maternity Home and its child placement agency operated.

After Dr. Durham retired as pastor of Arlington Heights Baptist Church, he continued to be active in the Tarrant Baptist Association, Community Voice, the Masonic Lodge, and the Moslah Temple Shrine. He also taught religion to students at Arlington Heights High School after the local board of education ruled that public high school students should receive two hours of religious education.

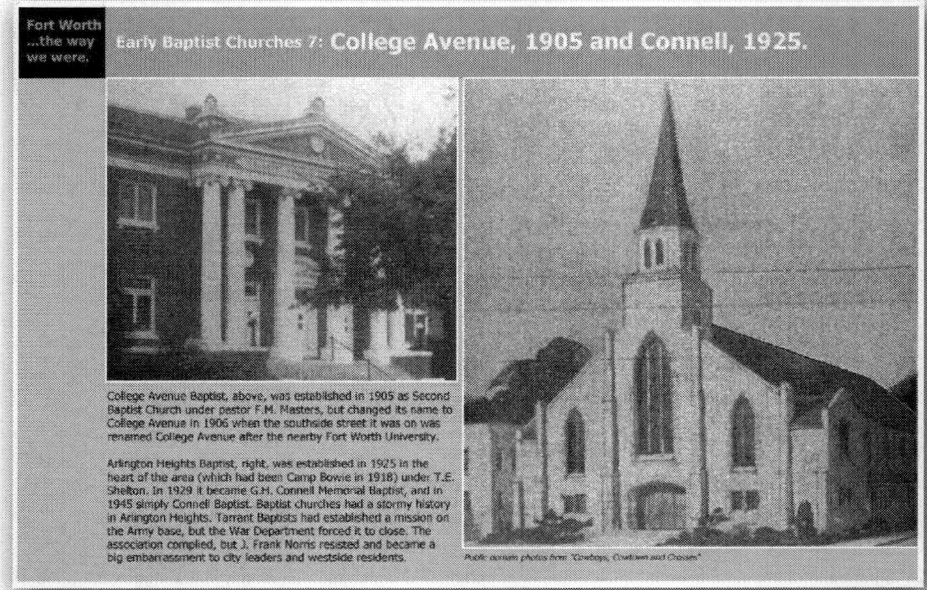

Fort Worth ...the way we were.
Early Baptist Churches 7: College Avenue, 1905 and Connell, 1925.
College Avenue Baptist, above, was established in 1905 as Second Baptist Church under pastor F.M. Masters, but changed its name to College Avenue in 1906 when the southside street it was on was renamed College Avenue after the nearby Fort Worth University.
Arlington Heights Baptist, right, was established in 1925 in the heart of the area (which had been Camp Bowie in 1918) under T.E. Shelton. In 1929 it became G.H. Connell Memorial Baptist, and in 1945 simply Connell Baptist. Baptist churches had a stormy history in Arlington Heights. Tarrant Baptists had established a mission on the Army base, but the War Department forced it to close. The association complied, but J. Frank Norris resisted and became a big embarrassment to city leaders and westside residents.

Arlington Heights Baptist Church, established 1925. Public Domain Photo, *"Cowboys, Cowtown, and Crosses."*

On September 18, 1978, Dr. Durham's lifelong marriage to Hassie Durham ended when she died as the result of a cerebral vascular accident with complications from pneumonia. According to an obituary published in Fort Worth's newspaper, the *Star Telegram*, Mrs. Durham had been a teacher of the Dorcas Class of Arlington Heights Baptist Church since 1930, and a leader of the Sunbeam Band for 35 years. Her years of employment consisted of *"superintendent of nurses at the Old Baptist Hospital in Fort Worth and superintendent of nurses at Furman University."* Mrs. Durham's employment as a nurse and as housemother of an *"unnamed maternity home,"* most likely Homestead, also were confirmed on her Texas-issued death certificate.

Dr. Durham had been a widower for slightly over a decade when he died in Fort Worth on February 2, 1989. The text of his obituary, written by Bill Verhines of the Fort Worth *Star Telegram* appears below:

T. E. Durham, pastor of Arlington Heights Baptist Church from the late 1920's to the early 1960's died Thursday at a Fort Worth Hospital. He was 97. Weather permitting, funeral will be at 3 p.m. tomorrow at Arlington Heights Baptist Church. Entombment will be at noon Monday in Greenwood Mausoleum. Haverson & Cole Funeral Home is in charge of arrangements. Dr. Durham was born in Buford, GA. He received a Bachelor's Degree from Furman University in Greenville, SC, and Master's degree and doctorate from the University of Arlington in Arlington, VA. He was pastor of the First Baptist Church in Greenville for a brief time in the early 1920s. Dr. Durham came to Fort Worth to attend Southwestern Baptist Theological Seminary in 1923. In 1924, he was appointed superintendent of the old Baptist Hospital in Fort Worth. Dr. Durham began as pastor of the Arlington Heights church in 1929 when the congregation had about 35 members. When he left in the early 1960s, the church had more than 1,000 members. "I knew him as a committed pastor, a warm personal friend, interested in all the churches and committed to the community," said Dr. Robert Naylor, a former president of Southwestern Baptist Theological Seminary. "He was a spirit for good in the community." The church gave a home to Dr. Durham and his wife, Hassie, in 1958. Visitors recall how Dr. Durham often could be found in his study, wearing a yarmulke and reading the Old Testament in Hebrew. He knew Hebrew and New Testament Greek. Dr. Durham was made pastor emeritus of the church when he retired in the early 1960s. He also spent much time in ministry in the community. Dr. Durham was originator and dean of a program sponsored by the Fort Worth General Ministers Association that offered Bible instruction to high school students. He taught two hours a day at Arlington Heights High School. He also was a past treasurer of the ministers' association. During an association luncheon honoring Dr. Durham on May 8, 1961, Fort Worth Mayor John Justin declared the day "Dr. T. E. Durham Day."

"Dr. Durham represents the highest ideals of the church and his Christian influence and spirit have been felt in Fort Worth for over 35 years," the Rev. A. E. Ellis, the association's incoming president, said in a 1961 *Star Telegram* article. Dr. Durham was president of Homestead Child Placement Agency, which cared for unwed mothers and helped place babies in homes. He also was active in the Tarrant Baptist Association for more than 50 years and was past president of the Community Voice, a Mason, and a member of the Moslah Temple Shrine. Dr. Durham was in charge of arrangements for the Billy Graham Crusade when the evangelist came to Fort Worth in 1951. He was the widower of Hassie Delia Durham. The family suggests memorials to Arlington Heights Baptist Church. Survivor: Daughter, Helen L. Spuhler of Fort Worth.

Dr. Durham and Homestead Maternity Home

The back story of how Dr. Durham and Pearl Slaughter met is unclear, and numerous theories of their meeting exist among those who were impacted by the maternity home and adoption services. The most likely scenarios are simple ones. Pearl and her husband may have attended Arlington Heights Baptist Church where Dr. Durham served as pastor, or Dr. Durham could have met Pearl when he stopped by her Colonial Hotel Café, a short walk from his home and from the church, for coffee or for lunch. Some individuals maintain the minister and the hotel owner, through their respective positions, forged an early, and somewhat unlikely, partnership. Pearl Slaughter owned and operated properties where unwed mothers could live in privacy until they delivered their babies. And Dr. Durham's contacts with church members and others in Fort Worth's business, medical, and legal communities facilitated the placement of babies born to these mothers with childless couples who wanted to adopt. Hints of rumors allegedly existed throughout the community that couples who wanted to adopt a baby could attend Sunday services at Arlington Heights Baptist Church and pick up a baby a few houses away at Dr. Durham's residence. Without a doubt, Dr. Durham's relationships with other Baptist ministers in Texas, South Carolina, his home state, and in cities throughout the South and Southwest, allowed him to recommend Homestead Maternity Home and its adoption agency to hundreds, if not thousands, of other ministers who counseled unwed mothers and childless couples.

Interestingly, Homestead documents from the late 1950's list Pearl Slaughter as the home's first Executive Director, but Dr. Durham's name is noticeably absent on any Homestead letterheads and in Fort Worth City Directory listings until the early 1960's. This fact can be explained by Mrs. Slaughter's dismissal by the Homestead Hospital and Child Placement Agency's Board of Directors, and Dr. Durham's apparent election by the Board as Executive Director of the former entity's successor organization, Homestead Maternity Home and Child Placement Agency. Between 1963 and 1971, Dr. Durham's name appeared in one or more listings in each Fort Worth City Directory and Polk's Directory published during that time. These listings show the minister's name associated with Homestead Maternity Home at 1250 W. Rosedale and with Homestead's Child Placement Agency at 1028 5th Street. In the advertisements, Dr. Durham's name was predominantly displayed as *"Director.* The section location of the directory listings varied according to the year the directory was published, but the advertisements most often appeared in the alphabetical white page listings and under section headings in the yellow page listings such as *"Maternity Homes, Child Placing Agencies, and Homes and Sanitariums."*

On June 24, 1966, Dr. Durham completed a state generated form entitled *"Information Sheet on Staff Members"* requested during a recertification of the child placement agency's license. The State Department of Public Welfare, Child Welfare Division Form 1, apparently completed in Dr. Durham's own handwriting, states he was a seventy-five year old man, whose job title as "Executive Director" included duties he described as "Full charge of all operations." Other information available on the form indicated Dr. Durham was paid $6,000.00 annually and that he had received a Bachelor's Degree and had attended Furman University and "Southwestern," where he received a Master's Degree in Theology and a PhD. His listed experience included thirty and one-half years as pastor of Arlington Heights Baptist Church, five years as a hospital superintendent, two years as superintendent of a high school, and a total of forty years of experience in counseling.

Chapter 5

Homestead Doctors

According to *Polk's City Directory*, there were three hundred and eight physicians practicing in Fort Worth in 1968. At least three of these physicians, Dr. Hugh Parchman, Jr., Dr. Jack Llewellyn Turner, and Dr. A. I. Goldberg, provided prenatal care to expectant mothers who lived at Homestead Maternity Home during the 1960s and delivered their babies in All Saints Hospital, Harris Hospital, and St. Joseph's Hospital in Fort Worth.

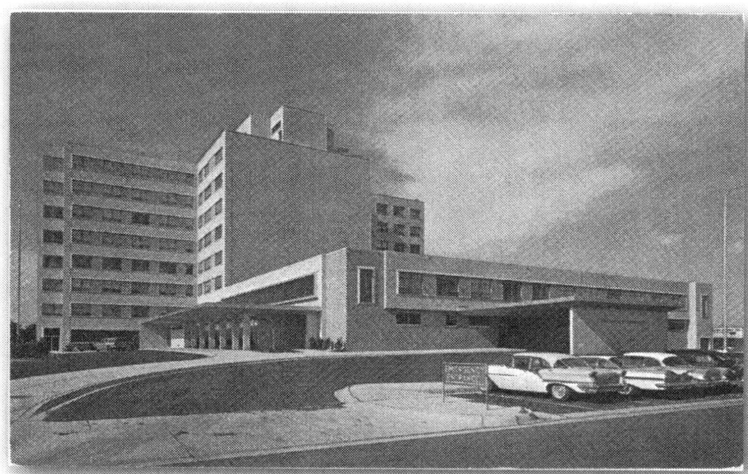

Harris Hospital, circa 1960. Photo Collections, Tarrant County Archives.

All Saints Hospital, circa 1965. Photo Collections, Tarrant County Archives.

St. Joseph's Hospital, circa 1960. Photo Collections, Tarrant County Archives.

Dr. Frank Cohen, M.D.

A Fort Worth pediatrician who allegedly examined and treated babies born during Homestead's early operation maintained a medical office for years at 715 S. Henderson near the city's hospital district. A Baylor Medical School graduate and World War II veteran, Dr. Cohen began practicing as a pediatric specialist in Fort Worth in 1946. Early twentieth century census records indicate Frank was born in Texas, one of eight children born to his Lithuanian-born parents, Mendel Cohen and his wife, Fannie Shimmer Cohen. Mendel Cohen supported his large family by operating a grocery store on Cleveland Street in Dallas, Texas. According to the *U.S. Census of 1940*, Frank, age 26, and his wife, the former Helen Gertrude Markusfeld were living in Chicago, Illinois, where he was a "resident intern" at the county hospital. Most likely, the hospital referenced was Cook County Hospital. Helen Cohen was born in 1916 in Bell County, Texas, to Russian-born parents, Sarah L. Robin and Phillip Markusfeld. Prior to her marriage to Frank, Helen had lived with her parents in Waco, Texas, where her father worked with his brother, Ben, in a produce company later named Markusfeld Banana Co. On July 29, 1975, Helen Cohen died in Harris Hospital at the age of 59, due to complications from a genetic disease diagnosed several months earlier. She was buried in the Beth-El Section of Greenwood Cemetery in Fort Worth. Less than a year later, on May 22, 1976, Dr. Cohen married Sara Elizabeth Goldblatt, a former Dallas teacher and widow of J. Morris Goldgar.

During the years Dr. Cohen was a resident of Fort Worth, he was a member and officer of several civic organizations, including the Underprivileged Child Committee, where he served as chairman. Dr. Cohen also served as vice president of the Tarrant County Medical Society, chairman of the Society's Public Health Advisory Committee, and past member of the Medical Committee of Tarrant County Citizens. In 1964, he was chairman of the final phase of "Operation Sugarcube," a program *"designed to provide mass polio immunization to Tarrant County citizens,"* and he was an active member of the Tarrant County Day Care Association. According to an article published in the

March 15, 1965 edition of Fort Worth's *Star Telegram*, Dr. Cohen was honored by the Sertoma Club in a ceremony at Hotel Texas, where he was presented with the 1965 Service-to-Mankind Award for his *"concentrated practice in the field of health and welfare for youth."* At the age of 92, Dr. Cohen passed away in Fort Worth.

Dr. Abraham Isaac Goldberg, M.D.

Early Homestead brochures confirm Dr. Goldberg's affiliation with Homestead Maternity Home when it was located at 3600 Crescent, but very little information exists about his actual association with the facility. At least one of the young women who lived at the Crescent location recalled someone on the Homestead staff drove her to Dr. Goldberg's office in downtown Fort Worth for prenatal checkups. Abraham Isaac Goldberg was born on May 10, 1901, in Maryland, where he lived with his Lithuanian-born parents, Benjamin Phillip Goldberg and Sarah Roddy Goldberg.

In 1930, young Dr. Goldberg was enumerated as a *"lodger"* in the West 4th Street home of James P. Anderson, a Fort Worth accountant, and his wife, Anna. Additional details on the *U.S. Census* recorded in 1930 showed A. I. Goldberg was a 28-year old unmarried physician who practiced medicine and surgery and that two other businessmen also rented rooms or apartments in the Anderson residence. Two years later, the *Fort Worth City Directory* identified Dr. A. I. Goldberg as a *"physician"* who practiced medicine at 906 Burkburnett Building in Fort Worth. That same city directory listing identified the doctor's wife as *"Florene,"* and the couple's residence address was shown as 522 W. 4th Street. A review of other publicly available information established that Mrs. Goldberg's maiden name was Florene Richardson and that she lived in Azle, Texas, prior to her marriage. By 1940, the couple had moved into a rented house at 1937 Forest Park Boulevard, and Dr. Goldberg continued to practice medicine in what was listed in the 1940 *U.S. Census* as a *"private practice."* Over thirty years later, Dr.

Goldberg's name appeared in a Fort Worth city directory published in 1971, where he was listed as a physician who practiced general medicine and hypnotherapy in his Summit Avenue office. The 1971 city directory listing also indicated Dr. Goldberg still lived with Florene at the Forest Park Boulevard address. After a long medical career in Fort Worth, it appears Dr. Goldberg may have practiced medicine until shortly before his death on May 10, 1976, at Harris Hospital.

Dr. Hugh Parchman, Jr., M.D.

Personal documents provided by a number of Homestead adoptive parents and adoptees indicate Dr. Parchman had an early association with Homestead Maternity Home and provided prenatal care to pregnant women after the facility opened at 1250 W. Rosedale. Available documents indicate he delivered Homestead babies at Fort Worth hospitals, including Harris Hospital and St. Joseph Hospital. Dr. Parchman was named for his father, a Lamar County, Texas, rural physician who was said to have allowed his young son to accompany him on visits to patients' homes in Lamar County, Texas. Observing his father's work must have inspired young Hugh Parchman to further follow in his father's footsteps by becoming a doctor himself. He received his medical degree from Baylor Medical College in Dallas, Texas, and married Rita Wheeling, also from Lamar County, Texas. In 1969, the couple divorced in Tarrant County, and later, Dr. Parchman and his former wife each remarried. According to Fort Worth city directory data, Dr. Hugh Parchman, Jr., practiced at 921 5th Avenue, just a block away from Homestead's Child Placement Agency at 1028 5th Avenue. Several birth moms interviewed for this book recalled walking the short distance from Homestead Maternity Home to the obstetrician's office for their prenatal check-ups, and one birth mother also recalled the doctor drove her to St. Joseph's Hospital after her water broke on the way to his office. Interestingly, several Homestead birth mothers also remembered Dr. Parchman as pleasant and quite *"good-looking."*

Dr. Jack Llewellyn Turner, M.D.

U. S. Census records establish Jack L. Turner was one of three sons born in Texas to Vivian Shropshire and Charley Turner. Vivian was the oldest child of Walter and Callie Shropshire who were living in Haywood, Georgia, when she was born in early 1900. The reason is unknown, but Walter Shropshire moved his family to Texas before Vivian was 10 years old. According to the *U. S. Census* recorded in 1910, the Shropshire family, including four additional children, lived on 3rd Street in Weatherford, Texas, just west of Fort Worth, where Walter Shropshire worked as a laborer in an ice cream factory. By 1920, Vivien was already married to 29-year old Charley Turner, a lumber salesman, and they were living in Fort Worth with their three-year old son, Charles Culbertson Turner. Between 1920 and 1930, Vivien gave birth to two more sons, Jack L. Turner in 1922, and Louis F. Turner in 1925. In 1930, it appears likely that Vivian and Charley Turner were separated, since she and her three sons were living with her parents, Walter and Callie Shropshire, in their home located at 108 Jessamine Street in Fort Worth. U. S. Census information showed Walter Shropshire was employed as a night watchman on a *"construction job."* Various public records indicate Vivian Turner may have remarried before 1940, since she was absent from the Shropshire household when the *U.S. Census* was recorded that same year. Jack Turner, age 17, and his younger brother, Louis, however, continued to live in their grandparents' household on Jessamine Street. In 1941, Jack Turner graduated from Paschal High School in Fort Worth, where he attained the rank of Lieutenant Colonel in the Cadet Corps. Turner's high school yearbook indicated he was a leader in the program and acted as executive officer of the city unit during a retreat parade held that year at Farrington Field. In the years that followed, Jack Turner attended Texas A&M University and was a member of the Cadet Corps. Turner served in the U.S. Army and later in the U. S. Air Force Medical Corps, where he remained a reserve officer for a number of years.

Turner married Eleanor Joan Urbanic, a former Army nurse, on August 22, 1947, in an Episcopal ceremony in Greenville, Texas. In

1948, he graduated from Tulane University School of Medicine in New Orleans, and on June 5, 1948, he received a license to practice medicine in Louisiana. Interestingly, he remained licensed in that state until December 31, 2008, a period spanning almost sixty years. Although the rationale is unclear, Dr. Turner also was licensed to practice medicine and surgery in California, and his name appeared in the *Board of Medical Examiners of the State of California* directory in 1949, 1955, 1962-63, and 1966-67. Around 1954, after fulfilling his military obligation, the young doctor began practicing obstetrics and gynecology in Fort Worth, Texas. Together, the doctor and former Army nurse raised a large Fort Worth family and were involved in numerous local society and civic activities. A Fort Worth newspaper article published in 1958 profiled Dr. Turner, praising his large obstetrical practice in Fort Worth and his many contributions to the community. In addition, the feature article discussed Dr. Turner's busy family life and his wife's child-rearing and volunteer activities. Eleanor Turner, the mother of the doctor's five children, passed away in early 1972, and later, the doctor married former Project HOPE employee, Barbara Wasciewicz, with whom he had a son.

The earliest listing found for Dr. Turner's medical practice appeared in a Fort Worth city directory published in 1959, when his office location was shown as 515 S. Summit Avenue. That same year, Dr. Turner's name appeared on the letterhead of Homestead Hospital and Child Placement Agency, 3600 Camp Bowie Blvd., stating he was the agency's obstetrician. In the years that followed, and as Dr. Turner's obstetrical practice increased, he established an office at 830 8th Avenue in an area that became Fort Worth's present hospital district. Although evidence of a professional relationship between Dr. Turner and Edna Gladney was not found, historic newspaper advertisements establish the obstetrician rented office space between April 1957 and December 1960 to the well-known founder of Gladney Children's Home. A newspaper article written about Mrs. Gladney and published in later years, indicated she may have rented space from Dr. Turner as early as 1952.

From January 4-9, 1962, Dr. Turner advertised in Fort Worth's *Star Telegram* newspaper announcing he had opened a new maternity center on 8th Ave. The ad read:

Jack L. Turner, MD,
Announces the opening of
Ft. Worth Maternity Center
Obstetrics-Diseases of Women
830 8th Ave ED 6-4716

Several decades later, the building in which Dr. Turner practiced was moved to another location, after he sold the land on which it was located. At least as early as 1959, while he was still in the early years of his practice, Dr. Turner began delivering babies born to Homestead Maternity Home residents at All Saints Episcopal Hospital and Harris Hospital in Fort Worth. Dr. Turner's name appeared on Homestead adoptees' original birth certificates filed with the State of Texas shortly after their births. But his name and the name of the hospital where the adoptees were born were omitted from amended birth certificates issued to adoptive parents after final adoption hearings were held in Tarrant County courts.

While Dr. Turner was seen by numerous members of the Fort Worth community as a socially involved and prominent physician, a few of the Homestead birth mothers interviewed for this book observed a different side of the doctor who delivered their babies. When these expectant mothers visited Dr. Turner for periodic prenatal visits, the man they remember was a serious one who rarely talked and spent very little time with his patients. Many of these young, pregnant women who were going through the most difficult months of their early lives, expected the doctor to talk to them about what to anticipate when they gave birth. Instead, many received only quick and perfunctory exams from an obstetrician they remembered as distant and uninterested.

In addition to his obstetrical practice, Dr. Turner was an active participant in Fort Worth civic affairs. In 1971, he ran for a seat on the Fort Worth

School Board and was defeated. But in 1976, when he ran again, he received sixty percent of the vote in a runoff election again Robert Starr. In March of 1980, an article written by Brian Howard and published in the March 8, 1980 edition of the Fort Worth *Star Telegram,* announced the doctor's *"11th hour"* filing for the school board seat occupied by incumbent board vice president, Mrs. Mollie Lasater. Howard also wrote *"During the two years as a trustee, Turner's outspoken and sometimes abrasive attacks on what he perceived as incompetent staff members, won him few backers among the district's teachers and administrators, an important force in board elections."*

Dr. Turner was a lifelong right-to-life advocate, something that may have been involved in his disagreements with Fort Worth hospitals in the early 1980's. A lawsuit he filed against several Fort Worth hospitals was chronicled in an article entitled *"Right to Life Doctor Sues Hospitals,"* written by Jane Martin and published in Fort Worth's *Star Telegram* on December 31, 1983:

> "A Fort Worth physician filed suit Friday against four hospitals that he contends conspired to terminate his hospital privileges because of his outspoken position against abortion. Doctor Jack L. Turner, an obstetrician-gynecologist and former Fort Worth School Board member, and his wife, Barbara Ann Turner, filed the lawsuit against All Saints Episcopal Hospital, Harris Hospital, St. Joseph Hospital, and Fort Worth Medical Plaza, Inc. Also named in the suit filed in U. S. District Court in Fort Worth are Stanley F. Hupfeld, Administrator of All Saints Hospital; Dr. Robb Rutledge, Chief of Staff at Harris Hospital; and 25 individual physicians at the institutions. Turner said in the lawsuit that on May 28, 1982, All Saints revoked his hospital privileges and then conspired with the three other hospitals to deny him access to those hospitals as well. St. Joseph terminated Turner's staff privileges Jan. 19, 1983. Harris Hospital refused him privileges on Dec. 8, 1982, as did Medical Plaza on Aug. 1, 1983. Turner contends the denials were based on All Saints Hospital's actions. Turner, who had been a member of the medical staff at All Saints for 28 years, asked a

federal judge to order the hospitals to reinstate his staff privileges so he can once more use the hospital facilities to treat his patients. He also seeks $10 million in damages as well as attorneys' fees and an unspecified amount in punitive damages. All Saints administrator Hupfeld said the hospital revoked Turner's privileges in accordance with its by-laws. 'Hospitals are required to routinely review the credentials and competence of their staff members as outlined by the courts and the Joint Commission on Accreditation of Hospitals,' he said. Hupfeld declined further comment. Turner could not be reached for comment Friday night. During his 1976-1978 tenure on the school board, he was a back-to-back conservative known for his classroom visits. He resigned from the board in 1978 to make way for the district's new single-member plan for electing board members. That year, he lost a bid for the board vice-presidency in a run-off election. Turner is represented in the suit by the Houston law firm of Richard "Racehorse" Haynes. In his suit, Turner said the 'group boycott' by the hospitals amounts to a violation of federal anti-trust laws, since the four hospitals monopolize hospital care in the Tarrant County area. 'By pooling their economic power in conspiring to bar Turner from admitting patients into local hospitals, the hospitals denied him his livelihood of practicing medicine in the county,' the suit says. Turner also contends he was denied his constitutional rights by being denied the opportunity of adequately answering charges lodged during meetings of the hospital's executive committee. In addition, his right of free speech was 'chilled' when hospital revoked his staff privileges for punishment 'for being a maverick and a right-to-life advocate,' says the lawsuit, which does not elaborate on Turner's anti-abortion activities. Turner also contends he was libeled and that his reputation was defamed as the result of the hospital's action. 'This has resulted in continuing financial injury and has impeached the reputation [of Turner] by casting doubts on [his] abilities as a doctor,' before his peers in the medical profession and his patients, the suit says."

The lawsuit was assigned to U.S. District Judge David O. Belew, and according to various accounts, Dr. Turner lost the suit. Throughout the years Dr. Turner practiced in Fort Worth, he must have delivered tens of thousands of infants in Tarrant County, Texas, including those born to Homestead mothers. On July 31, 2016, Dr. Turner passed away at the age of 93, and his numerous medical, military, and civic accomplishments were detailed in an extensive obituary published in Fort Worth's *Star-Telegram* on August 2, 2016.

Jack L. Turner, M.D., a retired physician, passed away Sunday, July 31, 2016, at his home. Service: 9 a.m. Friday, at St. John's Anglican Church, 2401 College Avenue, Fort Worth. The Rev. William T. Estes will officiate and The Rev. David F. Klein will assist. Entombment: Greenwood Mausoleum. Visitation: 4 to 6 p.m. Thursday at Harveson and Cole. Pallbearers will be David, Michael, and Patrick Pacheco, and Brad, Turner and Clayton Rejebian. Memorials: Should friends desire, gifts in his memory may be made to St. John's Anglican Church, 2401 College Avenue, Fort Worth, Texas 76110. Jack Llewellyn Turner was born Dec. 10, 1922, in Fort Worth to Charles C. Turner and Vivian Shropshire Turner. He graduated from R. L. Paschal High School in Fort Worth, Texas, A&M in 1946, and from Tulane University School of Medicine in 1948. He completed his internship and residency at Charity Hospital of Louisiana in New Orleans in 1954. He was in the ROTC at Texas A&M and called to active duty serving in the U.S. Army from 1943 to 1946 in the Heavy Weapons Division of the infantry. During this time, he was stationed at Camp Roberts. He was recalled to active duty as a Captain in the U.S. Air Force Medical Corps from 1951 to 1953 (Korean War) and was stationed at Keesler Air Force Base in Biloxi, Mississippi. Upon completion of his residency, he returned to Fort Worth in 1954 to begin private practice. He practiced obstetrics and gynecology (OB/GYN) for 50 years, retiring in 2004. For approximately ten years, from 1957 to 1967, he was an assistant professor of OB/GYN at Parkland Southwestern Medical School in Dallas. At the same time, he was the obstetrician for Homestead Child Placement Agency, which was under the direction of Pastor T. E. Durham, PhD. For years, he was a volunteer physician at the free clinics of John Peter Smith, St. Joseph, and Harris Hospitals, and was the obstetrician for Carswell Air Force Base. Dr. Turner was a member of many professional organizations including Tarrant County Medical Society (Life Member), Texas Medical Association (Life Member), American College of Surgeons, North Texas Chapter (Life Member), American College of OB/GYN (Life Member), Texas Association of OB/GYN (Life Member), Association of OB/GYN, Central Association of OB/GYN (Life Member), Southern Medical Association, American Society of Abdominal Surgeons, Tulane Medical Alumni Association, Conrad Collins Society of OB/GYN of Tulane University, Association of Professors of GYN/Obstetrics, Fellow of the American College of Obstetrics and Gynecology, and Fellow of the American College of Surgeons. Other affiliations include: American Red Cross (35 years), Family and Individual Services Agency, Tarrant County Mental Health Association, Tarrant County Arts Council, American Cancer Society, National Polio Foundation, Fort Worth Knife and Fork Club, and the Fort Worth Opera Association (18 years on the board and Vice-President). He was a member of the Board of Education for the Fort Worth Independent School District (1976-1978), serving during the time of the controversy over single-member districts. Dr. Turner was one of two members on the board who volunteered to resign, allowing Judge Mahon the authority to go ahead and implement the single member districts. Otherwise, Judge Mahon would have had to vacate all the seats on the board to satisfy the court order. Dr. Turner served several 2-month tours as a volunteer professor of OB/GYN Hospital Ship HOPE and Care-Medico between 1970 and 1990, teaching physicians, interns, and residents in the following countries: Afghanistan (two tours), Brazil (three tours), Indonesia, Jamaica, Tunisia, and St. Vincent Islands. He served as a volunteer physician and consultant at the Afghan OB/GYN Hospital for the Afghan Refugee Program in Peshawar, Pakistan. He loved to travel and traveled the globe, having visited over 50 countries. He recently talked fondly about one of his last trips, which was to China. He was also a 32nd Degree Scottish Rite Mason for over 70 years. Dr. Turner was a life-long and faithful member of St. John's Anglican Church, which he joined in 1947. He served several terms on the Vestry and as senior warden. We celebrate his life of service as a dedicated physician, loyal friend, and vibrant volunteer. He loved his medical practice and patients. He delivered thousands of babies and loved that aspect of his practice. Dr. Turner was also a pro-life physician that enjoyed politics and was a long-time member of the Republican Party. He had an outgoing personality with an intellectual and amiable sense of humor, often joking and laughing. Jack had a deep love for his country and could recite a wealth of history. Dr. Turner touched many thousands of lives through his medical practice and never met a stranger. The family would like to express a special thanks and appreciation to Dr. Allan Kelly and his staff for their compassionate and professional care over the years; Dr. Turner delivered Drs. Allan and Robert Kelly. A special thanks also to Mr. Jay King for his weekly visits and Bible study. Dr. Turner was preceded in death by his first wife, Eleanor; his son, Dr. Jack L. Turner II; his brothers, Charles and Louie Turner; and his mother and stepfather, Vivian and Calvin Smith. Survivors: Wife, Barbara; children, Dyer Ramahi, Daly Turner and Conrad Turner and wife, Irma, Sherwood Rejebian and husband, Brad, and Christopher Turner and wife, Holly; grandchildren, Ahmed Ramahi and wife, Rosa, Charlotte Stolzfus, Turner and Clayton Rejebian, and Carter, Gage, and Knox Turner; great-grandchildren, Zachariah and Arianna Ramahi, his Brazilian family, Nelson Macedo and wife, Tamara, and their children, Lucas and Lucy; special and devoted friend, George Joe, PhD; and nieces and nephews, Betty Pacheco, Jacki Turner, and Louie Turner.

Dr. Harry H. Womack, Jr., M.D.

Harry Hall Womack, Jr., Homestead's longtime pediatrician, was born on April 23, 1921, in the small east Grayson County town of Whitesboro, Texas. His parents were Harry H. Womack, a bookkeeper, and his wife, Dorothy Scheid Womack. Harry, Jr. was the couple's first child and as public records later established, he would be their only child. In 1930, as the country was still suffering aftershocks of the Great Depression, the *U.S.*

Census recorded that year showed Harry Sr. had moved his wife and eight-year old son to Orange, Texas. Harry Sr. managed a service station, and he lived with his wife and son on Cypress Street in a house they rented for thirty-five dollars per month. When the census was recorded, the Womack household also included Dorothy's 22-year old twin nephews, Horace Scheid, a clerk at the filling station, and Morris Scheid, who worked as an *"operator"* at a creosoting plant.

By April of 1940, Harry Womack, Sr. had moved his family back to north Texas, where they were listed as residents of Oakland Avenue in Denton, Texas, when the *U.S. Census* was recorded that month. At the time of the enumeration, Womack household residents included 46-year old Harry Sr., the proprietor of a milling company, his 45-year old wife, Dorothy, 18-year old Harry Jr., and John A. Womack, the elder Harry's 77-year old widowed father. Other census details indicated Harry Jr. was a third-year college student who worked as a biology assistant. The name of the college that Harry Jr. attended in 1940 likely was North Texas Teacher's College in Denton, now the University of North Texas, since he and his family lived near the college. An early 1940s listing in the *Fort Worth City Directory* showed Harry Jr., a student, and his mother, Dorothy, lived at 4400 James Avenue, near Paschal High School, the Baptist Theological Seminary campus, and Texas Christian University. Other available resources revealed the James Avenue address also was the residence of young Harry's paternal grandparents, John A. Womack and his wife, Elizabeth Hall Womack.

According to the Harry Hall Womack, Jr. Papers (1940-1948) in *The Texas Collection* at Baylor University, the young medical student began studying medicine at The University of Texas Medical Branch at Galveston in 1940. After graduating in 1943, Dr. Womack served an internship at the Kansas City (MO) General Hospital, and later, he joined the U.S. Army. Before leaving to go overseas, the young Army officer married Margaret Harris, a young woman he had met in Galveston. During his military tour, Dr. Womack served as a Captain in the U.S. Army Medical Corps in England. When the doctor completed his overseas assignment, he began a pediatric practice in Fort Worth that would continue for almost two decades.

A listing in the *Fort Worth City Directory* published in 1949 showed the young pediatrician's medical office was located at 1422 Pennsylvania Avenue, near the center of Fort Worth's current hospital district. This directory listing also indicated Dr. Womack and his wife, Margaret, lived at 2825 6th Avenue in a residential area of Fort Worth known then and now as Ryan Place. Other available public documents established that Margaret Womack was a daughter of Alabama-born Brantly Calloway Harris, a wealthy Galveston lawyer who once had served as the island's mayor. During the years Margaret Womack and her husband lived in Fort Worth, she raised four children, three sons and a daughter. In addition, Mrs. Womack taught high school English for a time, served for four years during the fifties as a junior editorial assistant for *Mademoiselle Magazine*, and organized and led a political organization known as *"Womanpower for Eisenhower."* By 1952, Harry and Margaret Womack had moved to 4811 E. Winthrop, one of several streets above West Vickery in Fort Worth, where newer housing was available. Built in the fifties, the housing area just east of Ridglea Country Club offered residents a convenient commute to downtown Fort Worth, the city's hospital district, and for Dr. Womack, a short drive to his growing pediatric practice in the 200 Professional Building. Interestingly, Dr. Womack's residence was a very short distance from Homestead Maternity Home's early location at 3600 Crescent. Apparently, Dr. Womack was a convert to the Catholic faith. Shortly after he was received into the Church, the following article appeared in the February 15, 1958 issue of *The Texas Catholic*:

> "Dr. Harry Womack was recently elected by the staff of doctors of St. Joseph Hospital to the position of chief of pediatrics department. Dr. Womack who lives with his wife and four children at 1520 Thomas Place, is also 1958 president of the Fort Worth Pediatric Society. He is a member of St. Patrick Co-Cathedral parish, having been received into the church a year ago by Msgr. Joseph P. Erbrick. The physician's office for the treatment of infants and children is at 1424 W. Peter Smith."

Homestead documents provided by adoptees and adoptive parents, some dating back to 1958, establish Dr. Womack served as staff pediatrician for Homestead Hospital and Child Placement Agency, later known as Homestead Maternity Hospital and Child Placement Agency. The exact date Dr. Womack's affiliation with Homestead began, however, is unknown. In the late fifties and throughout most of the sixties, Dr. Womack's name and pediatric specialty appeared on Homestead Child Placement Agency letterheads. A review of adoption expense statements given to Homestead adoptive parents and provided by adoptees during research for this book, indicated Dr. Womack initially charged a fifteen dollar fee for each newborn baby. That fee allegedly covered the initial hospital examination of each baby born to a Homestead mother and subsequently placed for adoption through Homestead's agency. Although Dr. Womack's newborn examination fee increased somewhat over the years, it was one of the lesser fees charged Homestead's adoptive parents.

Other information obtained from interviewees and documents in their possession establish the pediatrician's years of involvement with Homestead, and the pediatric care he provided babies placed for adoption through the child placement agency, continued until shortly before his death. Details included on Dr. Womack's Texas death certificate show the well-known Fort Worth pediatrician suffered a fatal heart attack in his home at 1520 Thomas Place in Fort Worth. Also, according to his death certificate, Dr. Womack was pronounced dead on August 12, 1968 at Harris Hospital. According to his obituary published in Fort Worth's *Star-Telegram* newspaper, *"He was a fellow of the American Academy of Pediatricians, and was a delegate to the State of Texas Medical Society in which he led a successful fight against liberalization of abortion laws."*

Chapter 6

The Lawyers

Throughout the history of Homestead Maternity Home and Child Placement Agency, available records show two Fort Worth attorneys, Mike Eugene Powell and Harold Valderas, primarily were responsible for the legal work adoptions required. The legal process for adopting a Homestead baby began when the birth mother signed a relinquishment form presented to her soon after she had given birth. Some birth mothers interviewed recalled Homestead staff members, usually the social worker and one other individual, brought the document to their hospital rooms. While many of these women signed the documents when they were presented to them, a few birth mothers recall delaying their signatures until just before discharge from the hospital. But what most of these women remember clearly were the tears they cried before, during, and after they signed the document declaring their newborn babies "wards of the state" and subsequently, allowing them to be placed for adoption.

Based on personal knowledge of Teri Davidson, a former Homestead foster mother who cared for babies between 1965 and 1967, the two staff members who obtained birth mothers' signatures on the relinquishment documents were Jeane Wilkerson, a Homestead secretary who also worked for Harold Valderas, a Fort Worth lawyer who handled agency adoptions in the mid-late 1960s, and Myrtle Swann, secretary to Dr. Durham, Homestead's Executive Director. Allegedly, Wilkerson and Swann visited the birth mother in her hospital room on the first day of her stay, and if she refused to sign the relinquishment document or said she was not yet ready to do so, the two women left and returned the following day. If the birth mother refused to sign the document on the second visit, the Homestead employees notified Dr. Durham, gave him the relinquishment document, and he obtained the birth mother's signature. Not one birth mother interviewed for this book recalls meeting with or being visited by an attorney or anyone else who acknowledged representing the attorney's office. And not any of these women remember anyone advising them of the six months' period each birth mother had to change her mind about giving up her baby for adoption. Birth mothers who did ask if they could change their minds about giving up their babies were told they would be required to pay all expenses incurred, including room and board at Homestead, prenatal care, labor and delivery charges, and hospital expenses for themselves and their babies. For most birth mothers, repayment of these expenses was an impossibility, and the hopelessness of the situation often compounded their feelings of sadness and helplessness.

Mike Eugene Powell, J.D.

As early as 1958, Mike E. Powell was listed on Homestead Maternity Home and adoption agency's brochures as the organization's attorney, and available documents prove Powell was Homestead's attorney of record until 1964. It is unclear how Powell's association with the maternity home and adoption service first began, but it is entirely possible he may have been offering legal services to prospective parents who were adopting through other Fort Worth agencies.

Powell was born in Oklahoma on November 5, 1915, to Otis H. Powell, 42, born in Kansas, and his French-born wife, Virginia Marshall Powell, age 39. By 1920, the Powell family had moved to Fort Worth where Otis Powell was employed as a superintendent for a pipeline company. According to the *U.S. Census* recorded in 1920, Otis H. Powell owned the house in which his family lived at 1100 Jennings, very near St. Patrick's Cathedral and the current location of Fort Worth's Omni Hotel. The Powell household included Bethany, Otis Powell's thirteen-year old daughter from a previous marriage, Marvin A. Lang, his thirteen-year old stepson, and four children by his current wife, Virginia. The younger children were identified on the census as Yula, 8; Patrick, 6; Mike E., 4; and Paul, 2 years old. In addition, Otis Powell's 68-year old widowed mother, Josephine Flynn, lived in the family's home on Jennings. In 1930, fourteen year old Mike E. Powell was enumerated in his father's household on the census recorded that year. Bethany Powell, Marvin Lang, and Yula Powell were absent from the household, an indication they were living on their own. In addition to Mike, the family included four more sons, Paul, 12; Pat, 10; John, 9; and the youngest son, Archibald, who was 7 years old. Census record details indicate Otis Powell was employed as superintendent of an oil company and had moved his bustling family to a larger residence at 1958 Hemphill Street in Fort Worth. Additional data included on the 1930 census showed the house on Hemphill was valued at $15,000.

Although very little is known about Mike E. Powell's teenage years, it appears he later enrolled at Southern Methodist University in Dallas, where he received a law degree. While attending law school, Powell met another SMU student named Anne Elizabeth Ambrose, whom he married. Anne was the daughter of Warren Delaware Ambrose, a successful Fort Worth oilman, and his wife, Anne Elizabeth Matthews Ambrose. In 1940, the *U.S. Census* listed Mike Powell as the 24-year old head of a household that included Anne E. Powell, his 21-year old wife, and their two-year old son, Mike, Jr. The couple lived next-door to Anne's parents, who had two children still living at home, Warren D. Ambrose, Jr. and Joe Ambrose. The address shown on the census indicated the Ambrose and Powell families lived near Azle, in the vicinity of Eagle Mountain Lake. According to a *Fort Worth City Directory* listing, Powell practiced law in downtown Fort Worth, in close proximity to his father-in-law's offices located at 614 Dan Waggoner Building. By 1945, Powell and his wife apparently had purchased a house at 3605 S. Bellaire Drive in Fort Worth, since the city directory published that year showed Powell, his wife, Annie E. Powell, and their three children as residents at that address. The directory also listed the Powell family's second residence at Eagle Mountain Lake. Since the residence was located near his in-laws' lake house known as the "Eagle's Nest," most likely it was the same house occupied by Mike and Annie Powell during the early years of their marriage.

Between 1945 and 1947, Mike and Ann Powell apparently separated and eventually divorced. Evidence of the separation and possible divorce appeared in a Fort Worth city directory published in 1947, when Mike E. Powell and *"Mavis"* were listed as residents of 3507 ½ Bellaire Drive. The exact date of Powell's divorce from Anne Ambrose Powell was not located, but available public information indicates Powell married Mavis Roberts following his divorce from Anne. Interestingly, Powell apparently moved his law office out of the Dan Waggoner Building between 1947, when Warren Ambrose passed away, and 1949. But according to the *Fort Worth City Directory* published in 1949, Powell's law office again was located in the Dan Waggoner Building in downtown Fort Worth. Interestingly, the law office was in close proximity to its former location and to the offices of Powell's former father-in-law, Warren Ambrose. In 1956, Fort Worth's city directory listed Powell's residence, where he lived with his second wife, Mavis Roberts Powell, as 3915 Clayton Road, and his office address as 614 Dan Waggoner Building. The 1960 city directory indicated Powell's office address was 206 W. 6th Street in Fort Worth, the street address for the Dan Waggoner Building.

W. T. Waggoner Building, Fort Worth, Texas. Photo Collections, Tarrant County Archives.

A review of correspondence from Powell to prospective Homestead adoptive parents during the early 1960's, confirmed the attorney's office address continued to be in the Dan Waggoner Building. Interviews with adoptees and their adoptive parents established that many Homestead clients received phone calls from Powell's Fort Worth law office asking them to meet at the office to pay adoption fees, sign paperwork and to pick up their babies. Several of these adoptive parents remember the babies were brought to the law office by a woman who wore a nurse's uniform and cap or more often, a Homestead social worker. In one instance, the adoptive mother identified the nurse as Ruth Hamilton, who worked at Harris Hospital. As Homestead's attorney, Powell performed legal services for the facility's adoption agency for at least five years, and without a doubt, he may have been involved with hundreds of Homestead adoptions that took place during the years the facility operated.

Attorney Powell's role in Homestead adoptions was mentioned in a document dated September 12, 1960 and signed by Mrs. Ruby Piester, Regional Child Welfare Supervisor, which alleged that Powell and Mrs. Slaughter, Homestead's director, were arranging placements of children according to the "financial ability" of adoptive parents. In addition, the document stated Miss Bradford, a Homestead social worker, said *"Mr. Powell offered a child to a couple at one price and a few hours later while heavily intoxicated, demanded larger payment."* The report also stated Miss Bradford reported *"the intoxication of the Executive and Attorney Powell while on duty is frequent."*

Also, in early September 1960, Richard Leon Pettigrew and his wife, Ruth Alice Pettigrew, of Lubbock, Texas, filed a lawsuit for an injunction in the 99th District Court in Lubbock, against Homestead Hospital and Child Placement Agency of Fort Worth. In the complaint, Mr. and Mrs. Pettigrew alleged Mike E. Powell, the attorney representing the Fort Worth child placement agency, had informed the couple the female minor child in their care, Linda Ruth, would be removed from their home without further notice. According to the complainants, Powell's warning came after he learned Mr. Pettigrew's salary had slipped below the required $6,000.00 annual income requirement, and Mrs. Pettigrew had continued to work part-time in the six months period after they took the child known as *"Baby Girl Locklear"* home with them. On September 6, 1960, Judge Howard C. Davison granted a temporary restraining order and ordered an independent home study by the Lubbock County Child Welfare office on the child's behalf. On September 16, 1960, Judge Davison signed a temporary injunction preventing Homestead from removing the child from the Pettigrew's home. And on October 14, 1960, the Judge ordered the Defendant to hold a final adoption hearing approximately six months in the future, and no later than April 1, 1961. Interestingly, Harold Valderas, a Fort Worth municipal judge at the time, represented the Defendant in the lawsuit, documenting the appearance that Valderas already may have been connected to the Homestead Child Placement Agency well before he became Homestead's official legal counsel.

In a later document, dated October 21, 1960 and entitled *"Discrepancies in the Operation of Homestead Agency,"* Mrs. Mary Barrett, Homestead Social Worker, who *"worked part-time for the agency doing adoptive studies…"* reported that she saw *"correspondence in Mr. Powell's office from Louis Bond Closser, Box 156, Ysleta Station, Texas."* According to Mrs. Barrett, Closser advised Attorney Powell that *"he had married a Mexican girl and he knew of high class Mexican people who would marry white girls who had made mistakes."* According to the report, the letter *"implied the Agency would send the girls to Mexico and pay $25.00 per month room and board until such time as permanent plans could be made for them."* The report also indicated Powell replied to Closser in a letter which *"listed all the Agency employees, including Mrs. Barrett, Miss Carolyn Bradford, and Mrs. Swann, Secretary, as well as Mrs. Slaughter, stating he was sending pictures when plans were completed"* and indicated a *"designated person would accompany the girls to Acapulco."* The October 1960 report indicates Mrs. Barrett believed *"the purpose of this is to take girls into Mexico to place their babies with Anglo Americans."* After Mrs. Barrett saw the correspondence, she *"became angry with Mr. Powell, stating he had no right to list her name and that she did not want to be involved in such activity, he denied any such plans."* Complete transcriptions of the discrepancy allegations and the report appear in the appendix of this book.

Interestingly, Powell and his second wife Mavis adopted a baby girl from Homestead, whom they named Michelle Eugenia Powell, apparently for her adoptive father. An interview with Michelle Powell, conducted by the author in mid-2016, appears later in this book, along with interviews of other Homestead adoptees. Sadly, Michelle was barely four years old when her father died of pancreatic cancer on July 22, 1964. Powell's obituary, reprinted below, appeared in Fort Worth's *Star Telegram* on July 24, 1964.

Mike Eugene Powell, 48, residence 3925 Clayton Rd. West, passed away Wednesday. Member of First Christian Church, Tarrant Bar Association, Texas Bar Association, American Bar Association, and Attorney-at-Law. Survivors: Wife, Mavis. Four sons, Mike Eugene Powell, Jr., Waco, Warren Ambrose Powell, Denton, Ronald Eugene Powell, TAFB, Oklahoma, Robert Eugene Powell, Fort Worth. Daughter, Michele Eugenia Powell, Fort Worth. Mother, Mrs. O. H. Powell. Four brothers, Marvin, and Archie Powell, Breckinridge, John Powell, Aztec, NM, Paul Powell, LeMarque. Sister, Mrs. John Harmon, Fort Worth. Three grandchildren, Mark Ambrose Powell, Mike Eugene Powell III, Paige Elizabeth Powell. Services 4 p.m. Friday, Robertson-Mueller-Harper Chapel, 1500 8th Ave., Dr. T. E. Durham, officiating. Internment: Greenwood. Arrangements: Ray Crowder, 2836 Hemphill, ED 5-1213.

Harold Luis Valderas, J.D.

Born in New York on December 17, 1923, Harold Luis Valderas likely experienced a childhood of uncertainties and may have been a foster child himself. The first time young Harold appeared on a *U.S. Census* was in 1930, when he was enumerated as a six-year old in a household headed by Clotilde J. Dietz, a fifty-eight year old widow. Mrs. Dietz's son, Edward A. Dietz, a clerk in a radiator shop, also lived in the household. Mrs. Dietz owned the house located at 118 Wabash Street in the Ozone Park area of Queens, New York, and its value was $6500. Since the census listed young Harold's relationship to the head of the household as *"boarder,"* it seems unlikely he is related to Mrs. Dietz or to her son. This particular *census record*, which lists place of birth for the individual enumerated and for the individual's parents, establishes Harold Valderas and his mother were born in New York, but his father had been born in Chile. The obvious question is this: Where were Harold's parents in 1930 when he was enumerated in Clotilde Dietz's household?

When the *U.S. Census* of 1940 was recorded for New York City, Harold Valderas, a U.S. born 16 year-old, was enumerated in a household headed by his 39-year old father, Louis Valderas, on W. 151st Street in New York City. Census details indicated the elder Valderas was born in Chile and was married to twenty-three year old, Puerto Rican born, Carmelina. Her 22-year old brother, Ivan Perez, also lived in the household. Harold's father worked as an assistant steward on a steamer ship, and his brother-in-law, Ivan, was employed as a laborer on the Beach Road trail crew. Other details included on the *census record* indicated Carmelina had lived in Ponce, P.R. in 1935, and Louis earned thirty dollars per month for forty-eight hours of work per week. Neighbors living near the Valderas family worked as elevator operators, clerks, stenographers, a church caretaker, and a Navy mechanic, and many of these individuals had been born in countries outside the United States, including Puerto Rico, Colombia, and Venezuela. According to Valderas family history information posted online by Valderas's son, Harold Michael Valderas, Carmelina Brun was his father's second wife. She was born on May 17, 1917, in Penuelas, P.R., to Maria Martinez and Angel P. Brun. It appears likely that Louis and Carmelina already were married when she arrived in the Port of New York City on May 17, 1939, on a vessel named the *"Puerto Rico."* Apparently, Louis Valderas and his first wife, New York born Elizabeth Cunningham, had separated when Harold was very young, and his biological mother's somewhat transient lifestyle apparently prevented him from living with her when he was a young child.

When young Valderas became old enough to do so, he joined the U. S. Air Force and began a career that culminated with his retirement many years later as a reserve officer in Tarrant County, Texas. World War II enlistment records establish Valderas lived in New York City when he volunteered for the U.S. Air Corps on April 9, 1942. The terms of his enlistment at the time were *"Enlistment for the duration of the War or other emergency, plus six months, subject to the discretion of the President or otherwise according to law."* Not only did Valderas's military service allow him to experience life outside his native New York City, it also offered him educational opportunities that may not have been available to him otherwise. He graduated college, attended law school, and received his law license in November 1954. The next year, Valderas opened his own law office. On December

30, 1965, Luis Harold Valderas married Spanish-born Marisa Louisa Garcia, and they had three children before divorcing in Dallas County on September 22, 1999.

For more than five decades, Harold Valderas practiced law, served as Fort Worth's City Judge, ran unsuccessfully for the office of Mayor of Fort Worth in 1969, and continued to serve as a distinguished Air Force Reserve Officer, retiring as a Lieutenant Colonel. In 1977, Texas Governor Dolph Briscoe rewarded Valderas for his legal and civic accomplishments when he appointed him to the office of State District Judge. An article written by Jim Atkinson and Rowland Stiteler and published in the August 1979 edition of *D Magazine*, indicated not everyone, however, was pleased with the Judge's personal and professional habits or with his legal decisions.

WORST JUDGE IN FORT WORTH
HAROLD L. VALDERAS
233rd District Court
SMU law school. Admitted to bar 1954.
Appointed to bench 1977.

It is fitting that Gov. Dolph Briscoe appointed Judge Valderas to the district bench on April 1, 1977. Motivated by a massive ego for which there is scant basis, his accomplishments or his abilities, Judge Valderas makes it obvious that he sees the courtroom as merely another step on the political ladder. Lawyers who have tried cases in his court say he treats attorneys for both sides of each case like unwanted step-children and takes an incredibly long time to make the simplest of decisions. That's possibly because he spends most of his time and talents promoting himself. Valderas obviously decided long ago that the road to success was not in his limited legal abilities, but in the political arena. He's done everything to build his image from becoming the consummate club-joiner to getting a hair transplant. That strategy has obviously worked. He was able to use his connections to propel himself from a mediocre career as a Fort Worth municipal judge to the district bench. Critics contend he has gained a lot of mileage from his Mexican-American-sounding surname (he is actually of Puerto Rican descent), while being one of the least tolerant judges in the county towards minorities.

In addition to his military and legal duties, Judge Valderas also served as the attorney for Homestead Maternity Home and Child Placement Agency. According to individuals interviewed for this book and Homestead letterheads bearing his name, Harold Valderas became Homestead's attorney after Mike E. Powell died. The earliest proof of Valderas's involvement with Homestead was in September of 1960, when he represented Mike E. Powell, Homestead's attorney, in a lawsuit filed by adoptive parents in Lubbock, Texas, against the adoption agency and Powell. In August of 1964, shortly after Powell's death, Valderas again represented Homestead Hospital and Child Placement Agency in a lawsuit filed against the organization by Pearl Slaughter, after the former Executive Director claimed she had been illegally discharged and dismissed by less than a quorum of board members. In the years that followed, Valderas continued to represent Homestead, until it closed in the early 1970s, in adoption proceedings for babies born to mothers living at the maternity home and to others who used the services of its child placement agency.

According to many Homestead adoptees who have attempted to gain access to their adoption records throughout the past several decades, the years that Harold Valderas worked as Homestead's attorney represent a period of much uncertainty and many unanswered questions. A number of these concerns continue to exist today, including the possibility Valderas may have issued an unknown number of adoptees' amended birth certificates directly from the bench. This probability arose during the past decade as search angels and others who assist adoptees in finding their birth mothers discovered some birth certificates issued to adoptive parents have numbers and dates that conflict with those shown on corresponding original birth certificates. Another unresolved issue involves an unproven allegation that Judge Valderas may have been involved or at least have had knowledge of the alleged destruction of Homestead adoption documents before the maternity home and child placement agency closed its doors in the early 1970s. In 2006, a small group of Homestead birth mothers met with and spoke directly to Judge Valderas after he attended a reunion of Homestead adoptees, adoptive parents, and birth mothers held in Fort Worth. During the meeting, these women asked the former Homestead attorney about a long-standing allegation that records documenting Homestead's maternity care and adoption services were destroyed when the organization closed its doors. According to Mary Schwitters Knudsen, one of the Homestead birth mothers present during that meeting, Judge Valderas acknowledged that a Homestead board member took the organization's records to a ranch near Fort Worth, where the documents allegedly were burned.

During research for this book, Harold Michael Valderas, was kind enough to be interviewed about his father's life and his legal and civic work in Fort Worth. Although Valderas is too young to recall anything at all about his father's connection with Homestead Maternity Home and Child Placement Agency and the legal work he performed for the organization, he willingly shared personal memories of his late father. According to Valderas, his father was a *"dedicated and loving family man,"* whose honesty and integrity he admired and respected. His father's military service and his civic involvement, in addition to his children, Valderas added, were the most important parts of his life. A copy of Judge Valderas's obituary is reprinted below, as it appeared in local newspapers.

> *VALDERAS, JUDGE HAROLD L. 83, passed away Saturday, March 31, 2007, in Fort Worth. Funeral: 12:05 p.m. Tuesday at St. Patrick Cathedral. Burial: Mount Olivet Cemetery. Rosary: 6 p.m. Monday in Mount Olivet Chapel. A man whose life's hallmark will forever be written in the service of his county, community and fellow man....A man who came from a humble beginning as the son of a merchant marine from Chile and a mother of high expectations but with few worldly means. Harold L. Valderas began his career as a private in World War II and with God's grace and given talent rose through the ranks during the subsequent conflicts in Korea and Vietnam,*

eventually rising to the rank of lieutenant colonel in the United States Air Force. During the pause in our nation's conflicts he achieved the degree of juris doctor from Southern Methodist University. While attending university, he helped to establish the fraternity of Sigma Chi at SMU. Later he also assisted in the establishment of the Sigma Chi Chapter at Texas Christian University. At the time when it was a challenge for a man of Hispanic origin to rise to political prominence in the state of Texas, he achieved just that with his ascension to civil and then district judge of Tarrant County. He helped to break down barriers, carving the way for other Hispanics, allowing them the opportunity to serve their community as he did. The following quote summarizes his lifelong dedication to service and country: "If there's a war going on, and it's my country, I want to be a part of it. When our country is in trouble and needs me, that's where I want to be." --Harold L. Valderas Lt. Colonel USAF Senior District Judge in Texas. www.valderas.com/bio-education.htm

Chapter 7

Homestead Social Workers and Other Staff

Homestead Maternity Home and Child Placement Agency employed dozens of people over the years the facility and adoption agency operated. Names of Social workers and other staff members who worked at 3600 Crescent during the time the apartment hotel operated as a maternity home were not located during research for this book. Names of individuals who were employed at the West Rosedale Street location, however, were discovered during a review of various Homestead correspondence and other business documents provided by adoptees and adoptive parents interviewed. The largest number of individuals employed by Homestead during the years the residence and adoption agency operated appear to be social workers. With the exception of Robert J. Gilchrist, whose title in 1960 was *"Supervisor of Social Work,"* all Homestead social workers identified were women. The names of Mary Jo Maruda, Carol L. Frank, Judith A. Kelley, and Mary F. Barrett appeared frequently in Homestead correspondence. Old correspondence mailed to adoptive parents and now in the hands of adoptees indicates Ms. Maruda may have been employed by Homestead as a social worker longer than others identified during research for this book. In addition, a college student, Jaye Skaggs, who interned for a brief period at the maternity home's West Rosedale location, allegedly assisted Homestead social workers in performing their duties.

Robert J. Gilchrist, Social Worker

A former Homestead social worker, Robert J. Gilchrist, made an unusual career move when he became a social worker after working for over a decade as a journalist. Gilchrist was born and raised in New Jersey, and he graduated from Randolph-Macon College in 1939. In 1940, Gilchrist received a Master's degree in journalism from Columbia University. Details about why Gilchrist went back to college to obtain another degree are unknown, but available information shows he received a Master of Science in Social Work from the University of Oklahoma in 1953. Although it is unclear where Gilchrist was employed after obtaining his Master's degree in 1940, an advertisement published in an East Texas newspaper in late 1958 listed Gilchrist as the Supervisor of Social Work at Homestead Maternity Home and Child Placement Agency in Fort Worth, Texas. In 1960, a Fort Worth city directory listed Gilchrist as a case worker at Homestead Child Placement Agency. That same directory also indicated Gilchrist and his wife, Florence, lived in Haltom City, a suburb just east of downtown Fort Worth. Although the exact date is unclear, it appears Gilchrist left his job at Homestead in the early 1960's, shortly before Homestead hired social worker, Mary Jo Maruda. It is interesting to note that Gilchrist's employment at Homestead is absent from his obituary, while other details of his lifelong career in social work are well-covered. According to the obituary, Gilchrist worked as a social worker for the Prisoner's Aid Associations in Baltimore, Maryland and in Wilmington, Delaware, and he served as a probation officer for the State of Delaware. In later years, Gilchrist was employed as a supervisor of psychiatric social work at the Willowbrook State School in Staten Island, New York, and at the Maryland Training School for Boys at Holly Center in Salisbury, Maryland. In his last position, Gilchrist served as academic advisor at Cecil County Community College in northeast Maryland.

Mary Jo Hurtt Maruda, Social Worker

A graduate of Tulane University School of Social Work in New Orleans, Louisiana, Mary Jo Hurtt, later Mary Jo Maruda, was born in Louisiana in

1925. Based on interviews with adoptive parents and the stories that some told their adopted children, Maruda appears to have been the first Homestead staff member many couples initially met when they applied to adopt a baby. At the time Maruda worked for Homestead, she was an unmarried woman, likely divorced, who apparently had no children. Interestingly, Ms. Maruda lived in an apartment in Fort Worth's Arlington Heights neighborhood, in very close proximity to Dr. Durham's church and home, Pearl Slaughter's residence and apartments on Dorothy Lane, and to the Colonial Hotel and Café on Camp Bowie Boulevard. Whether Ms. Maruda was acquainted with Dr. Durham, Mrs. Slaughter, or other Homestead staff members before she was hired as a social worker at the maternity home and its child placement agency remains unclear.

Maruda's signature appeared on many pieces of Homestead correspondence kept throughout the years by adoptive parents and passed on to their adopted children. In addition, a few of the adoptive parents interviewed for this book, as well as a foster parent, remember Ms. Maruda as their primary Homestead contact at Homestead during the early-mid 1960s. According to the individuals who recalled interacting with Maruda, she was kind and helpful. Several adoptive parents whom Maruda assisted with their adoptions recalled farewell letters they received from the social worker after she became engaged to marry Charles Vance Welch, Sr. Maruda's letters included her new married name and the couple's address after their marriage, signifying her desire to remain in touch with Homestead adoptive parents even after her resignation from Homestead. Sadly, Mary Jo Maruda Welch, who had no children with her husband, died a little more than a decade after she married Mr. Welch. A Texas certificate of death shows that Maruda-Welch died unexpectedly at home on July 28, 1978, and an inquest was held. According to the document, her sudden death was attributed to complications caused by an enlarged liver. Mary Jo Hurtt Maruda Welch was buried at Greenwood Memorial Park and Mausoleum in Fort Worth, Texas. Charles Vance Welch, Sr., who died on May 22, 2000, is also buried in Greenwood Memorial Park. A somewhat puzzling inscription, apparently written by her husband, appears on his late wife's flat grave marker.

Mary Jo Welch
1925 – 1978
Salute to M.J. Cowtown U.S.A. Texas
Just a Little Irish Colleen, she was always a step behind!
I found a scar across my wrist today, Amen.
Love, Love, Love!
Charley V. Welch, Sr.
Feb. 14, 1997 Valentine's Day

Mrs. Mary F. Barrett, Social Worker

Also known as Mrs. Oscar L. Barrett, Mrs. Mary Barrett served as Supervisor of Social Work at Homestead during the mid-1960 time period. Mrs. Barrett originally was from Atchison, Kansas, and her husband, an employee of a large Fort Worth Lumber Company, had roots in West Virginia. Like many other individuals who were associated with Homestead in the 1960's, the social worker and her husband lived in the Arlington Heights section of Fort Worth. Mrs. Barrett previously was employed by Edna Gladney Home and by the Texas Department of Public Welfare in Fort Worth, Texas. A report documenting *"Discrepancies in the Operation of Homestead Agency"* dated October 12, 1960, mentioned Mrs. Barrett's concern that Mike E. Powell, Homestead's attorney, was involved in a questionable adoption arrangement with an Ysleta Station, Texas, man named Louis Bond Closser, an El Paso high school principal. The report appears in its entirety in the Appendix to this book. Also included in the Appendix are two additional reports prepared earlier in 1960 and in June of 1966. Each report discusses the state's concerns about the facility's adoption practices, as well as its concerns with the agency's licensing. According to one social worker who was employed by Homestead in the mid-1960s, Mrs. Barrett's interpersonal skills often created difficult working relationships with social workers she supervised.

Homestead Foster Parents

At least four Fort Worth couples fostered babies born to Homestead mothers in the 1960s. According to Teri Davidson, who currently lives in New Hampshire, she and her husband John Davidson fostered over thirty Homestead babies between December of 1966 and late 1967. The couple learned about the need for additional foster parents for Homestead infants available for adoption from another foster couple, Mary and Bill Johnson. Teri and John met the Johnson couple at their church, Castleberry Baptist, in the River Oaks section of Fort Worth. Teri explained that two other Castleberry couples, Reed and Joanne Jenson and Carol and Ray Stone, also fostered Homestead babies during the same time period. Based on Carol Stone's records, now in Teri's possession, she and her husband fostered almost fifty babies during the late 1960s. When Teri and John first became Homestead foster parents, they already had four children of their own, and several years later, they adopted a baby girl from Homestead.

John Davidson was stationed at nearby Carswell Air Force Base, and the couple lived in the River Oaks section of Fort Worth, near the military installation. According to Teri, Dr. Victor E. Sears, pastor of Castleberry Baptist Church between 1963 and 1970, and his wife, Carolyn, were friends of Dr. Thomas E. Durham, Homestead's executive director. Interestingly, several adoptees interviewed for this book were told by their adoptive parents that Dr. Sears referred them to Dr. Durham and Homestead's adoption agency during the time they attended Castleberry Baptist. When Teri accepted the job of fostering Homestead babies, she recalled specifically asking Dr. Durham to allow her to care for babies who were "*less likely to be adopted soon after birth or who might have had problems caused by labor and delivery.*" Teri's preference for providing longer-term care for these infants worked well for her and for Homestead, and she believes that she provided individualized care to the babies she fostered.

Teri ended her foster mother duties shortly before she enrolled in the newly offered two-year Associate's Degree nursing program at Tarrant County Junior College in Fort Worth. During the last two years she lived in Fort Worth, Teri completed clinical assignments in labor and delivery at All Saints Hospital, one of three known area hospitals where Homestead mothers gave birth. During her work at All Saints Hospital, Teri recalled the details of one baby boy involved in a very unusual Homestead adoption during the time she was at All Saints. According to Teri, the infant born to a Homestead mother required several extended stays in the neonatal intensive care unit at the hospital. During his lengthy stay, nurses who cared for the baby boy named him "Eric." Since labor and delivery costs for Homestead babies, as well as the cost of an initial pediatric examination and other early medical expenses were passed on to the adoptive parents, Dr. Durham and Homestead officials became very concerned about the baby's accumulating medical expenses. In fact, Homestead staff began to wonder if Eric's medical issues made him "unadoptable." Certainly, there were no adoptive parents waiting for him when he was released from the hospital.

As Dr. Durham and Homestead board members continued to wonder about Eric's fate in life and how the organization would pay the five-figure hospital bill, an older couple, Stanley and Naomi Ross Cheslock, saw Eric and decided to adopt him. The couple, along with their nineteen year old daughter, a local nursing student and their only other living child, first saw Eric when they visited their baby girl in the same neonatal unit before her death. The grieving couple longed for another child, and with their daughter, apparently fell in love with Eric in spite of his medical condition. Subsequently, the couple contacted Homestead, and although the two were older than most adoptive parents, their application to adopt was approved. According to Teri, who fostered Eric for a time and had personal knowledge of his adoption, Mr. and Mrs. Cheslock paid Homestead sixteen thousand dollars to adopt the baby boy. Eric's adoption, Teri added, was considered a major success by Homestead officials. The couple wanted the baby, their nursing student daughter was willing to help her parents care for her adopted baby brother, and Homestead could pay the unusually large bill owed All-Saints Hospital.

Note: Young Eric, later renamed "Taub," and his adoptive parents were no longer living when interviews were conducted for this book. His adoptive sister, however, volunteered additional information about her brother's adoption and his life, and details from her interview are included in a later chapter entitled Homestead Adoptees.

Mrs. Anna D. Urban, Secretary and Board Member

The widow of A. F. Urban, Mrs. Urban was employed in 1966 as a secretary at Homestead Maternity Home and Child Placement Agency at 1250 West Rosedale. Public records reviewed in connection with Homestead's operation established that Mrs. Urban also served on the organization's board of directors in 1968. According to the Fort Worth City Directory, Mrs. Urban had lived in the city since at least 1949 and was a former employee of Niblack Slenderizing Systems, located at 710 Carroll Street in Fort Worth. In 1966, *The Lepanto*, the yearbook for Our Lady of Victory Catholic School, listed Mrs. Urban as a donor for contributing to the school in honor of her grandchildren. Later city directory information indicated Mrs. Urban's association with Homestead had ended, and she had returned to work at the Fort Worth reducing salon on Carroll Street. Texas death records establish the former Homestead secretary and board member died of pancreatic cancer on March 8, 1974.

Carol Lee Frank, Social Worker

A native of Dallas, Texas, Ms. Frank was born on September 15, 1934 to Rev. Mervyn Davis Frank and Beatrice F. Frank. She attended Woodrow Wilson High School in Dallas and was a 1956 graduate of the University of Mary Hardin – Baylor, where she received The Distinguished Alumni Award. Ms. Frank was awarded her Master of Science in Social Work degree at the University of Texas in Austin, and later she attended graduate classes on aging at North Texas State University in Denton, Texas. Exact dates of her employment at Homestead are unknown, but it appears she left before 1968, when she is listed that year in the Dallas City Directory as a supervisor for the Dallas County child welfare office. In later years, Ms. Frank worked for the Salvation Army in Dallas, and in 1992, she was named Executive Director of the Salvation Army Carr P. Collins Social Services Center in Dallas. At the time of her retirement, Ms. Frank was the Texas Divisional Social Service and Pre-Release Director. Interestingly, a Homestead adoptee interviewed for this book was adopted by one of Carol Frank's sisters, and his story appears in a later chapter. Carol Frank died on May 1, 2004, after devoting her entire career to helping others.

Mrs. Corine M. Gray, Housemother

Mrs. Gray, as she was called by Homestead birth mothers, was employed during the 1960's by the maternity home as a live-in "housemother" at the West Rosedale Street location. Biographical details about Mrs. Gray are scarce at best, but early census records indicate she likely grew up in West Texas and that she may have remarried later in life and after Homestead closed its doors. On May 12, 1966, during the state's investigation and recertification of the agency's license, Mrs. Gray completed a Texas State Department of Public Welfare, Child Welfare Division *"Information Sheet on Staff Members."* According to her own handwritten statement, Mrs. Gray's job title was *"Housemother,"* and her salary was *"$100/per month"* plus room and board. She was sixty-three years old when the form was completed on May 12, 1966, by her own statement, she had completed four years of college, and she had been in her position at Homestead for seven years. On the same state generated form, Mrs. Gray listed her job duties as *"Supervising girls/making Doctor appts/Go with them to hospital when they are in labor."*

By most accounts, Mrs. Gray was not the most-liked Homestead staff member. One birth mother, to whom the housemother gave a small red pill called a "red devil" by other residents, went into labor at the maternity home and remembered how difficult it was for her to walk down the home's steps to get into a taxicab waiting to drive her to the hospital. Allegedly, Mrs. Gray did not accompany her to the hospital. According to another birth mother, Mrs. Gray frightened her when she ordered her on several occasions to visit the housemother's private apartment. In the privacy of Mrs. Gray's room, and with the door closed, the elderly woman allegedly made veiled threats about knowing the young woman's boyfriend and the father of her unborn baby. The young woman never understood why she was singled out by Mrs. Gray to be the target of these threats, and she still remembers how afraid she was the housemother would retaliate in some way if she told anyone about the incidents. Another young woman who went into premature labor and allegedly gave birth in a room at Homestead, still remembers the lack of concern and kindness shown her by Mrs. Gray when she told the housemother she was experiencing spontaneous bleeding. Later, the young woman gave birth to a premature infant, allegedly in a vacant room at the maternity home on W. Rosedale.

Although many pregnant women who lived at Homestead Maternity Home and knew Mrs. Gray saw her as a stern and formidable woman, several other birth mothers interviewed for this book remember the elderly housemother as kind and caring. Each of these young women recalled a letter Mrs. Gray wrote to her after she had returned home from Homestead. In the letters, Mrs. Gray wished the young women well in their future lives and endeavors and thanked them for being pleasant and kind to her during the time they spent at the maternity home.

Mrs. Madge Gregory Hoskins, Homestead Housemother

One of six children born to Thaddeus Gregory, a Mississippi-born physician and his wife, Emma, Madge grew up in Delta County, Texas, near where she was born and where her father practiced medicine. According to the *U.S. Census* of 1900, it seems likely Dr. Gregory moved his family to Texas shortly after 1890, since Madge, born in 1891, appeared to be the first of his children to have been born in Texas. By the time Madge was eighteen years old, she was employed as a PBX operator at The Coffey Clinic, 306 W. Broadway in Fort Worth. Dr. Gregory apparently died before the *U.S. Census* was recorded in 1920, and the family had moved to 1620 West Oleander Street in Fort Worth. Madge's widowed mother, Emma Hoskins, was shown as the head of a large household made up of several older children and young grandchildren. According to the same census record, Madge was a 28 year old widow with two children, Loretta, age 6, and Wayne, 8 years old. Fort Worth city directory listings published in later years indicate Madge was the widow of Horace Hoskins. Apparently, Madge and her younger sister, Hattie, were the only members of Emma Hoskins's household who were employed in 1920 when the census was recorded. Other census details indicated Madge worked as a supervisor of telephone operators, and 20 year old Hattie was employed by Southwestern Bell as a telephone operator. Although the date Madge went to work at Homestead is uncertain, one of the birth mothers interviewed for this book remembered her as the first Homestead employee she met upon her arrival in Fort Worth from North Carolina. She explained he older woman, known simply as "Mrs. Hoskins," was the Homestead housemother who met her at the Fort Worth bus station in 1962 and drove her to the maternity home. A certificate of death filed with the State of Texas indicated Mrs. Hoskins died on May 24, 1979.

Ruth N. Hamilton, Director of Nurses, Harris Hospital

According to the Fort Worth City Directory, Ruth N. Hamilton served as Director of Nurses at Harris Hospital between 1955 and 1959. In 1962, According to "Barbara," mother of a Homestead adoptee born in December of 1962, Hamilton was the nurse who brought her adopted baby known as "Baby South" to the law office of Mike Powell, where she and her husband finalized Homestead paperwork allowing them to take the baby home. A Homestead staff member told "Barbara" that her adopted son's mother was a 24-year old Native American woman named "Carmen South," who was a member of the Coushatta Tribe near the Texas-Louisiana state line. The staff member told "Barbara" her baby boy's birth mother also had French ancestry. It is interesting to note that Ruth N. Hamilton's occupation, according to the *Fort Worth City Directory* published in 1963, listed Ruth N. Hamilton's occupation as the Assistant Director of Nurses at Harris Hospital. By 1968, Hamilton's title at the hospital had changed in the city directory's listing to *"Assistant Education Director,"* and in 1971, her occupation was shown simply as *"nurse."*

Mrs. Judith Kelley, Social Worker

Copies of Homestead correspondence from the mid-1960s indicates Mrs. Kelley worked as a social worker at the West Rosedale Street location in Fort Worth. At least one adoptive parent interviewed for this book remembered Mrs. Kelley as knowledgeable, friendly, and helpful in hers and her husband's effort to adopt a Homestead baby. She also recalled Mrs. Kelley was pregnant with her first child and that she did not return to Homestead after the baby was born. According to public records, Mrs. Kelley last lived in Arlington, Texas, and is now deceased.

Sharon K. Dowden, Social Work Intern

Sharon, a graduate of Eastern Hills High School near the Meadowbrook area of Fort Worth, appears to have worked for a short time at Homestead after she graduated high school. During the time she was employed by Homestead, Sharon lived in east Fort Worth near her parents, in an apartment in a fairly new complex located on Handley-Ederville Road. Interestingly, the married birth mother of an adoptee interviewed for this book also lived in the same apartment complex during her pregnancy. Research for this book failed to uncover a personal or professional relationship between that birth mother and Ms. Dowden.

Dorothy Harris Haskins Scheidt, Harris Hospital Nurse

In early January of 1964, Dorothy Haskins Scheidt signed an original Texas birth certificate issued for a baby girl born in late December of 1963 to a Homestead resident from North Carolina. Mrs. Scheidt signed the document in the space provided for the *"attending physician,"* and included her title as *"Director of Nursing Service."* Exactly why Mrs. Scheidt signed the original birth certificate, instead of the attending physician, remains a mystery, especially since the birth mother believes she delivered her baby in a room at Homestead, instead of a local hospital. A Fort Worth city directory published in 1968 lists Dorothy Harris Haskins as an employee of Harris Hospital, and her residence was shown as *"3552 Kent St Apt 2."* Current maps of Fort Worth indicate the location is now part of the Texas Christian University campus. The name "Scheidt," remains a mystery, however, since neither marriage nor divorce records for Dorothy Harris Haskins and a Mr. Scheidt were located in Tarrant County or other locations in Texas.

Miss Jaye Skaggs, Social Work Intern

According to Teri Davidson, a former Homestead foster mother, Miss Skaggs worked as an intern at Homestead during the summer or maybe during a semester when she attended Texas Christian University in Fort Worth. Mrs. Davidson specifically remembered the young woman, since she drove some of the Homestead babies from the hospital to the Davidson's foster home. According to Mrs. Davidson, Miss Skaggs also picked up babies from her foster home and drove them to Homestead where adoptive parents were waiting to take their babies home. Available public records indicate Miss Skaggs completed her college studies and became a talented and well-known interior decorator in Fort Worth.

*Ann, Social Worker

After Ann relocated to Fort Worth with her husband, she answered an employment advertisement placed by Homestead Child Placement Agency. In early 1965, Dr. Durham, Homestead's Executive Director, interviewed and hired Ann who had earned a sociology degree in California. She joined Homestead's staff at the office located at 1028 5th Avenue as a social worker whose supervisor was Mary V. Barrett. Ann's job duties involved administrative tasks, contacts with prospective adoptive parents, and making pre-adoption and post-adoption home visits, primarily outside of Fort Worth. Shortly after she was hired, Ann began developing certification procedures for private homes that served as foster homes for Homestead babies, something she said had never been done before. In addition, Ann picked up Homestead babies when they were dismissed from All Saints Hospital, usually when they were about 2-3 days old, and drove them to their assigned foster homes. Most of the babies she transported to foster homes, Ann recalled, were adopted before they were a week old. Ann said her duties did not involve interactions with the maternity home's residents or with the housemother, and she was aware that Mrs. Barrett and Dr. Durham made a deliberate effort to keep the social work and administrative staff away from the young women. Out of town visits to the homes of prospective adoptive parents were part of her duties, Ann added, and since Mrs. Barrett did not drive, she drove to the various locations and was accompanied by Mrs. Barrett. Although Ann was capable of completing the home visits herself, she said Mrs. Barrett enjoyed leaving the office and making the out of town trips. Although the elderly widow had never learned to drive, Ann recalled that Mrs. Barrett frequently gave her advice about driving, and she closely supervised the home visits. Although Ann enjoyed interacting with adoptive parents and being part of one of the happiest events of their lives, she admitted that she found it very difficult to work for Mrs. Barrett.

Ann said she talked with Dr. Durham from time to time, but Mrs. Barrett supervised her day-to-day duties. She never met Dr. Durham's wife nor Homestead's housemother. And even though she did not work directly with Harold Valderas, Homestead's attorney, she did see him at the agency's office on more than several occasions when he would drop off adoption paperwork. Ann also was aware that Dr. Jack Turner, Homestead's obstetrician, made frequent visits to the maternity home, and she often observed him entering and leaving through the maternity home's separate outside entrance. Although Ann assumed Dr. Turner was visiting with Homestead girls, she said he could have been meeting with Dr. Durham, as well. Ann believed her job was the perfect one for her. When Ann resigned from her position less than a year after she joined Homestead's staff, she remembered Dr. Durham pulling her aside and praising her for lasting longer than anyone else Mrs. Barrett had supervised.

Chapter 8

Homestead Birth Mothers

"The truth is rarely pure, and never simple."

– Oscar Wilde, in "The Importance of Being Earnest."

During the fifties, sixties and seventies, in what some have referred to as the "Baby Scoop Era, tens of thousands of young pregnant women came to Fort Worth, Texas, to live in facilities known as "unwed mothers' homes," or "maternity homes." Homestead Maternity Home, first located at 3600 Crescent and later at 1250 West Rosedale, was one of several similar organizations located in Fort Worth. Although Volunteers of America (VOA) with funding from the Salvation Army and the privately-run Edna Gladney home were Homestead's competitors, each of the three facilities was somewhat different. According to birth mothers interviewed for this book, Homestead offered maternity home residents "work privileges" as long as their pregnancies allowed them to stay employed, while the Edna Gladney home did not. New mothers often remained at Edna Gladney and cared for their babies until they were adopted, and with approval, a young woman could continue to live at the home until she found employment and transitioned to outside housing. Volunteers of America had no central residential facility. Instead, the organization offered assistance to pregnant women by placing them in private homes where they lived until they gave birth. After giving birth, some of these women returned to live in the private homes until they became gainfully employed and were able to afford a place of their own.

According to early brochures and advertisements, Homestead Hospital and Child Placement Agency, the organization's early name, and later, Homestead Maternity Home and Child Placement Agency was organized as a non-profit organization and operated by a board of directors. The board was comprised of local citizens who were members of Fort Worth's business and professional community and included at least one doctor and a lawyer. The individual who made decisions about Homestead's day-to-day operation was the Executive Director, Pearl (Mrs. W. W.) Slaughter, and later, Dr. Thomas E. Durham, a retired Baptist minister. Prior to 1958, it appears that Homestead was not licensed by the State of Texas to operate an adoption agency. Throughout the years that Homestead operated, the organization promoted its maternity and adoption services in newspaper advertisements appearing in Sunday newspapers published throughout Texas and a dozen or more large cities in the United States. A review of the numbers of advertisements printed in U.S. cities, revealed a large percentage were published in Shreveport, Louisiana, St. Louis, Missouri, and Jackson, Mississippi newspapers. The ads primarily appeared in the classified section and frequently were listed in the "Personals" column. In addition, Mike E. Powell, Homestead's first known legal counsel, allegedly traveled to various locations in Texas, Oklahoma, and New Mexico, where he is said to have met with officials at colleges, Indian reservations, and military installations. During these marketing meetings, Powell allegedly offered brochures and other information about Homestead Maternity Home and its adoption service.

There are no records available to tell the exact number of birth mothers who lived at Homestead Maternity Home during the years the facility was open. And there are no official records to verify the number of babies born to these mothers and adopted through Homestead's child placement agency. In fact, no Homestead business records exist at all. Simply based on "baby numbers" appearing near the top of non-id information sheets provided by Homestead staff to adoptive parents, the total number of babies adopted through Homestead's agency may have at exceeded fifteen thousand. This number cannot be proven, however, since the date the numbering system began, and the number used to begin the series cannot be determined. Numerous rumors have existed for more than a decade, alleging the destruction of the facility's records by one or more of its officials. But those who may have had first-hand knowledge of the destruction are now deceased. However, the State of Texas through its Bureau of Vital Statistics currently acknowledges the alleged destruction of Homestead's records. During research for this book, two adoptees who requested their original birth certificates from the Texas Bureau of Vital Statistics in Austin in 2014 and in 2015, received official letters stating that records likely were destroyed or even burned.

Throughout the next pages of this book, you will read the stories of the Homestead birth mothers who experienced them. These women represent a very small percentage of thousands of Homestead mothers who gave birth to babies that many were forced to give up for adoption. An extremely large number of Homestead birth mothers still find their experiences are too painful to share with anyone. Sadly, many of these young women were not allowed to talk about their pregnancy, labor, or delivery of a baby they never saw, touched, or held, when they returned home. One particular commonality exists with mothers who gave up babies for adoption – their experiences often impacted their lives in similar ways. A large percentage of Homestead birth mothers married very soon after giving birth and gave birth to another child early in the marriage, possibly to replace the baby they gave up for adoption. Some women never married at all, and others who did marry, often had no other children.

Becky George Eminger

Growing up on a ranch in Portales, New Mexico, Becky was part of a large, extended family whose members lived in houses near the one she shared with her parents. Becky said she was seventeen years old and had just graduated from high school when she learned she was pregnant. The father of her baby was her steady boyfriend, a young man who lived in the same area and who she had dated for one and a half years. Becky said their dates were primarily scheduled around activities at school or church and in their community and involved many other people. She explained that she had sex only once with her boyfriend before she became pregnant. By June of 1965, Becky believed she might be pregnant and broke the news to her boyfriend. He was "terrified," Becky said, and told her "I don't know what I'm going to do." According to Becky, her baby's father was in his second year of college and was very afraid of telling his mother, a teacher who placed much importance on higher education.

Although Becky had broken the news that she might be pregnant to David, her boyfriend, she had not told her mother. She vividly recalled the day her mother mentioned that she had not seen evidence of Becky's period, and how she admitted to her mother that she thought she might be pregnant. In the following weeks, other family members, including her grandmother and an uncle who was home from the military, noticed changes in Becky's appearance. But it was not until Becky's relatives gathered for a family funeral in early fall that her "Granny" asked her directly if she was pregnant and said, "Don't you lie to me." Becky's grandmother, who also lived on the ranch, soon talked to her son about his daughter's pregnancy. A few days after Becky's Dad talked to his mother, he came home from working in the fields and told Becky to "get dressed," quickly adding, "We're going to see David's family." Less than an hour later, Becky and her parents arrived at the young man's house. Soon after they were inside the house, David walked in with another girl who "had a diamond on her finger," and Becky recalled the visit "went downhill from there." She remembered clearly how loud, chaotic, and out of control the situation became. At one point, Becky said, a fight almost broke out between her mother and David's mother, when she claimed her son could not be the father of Becky's baby. His mother justified her statement by saying that David had been "dating that girl" with the diamond on her finger for "six months."

Very soon after the awful scene took place at David's house, Becky's father met with the pastor of their Baptist church and asked for advice. According to Becky, the pastor told her father "You cannot allow her to keep this baby, because it will be ostracized." During the visit, the pastor advised Becky's father to contact Homestead Maternity Home in Fort Worth, Texas, but Becky never knew when her father talked to Homestead staff or what details were discussed during the conversation. Her father did tell her, however, that she would be living at Homestead until the baby was born, and the child would be placed for adoption by the maternity home's agency. Becky believes Homestead officials may have recommended that her admittance be delayed until after the holidays were over, because she did not leave right away. When asked if she had siblings who knew she was pregnant, Becky said her brother, twenty months younger, knew about her pregnancy. She added that her brother was aware she would be going to Fort Worth to live until she had her baby, and he also understood the baby would be placed for adoption. Becky turned eighteen in December, and at Christmas that year, her parents and relatives had a "big family Christmas" that included parties at several of their houses on the ranch. Becky still remembers the gold lame' dress with an empire waist her grandmother bought for her to wear to holiday gatherings since her other festive dresses no longer fit. Becky remembers these holiday parties well, since she would not see most of her relatives again until after she gave birth the next year. She recalled a video made at one of these events, one that included Becky in the gold lame' dress, mysteriously disappeared from her family's video collection.

Becky said her father drove her to Fort Worth, and since it was late in the day, they spent the night in a local hotel. The next morning, her father drove her to Dr. Jack Turner's medical office where she received her first physical exam. After she and her father left the doctor's office, they drove to Homestead Maternity Home on West Rosedale. When they arrived at the large three-story brick building, Becky remembers her father saying that he was "impressed" by what he saw. A Homestead staff member instructed Becky's father to escort his daughter to Mrs. Gray's room, so he carried Becky's suitcase, and Becky said she followed her father down the hall. When he knocked on Mrs. Gray's door, the housemother answered. But before her father could pick up Becky's suitcase, Mrs. Gray adamantly told him "no men are allowed in here," and immediately asked him to leave. As soon as her father turned to leave, Mrs. Gray walked Becky to her assigned room. According to Becky's recollection, Mrs. Gray was "short and heavy-set," and "probably in her fifties or sixties." Becky added, "She was not very nice." Later, Becky learned that Mrs. Gray was a "no-nonsense woman who did not have a maternal side."

Becky recalled her father had been assured by a Homestead official that no girl who lived within fifty miles of Portales, New Mexico, would be in residence at Homestead while his daughter lived there. But as Becky settled in, she was shocked to hear a familiar voice of another girl from Portales. According to Becky, her father paid fifty dollars per month to Homestead for her room and board, and she was assigned a few chores that included assisting with food preparation in the basement kitchen. The girls ate at a long table in a dining room near the kitchen, and she recalled the furniture in the dining room was "institutional stuff." The maternity home's rooms were "bad," she recalled, and there was a closet on the first floor that had a "pile of maternity clothes" that former residents had donated for the other girls to wear if they chose to do so. Becky did not remember how she did her laundry, but she did recall taking her turn at cleaning the refrigerator and freezer. The latter chore is forever burned into her memory of Homestead, Becky added, since she went into labor while performing that particular task.

Homestead's practices required the girls to tell Mrs. Gray when they went into labor, but Becky was uncomfortable around the housemother and did not immediately tell her when she began to experience labor pains. Instead, she told another Homestead resident, with whom she had developed a friendship, and the friend sat in a rocking chair in Becky's room and monitored her labor pains. Soon after midnight, Becky's pains had become more frequent, and her friend convinced her to tell Mrs. Gray. When she and her friend knocked on the housemother's door and told her it was time to go to the hospital, Mrs. Gray's response was "Why in the hell didn't you tell me you were in labor?" A few minutes later, Mrs. Gray gave Becky "some sort of pill" that made her "sick and woozy." The last thing Becky remembered at Homestead was "looking at the taxi" waiting outside the building, ready to take her to All Saints Hospital. The next thing Becky knew she was already at the hospital, and when she was aware of her surroundings again, she was being "wheeled out of the delivery room." That night, about 9:30 p.m., Becky asked to call her mother, and the nurses refused to allow her to make the phone call. Later, when she told the nurses she was hungry, they were "not nice to me and gave me only Dr. Pepper and crackers." A member of the nursing staff, however, did allow Becky to phone her mother in New Mexico the next day. During that phone call, Becky recalled telling her mother about the other Homestead girl from Portales, and she gave her the girl's name. About two to three days after Becky gave birth, Dr. Turner came to her hospital room and told her she had given birth to a six pound, nine ounce baby boy with blonde hair and blue eyes. Becky said Dr. Durham did not visit her at all while she was in the hospital, and she added that she had seen the maternity home director only once during the roughly three month period she lived at Homestead.

After a four to five day hospital stay, Becky was discharged from the hospital and driven back to Homestead in a taxi. No one told her anything, and she didn't ask, but Becky assumed that she had no problems relating to labor and delivery when she left the hospital. Although Becky did not recall the exact length of time she remained at Homestead, she said it could not have been more than a few days. With very little notice, Mrs. Gray informed Becky that she would be "flying home," and a limousine would take her to the airport. When the airport limousine was late in arriving at the airport, Becky was forced to run with her suitcase in tow to the gate. But she did not make it in time and missed her plane. Becky said she was frightened because she had never been inside an airport until then. In addition, she dreaded calling her father to tell him she would not be arriving at the Lubbock airport when he expected. Several long hours later, Becky left the airport on another flight, and her father was waiting at the Lubbock airport when she arrived. She said she felt "starved" after the long trip and no food, so she asked her father if he would stop at a restaurant on the way home. He refused, she said, and told her there was "food at home." The rest of the trip was spent in silence, she added.

Once Becky was back at the family's ranch in New Mexico, neither her parents or other family members asked about her stay at Homestead or about the baby she gave up for adoption. Years later, however, her mother said that Becky's father made the decision to send her to Homestead in Fort Worth and added that she had "no control over what happened." Interestingly, a few weeks after Becky returned home, one of the social workers at Homestead mailed a letter to her home address in New Mexico. When Becky opened the envelope, she was quite surprised to find two pictures of her infant son tucked inside the letter. Years later, after Becky discovered her son's foster parents were Teri and John Davidson, she learned that Teri had taken the pictures in the letter she had written and asked the social worker to mail.

In the weeks that followed, Becky resumed her life and began socializing with her friends. On one of these evenings out, when she and some friends drove to Clovis to dance, she was very surprised to see her baby's father there. She was even more surprised when he asked her to dance. She agreed, and after the dance was over, the two of them talked. David told her he had broken off his engagement and was no longer dating the young woman she had seen at his parents' house. During the conversation, David asked Becky to marry him, and she told him "no" and tearfully added, "I had to give my baby away." David continued in his attempt to convince Becky that she should marry him, told her they could have more children, and even promised that he would help her find their son. But Becky refused to change her mind, and she left the dance with her friends. Later, Becky discovered that David's step-father, who operated the dairy farm where his family lived, had told David that if he ever found out Becky's baby was his, David would "lose everything." And "true enough," Becky said, "David had been cut out of the will." Not long after she returned to Portales, Becky married a man who was seven years older. The marriage ended in divorce, she said, because her husband was abusive. In hindsight, Becky feels she married the man simply because she believed she did not deserve better.

Becky always knew she would try to locate her son, and in the mid-1990's, she joined an adoption group in Reno, Nevada, near where she lived at the time. She recalled that someone in the group directed her to Pat Palmer in Irving, Texas, and in 1996, with Palmer's help, Becky was reunited with her son, James, who had been adopted by a Corpus Christi, Texas, couple. A short time later, Becky traveled to the Texas gulf coast city where James was raised, and she met her son in person for the very first time. Later, Becky met her son's wife and their two children, and eventually, James met Becky's family, including his two half-sisters. At the time Becky shared her story, James and his father had not met. In retrospect, Becky believes her experience as an unwed teenage mother taught her a "valuable lesson." She continued by saying "None of us at Homestead were bad girls. There were so many of us there who were just naïve girls who fell in love and believed our boyfriends when they said they loved us and that (our relationships) would end in marriage. So we had sex with them believing that if we got pregnant, we would get married."

Beth R.

Beth was born in Paducah, Kentucky in 1944, just before World War II ended. Her father worked for American Bridge, and he was transferred twice, to the Houston, Texas area, where she graduated high school, and to Texarkana, Texas, the day after her graduation. According to Beth, she had a steady boyfriend in high school who enlisted in the military before she graduated. After the young man left town, Beth began dating another young man named "John M."

In the spring of 1962, Beth attended the Senior Prom with John, and she believes she became pregnant on prom night. Although Beth told her mother she was pregnant, she waited about two to three months to tell her boyfriend about her pregnancy. After John told his mother, she took Beth to a doctor in Orange to confirm the pregnancy. Once the pregnancy was confirmed, the young couple decided they should get married, and Beth's mother began making her daughter's wedding dress. About the same time,

John drove up to Texarkana to see Beth, checked into a local hotel, and called Beth to let her know where he was staying. Beth was happy to hear he was in town, and drove over to the hotel to see him. But her happiness turned into tears, when John broke the news that he was calling off the wedding. Beth asked why, and John explained that men at work had begun asking him if he knew for certain the baby Beth was carrying was really his. They even chided him, he said, saying the baby's father could have been someone else in the Houston area. Beth still recalls how upset she was at the time and how she drove home in tears and told her parents that John did not want to marry her.

Beth's mother also was upset, and she remembered how her mother couldn't understand why John did not want the baby. Her father was upset and angry and even suggested he should "take her to Shreveport," to "get this taken care off." But Beth's mother soon took control and began searching for an unwed mothers' home that would accept her daughter. Beth said her mother was reading the Sunday paper when she saw an advertisement for Homestead Maternity Home in Fort Worth. The next day, Beth recalled, her mother phoned Homestead and talked to a staff member who provided details about the facility, including the amount she and her husband would be required to pay for Beth's room and board. Beth's mother immediately said "no," and adamantly told the individual she and her husband would *not* be paying Beth's room and board, since Homestead was getting her daughter's baby. Before the phone conversation ended, the Homestead official agreed to waive the cost of Beth's room and board. And as it turned out, Beth lived at Homestead cost-free for about four months.

Various dates exist for the closing of Homestead Maternity Home's location at 3600 Crescent and the opening of the three-story red brick building on West Rosedale. But Beth's recollections of her stay at Homestead's location on Crescent indicate the two facilities may have operated concurrently for at least a couple of years in the early 1960's. For the last five months of her pregnancy, Beth lived at the 3600 Crescent location, which she described as a *"big, old 2-story house near the railroad tracks."* To the side of the big house was a *"smaller brick house, similar to a guest house, where married women or women who already had children,"* lived until they delivered their babies. Beth's father drove her to their local bus station and watched as she boarded the bus headed to Fort Worth. When she arrived, Beth remembered she had to wait for several hours until someone from Homestead arrived to drive her to the maternity home. Since Beth had traveled very little, she remembered how uneasy she felt during the long bus ride and the extended wait in the Fort Worth bus terminal. When she arrived at Homestead on Crescent, she was assigned her own room and bath. Beth remembered how surprised she was to learn that several of the girls in the main house were only 12-13 years old. She also met another woman, older than she was, who had driven her own car from California. Beth recalled the woman "had a wallet full of money."

An older woman named Mrs. Gray lived onsite and served as the facility's housemother. Although Mrs. Gray spent much of her time in her own room, she did allow the girls to visit her there or in her office, where she assured them that giving up their babies for adoption "was a good thing." A minister and his wife regularly visited the maternity home, prayed with the girls and women, and told them what *"a good thing"* they were doing to help couples who could not have children of their own. When she was asked during the interview about pregnancy and childbirth classes or counseling available to Homestead residents, Beth said she had no memory of any classes at all.

According to Beth, living at Homestead overall was a pleasant experience. The residents prepared all the meals, primarily from frozen items kept in big lockers in a small building behind the big house. At the time, she believed the food was donated by various individuals and organizations, because she witnessed some of the deliveries when she took walks around the grounds. Beth said the meals at Homestead included some of the best meat and vegetables she had ever tasted. Mrs. Gray made certain all the pregnant women took daily pre-natal vitamins provided by the facility. Although Beth could not remember the social worker's name, she did recall the individual "took us to the store to buy personal items, like bras, cosmetics, etc., and drove us to our doctors' appointments." The women went to Dr. Turner's office for their prenatal exams, and they were told from the beginning that he would deliver their babies. Beth laughingly recalled the time Dr. Turner wrote a prescription for "something to bleach hair" for "Daphne, a blonde from Shreveport."

When asked if anyone was allowed to visit her at the maternity home, Beth said her parents visited her twice, and her baby's paternal grandmother visited once. Beth's baby was due in January of 1963, and since she told Dr. Turner that she needed to enroll in college in time to attend the spring semester, he agreed to induce her labor. Homestead mothers were not allowed visitors while they were in the hospital, Beth recalled, but she did phone her mother before she left for the hospital. After Beth was admitted, the nurses who cared for her told her it would be best if she did not see or hold her baby after she gave birth. In an attempt to ensure their privacy, Beth said Homestead mothers were assigned rooms on a different floor of the hospital from other maternity patients. She recalled staying in the hospital for two to three days before she was sent back to Homestead with only a bottle of perineal cleanser. According to Beth, she had no follow-up visit with the doctor, and she remained at the maternity home for about a week before leaving Fort Worth on a train to return to her parents' home. Beth's mother and aunt met her at the train station, but there was no discussion during the drive home about Beth's delivery or the baby she gave up for adoption. She added that her mother never again mentioned her daughter's pregnancy or the baby placed for adoption. In 1964, Beth and her current husband were married. Twenty years ago, Beth began searching for her daughter, and they were happily reunited about five years ago.

Beverly Wilkerson Benn

A native of Bryan, Texas, "Bev," as she prefers to be known, still lives near the house where she lived with her family when she became pregnant at eighteen years old. Although Bev did not remember all the details about her stay at Homestead Maternity Home and explained that she believes she "has blocked out some of those memories," she believes that overall, she received good care while at Homestead. Bev added, "The meals and snacks were nutritious, and my dorm room was comfortable. At the beginning of my 9th month, I was moved to a private room on the first floor. For the most part, the staff at Homestead were good to us. We were allowed to go shopping in town, we had ice cream, watermelon, and soda and iced tea parties in the back yard of the home." Although Bev did not remember the housemother's name, she said the woman taught Homestead girls "to crochet, knit, do needlework, etc." At some point, Bev remembered being interviewed by a Homestead staff member, whose name she doesn't recall, and she "asked a lot of background and medical questions about me and the father of my baby." She said the staff member also briefly explaining the Affidavit of Voluntary Relinquishment of Parental rights and the adoption process. That same individual warned Bev that if she refused to sign the relinquishment document after she gave birth, she would be required "to pay the doctor and hospital bills."

Bev said Dr. and Mrs. Durham were in charge of Homestead Maternity Home in Fort Worth when she lived there in 1968. Dr. Hugh Parchman, she added, delivered her baby at All Saints Hospital. When asked if she received counseling before or after she gave birth, Bev said "there was no counseling provided after we gave birth," and added, "There should have been counseling. I was depressed and cried constantly for a year or more after I gave up my daughter for adoption." Bev summarized her experience as an unwed mother in the 1960's by saying "If the times in 1969 in my small town in southeast Texas were the same as today, I would have kept my baby. I agonized over my decision to give up my daughter for adoption ever since that day after her birth when I signed the papers."

Bev always knew she would search for her child, and over three decades after giving birth in Fort Worth, she registered with the Central Adoption Registry, a matching service set up by the State of Texas. Sometime later, with the help of another Homestead birth mother who had already found her child, Bev was reunited with the daughter she had given up for adoption.

"Celia"

A resident of Parker County, Texas, Celia became pregnant at eighteen, just before she graduated from high school. Her baby's father knew Celia was pregnant, but he was "not interested," she said. When Celia told her parents about her pregnancy, they decided she should go to the Edna Gladney home in Fort Worth, where Celia would live until she gave birth and the baby could be placed with adoptive parents. When Celia's parents contacted the Fort Worth maternity home, they were advised their daughter's room and board would be based on Celia's father's income. Since her parents believed the cost of staying at Edna Gladney was excessive, they chose to admit Celia to Homestead Maternity Home in Fort Worth, where they were required to pay only sixty-five dollars a month. When asked how her parents found out about Homestead, Celia said they read an ad in the local newspaper. Celia recalled her mother, who was more supportive than her father, drove her to Homestead. When she was admitted to the maternity home, Celia was already seven months pregnant with a due date of late January 1971. She was assigned a private room on the second floor and shared a bath with the girl who lived in the room next door. During her stay at Homestead, Celia and other residents walked in small groups to Dr. Hugh Parchman's office located nearby on 5th Avenue. "I just loved Dr. Parchman. He was such a lovely man," Celia recalled.

According to Celia, Homestead staff, including Dr. and Mrs. Durham and the cook who prepared meals in the basement kitchen, were good to her. Meal preparation, Celia said, was the cook's primary responsibility, but she and the other girls assisted in minor ways. Meals were served at a long table in the basement dining area. Since Celia lived at Homestead during Thanksgiving, she recalled going with a group of about ten girls to Dr. and Mrs. Durham's home for Thanksgiving dinner. One of the more unusual memories Celia has of her stay at Homestead involved another young resident, a local Fort Worth girl, whose boyfriend climbed the second floor fire escape steps after dark to visit the girl on the landing outside her window.

In early December, Celia's water broke, but she did not go into labor until a week later. On December 11, 1970, Dr. Parchman delivered her premature baby at All Saints Hospital. She recalls nothing about her labor and delivery experience, since she was heavily sedated. Although a social worker told Celia she had given birth to a daughter, she said she never saw or held her baby girl. Within a short time after her baby's delivery, someone brought the relinquishment paper to her hospital room, where she remembers signing the document without a witness present. Although she did not remember the total number of days she remained in the hospital after giving birth, Celia does recall returning to Homestead and staying for three days before her mother drove to Fort Worth to take her back home to Parker County.

Celia's life was different, she said, after she returned home, and she continued to live with her parents for less than a year before she found a job in Fort Worth and moved out. About three years later, she married and had another child. Although Celia continued to be a patient of Dr. Parchman, by the time she became pregnant again, much to her disappointment, Dr. Parchman had stopped delivering babies.

After the internet became available, Celia began searching for the daughter she gave up for adoption in December of 1970. Initially, her searches yielded no results, but after lots of diligence and much patience, Celia discovered her daughter's death certificate. Shocked and saddened from learning that her daughter had passed away when she was only nine years old, Celia's emotions were intensified by information on the death certificate showing her child had been a resident of the Denton (TX) State School at the time of her death. At the recommendations of adoption search angels, Celia obtained a copy of her daughter's original birth certificate from the Texas state birth registry in Austin. She also contacted officials at the state school in Denton, Texas, who informed her that her child was buried in a cemetery nearby. Later, Celia visited the school and met with officials, who directed her to her daughter's grave site, where she said goodbye to the baby she never saw or touched.

At the time Celia's daughter was born, she was aware her baby was several weeks premature and understood that she would remain in the hospital for an undetermined length of time. But no one at All Saints Hospital, including Dr. Parchman, the baby's pediatrician, nurses, or social workers, or even staff members at Homestead Maternity Home and its child placement agency, ever told Celia her baby was born with a serious medical condition. As she attempted to come to terms with the revelation that her baby was never adopted, as she had always believed, and that her daughter had lived almost all of her life in a state school environment, Celia began to search for details and explanations. First, she obtained medical records documenting her stay at All Saints Hospital in December of 1970. These documents included labor and delivery records, as well as postpartum notes for herself and the baby. At the same time, Celia requested and received copies of medical records for the eight years her daughter had lived at the Denton State School. After reviewing and analyzing the documents, Celia learned the baby was diagnosed with microcephaly soon after she was born. She also discovered her daughter remained in foster care for about one year before she was admitted to the Denton State School.

Today, Celia still remembers well the weeks she spent at Homestead and all the years she hoped to meet her daughter one day. But she says the past is the past, and she has learned to deal with it in her own way.

Donna

Donna was sixteen years old and living with her parents in Killeen, Texas when she became pregnant in the fall of 1964. Her father was a government employee and had first moved to Texas while he was in the U.S. Army. Donna's parents met and married in New York, where her mother worked as a practical nurse, and she was their only child. Donna first met "Sonny," her baby's father, when he was a young Air Force recruit. According to Donna, when "Sonny" had military leave, he visited his sister who lived in Donna's neighborhood next door to a married girlfriend of hers. Because her friend was pregnant and the woman's husband was away in the Army, Donna often visited the friend to help her with household chores.

Donna wasn't dating anyone when she met Sonny, but when he initially asked her for a date she refused, primarily because she was interested in another guy. But the "nice, attractive guy" continued to visit his sister in Killeen, and "he kept pursuing me," Donna explained. By August, the two were dating. In retrospect, Donna described their relationship as a "summer romance" that ended when "he was discharged from military service around Christmas." By then, she was already pregnant with Sonny's child, and when her father found out, he "hit the roof," Donna recalled. In hindsight, Donna believes she and Sonny were just "young, stupid, and very naïve."

Although her parents were raised Catholic, Donna and her family attended other churches, including a local Baptist church in Killeen. Donna doesn't know for sure, but her mother may have learned about Homestead Maternity Home in Fort Worth from someone at the church. When her mother told Donna about Homestead, she also mentioned the Edna Gladney Home in Fort Worth. In the following weeks, Donna and her parents visited both maternity homes. After they had visited each home, Donna's parents allowed her to choose between the two, and she chose Homestead. When asked about her decision, Donna explained the Edna Gladney Home offered a more "social environment" than what she envisioned or wanted. Before Donna was scheduled to leave Killeen for Homestead, her mother told her she did not have to give up her baby. Although Donna considered keeping her baby, she realized that she was not old enough to raise a child herself, and her mother would have "taken over as the baby's mother." Donna further explained her parents were "good people," but they were "old-fashioned in their belief system," and she didn't want that for her child.

About six weeks before her June 1963 due date, Donna and her mother left Killeen on a bus headed to Fort Worth. According to Donna's account, her mother was with her when she was admitted to the maternity home at 1250 West Rosedale. The process was a short one, since her parents already had talked to a Homestead social worker and to Dr. Thomas Durham, the maternity home's director, when they had previously visited the Fort Worth facility. Donna was quickly assigned a room on the "mostly empty" third or top floor of the red brick building. A Homestead official, Donna said, explained to her that all first and second floors were filled to capacity with other women who were farther along in their pregnancies. Donna was told she would be moved to a lower floor when a room became available, and when she was closer to term, she would be assigned a first floor room. The room assignment procedure at Homestead, Donna explained, reduced the number of flights of stairs the women needed to climb, since steep stairs were the only means of access between the facility's floors. And as Donna summarized the process, "the closer to term or the bigger you were, the lower the floor."

Fairly soon after she arrived at Homestead, Donna developed her own personal routine. She said she kept to herself for most of the time she lived at the facility and explained how she preferred to "stay away from the boisterous bridge games and the occasional cat fights" that took place on the first floor. Instead, she kept busy by sewing curtains from old sheets that she used to cover the big, old windows in her room. In the evenings, Donna said she wrote letters to her mother, who regularly corresponded with her. As word spread that Donna was a very good seamstress, other residents asked her to teach them to sew on the machines located in Homestead's first floor sewing room. When asked if she was responsible for any chores at Homestead, Donna said she and the other residents cleaned their own rooms, did their own laundry, and sometimes peeled potatoes for dinner and washed dishes after evening meals. Pregnant women were not responsible for any heavy cleaning, such as scrubbing floors or washing windows, and she explained that Homestead hired individuals to prepare meals in the basement kitchen and to clean the common areas in the maternity home.

During her stay at Homestead, Donna became friends with another resident, "Yvonne," a pregnant 14-year old who already had an 18-month old baby. Donna said she and Yvonne craved watermelon and often walked a short distance down the street to a convenience store where they bought a melon and shared it back at Homestead. A few of the other girls became upset when Donna and Yvonne did not offer them a piece of the watermelon. On their next trip to the store, the two girls noticed a sign advertising watermelons at half-price over the weekend, so they returned to the store later and bought two watermelons for the price of one. Each of the girls carried a watermelon back to Homestead, where they shared them with a few other residents at the picnic tables out back. Since there was not enough watermelon to go around, some of the girls who were left out talked to Mrs. Gray, Homestead's housemother. After the girls had eaten the watermelons, Mrs. Gray called Donna and Yvonne to her room, where she told them two of the girls who were not included in the watermelon party had complained that Donna and Yvonne had exchanged sex for the two watermelons. Donna said Mrs. Gray's face was "all screwed-up and she looked like the Evil Witch of the West," when she questioned them. Donna explained that she looked Mrs. Gray in the eye and said, "Just look at us. Does this story really sound reasonable?" After a few moments of silence and a deep stare, Mrs. Gray dropped the questioning. After the incident, Donna said she and Yvonne "stayed by ourselves."

Donna moved to the first floor less than a week before her due date in mid-June of 1965. In addition to sleeping rooms, which were not air-conditioned, the first floor housed the laundry area where a washer and dryer were located, an air-conditioned library with a television, an exam room, and the sewing room mentioned earlier. Mrs. Gray also lived on the first floor. When asked to describe Homestead's housemother, Donna recalled she was "a heavy-set, gray-haired, older lady, about five-two or three, who weighed between 160-170 pounds." She added that Mrs. Gray "carried a big key ring with lots of keys" causing her to "jingle when she walked." Although Mrs. Gray enjoyed small conversations with some of the girls, Donna remembered she had a "chilly side, not mean, but she was not warm and fuzzy or the motherly type." Some of the girls liked her, Donna said, but she stayed away.

The evening that Donna went into labor is still etched firmly in her mind. Dinner that night was fried chicken and mashed potatoes, one of her favorites. And even though she felt some mild pains before dinner was served, Donna kept her discomfort to herself, primarily because she wanted to eat fried chicken. The pains continued after dinner, she recalled, and one of the other girls, whose room was nearby, finally told Donna she needed to "time" the pains, since they were happening more often. The other resident also attempted to convince Donna that she should notify Mrs. Gray. Donna admitted that she delayed telling Mrs. Gray about the labor pains until she absolutely knew she couldn't wait any longer. Her rationale was that she simply didn't want to deal with the woman she disliked so much. Once Donna told Mrs. Gray she was in labor, the housemother gave her a pill the other girls called a "red devil." Almost immediately, Donna said she "got loopy and started talking my head off." She also remembered having difficulty walking down the steps to a taxi waiting outside that drove her to the hospital. When asked who rode with her in the taxi, Donna said no one accompanied her on the trip to the hospital.

At the hospital, the nurses were very nice, and they called her "Little Bit," because she was only five feet two inches tall and tiny, even though she was nine months pregnant. Donna recalled telling the nurses they should not put her to sleep because she had eaten a big dinner. She said, "Someone must have given me some sort of anesthetic, because I don't remember any pain, or pushing, or hearing the baby cry." She described her overall condition as being "bombed out of my gourd." At some point after her baby was born, Donna heard the doctor telling her he was going to cut off a mole and would "stitch her up." She said she does remember telling him to "stitch it all up – I'm not going to use it again."

After Donna gave birth, hospital staff moved her to a room with two beds, but she was the only patient in the room. Although her mother was not there when she gave birth, she did visit Donna the next day. Shortly after her mother arrived, one of the nurses told her that neither she nor her daughter should go to the nursery. Her mother did go to the nursery, however, and returned to tell Donna she had given birth to a baby girl with a "head full of dark hair." A couple of days after her daughter was born, Donna said someone she had never met – maybe a social worker – came to her hospital room to get the relinquishment paper signed. The individual did not tell Donna she was required to sign the paper nor did she explain that she could refuse to sign it. When asked if anyone advised her that she could change her mind within the six-month period leading up to the final adoption, Donna said "no." She did recall Dr. Durham saying that Homestead took care of all our needs before we gave birth. He also said that if we changed our minds about giving our babies up for adoption, we would be required to repay the money Homestead had spent for our care and medical expenses.

Donna returned to her parents' home in Killeen about a week after her daughter was born. Within a few days, Sonny called her and asked if she would meet him somewhere to talk. Donna reluctantly agreed to meet at a local soda shop, where she pointedly asked him, "What do you want? She's already gone." Donna said he did not answer or say anything at all, and at that point, she got up and walked out. Donna said she didn't know at the time that Sonny had stopped by her parents' house a time or two while she was at Homestead to talk to her mother and to ask about her. Later, she learned that during one of these visits, Sonny talked to her mother about their relationship and had given her a letter he had written to Donna that he asked her to send to her in Fort Worth. According to Donna, she never received the letter. Donna has wondered from time to time if her life, Sonny's life, and the life of their daughter would have been different if she had known exactly how Sonny felt about their relationship. But she still believes Homestead was where she needed to be at the time.

Back at home in Killeen, Donna attempted to resume her life by going to work at a local restaurant. Soon she met a young military guy who frequented the restaurant, and they became friends. The young man made quite an impression on Donna and her parents, because he followed her home in his car after she worked the late shift, saying he wanted to make sure she arrived at home safely. Their friendship grew, and by the end of the year, when she was seventeen and a half years old, the couple married and moved to Maryland. Donna said the marriage lasted seven years before it ended in divorce. After a brief second marriage and a subsequent divorce, Donna began a relationship that lasted over thirty-four years before it ended a few years ago. In hindsight, Donna believes Homestead was "the best choice" for her and for her baby, since her mother would have attempted to take over and try to be the child's mother, rather than her grandmother.

Donna had no other children, and she never forgot the baby she gave up for adoption in Fort Worth in 1965. She always knew that one day she would be reunited with her daughter. It took over four decades, but a few years ago, Donna received the call she had been expecting for years. Her daughter found her, and the relationship that developed after the two were reunited continues to be a special one.

"Essie"

Born in the Piedmont area of North Carolina in 1944, Essie dropped out of high school when she was seventeen years old. "We were poor," Essie said, "and I just didn't fit in with the other girls." She explained that her father moved their family from North Carolina to Georgia when she was six years old, and she had developed some friendships there. But when she was a young teenager, the family moved back to North Carolina. Back in North Carolina, Essie said she felt as if she "wasn't good enough" to become close friends with most of the girls at her high school, because the other girls ran with "a different crowd." Essie's lack of friendships with other girls at her high school, however, was offset by her popularity with the town's young men. Essie said she worked on local tobacco farms and as a babysitter in town during the two years after she left high school. When she wasn't working, Essie recalled, she spent her free time hanging out at the local skating rink or partying at various places around town. She admitted that she enjoyed the attention from the guys she met, but at nineteen, she discovered she was pregnant. Since she had no strong connection with her baby's father, Essie said she kept the pregnancy to herself.

Afraid to tell her parents that she was pregnant, Essie told her sister, who lived in a nearby town, and her sister and brother-in-law offered her a room in their house. Essie also told her sister that she wanted to keep her baby, and her sister agreed to help her care for the baby after she gave birth. While

Essie lived with her sister, she worked in the tobacco fields nearby, alongside her sister and brother-in-law, but as her pregnancy advanced, she found it increasingly difficult to keep working. When she could work no longer, Essie applied for public assistance for herself and her unborn child, but she said she was denied. With no job and no other income, Essie said her only choice was to move back in with her parents and to tell them she was pregnant. Essie explained that she was "a skinny girl," and her pregnancy became visible very fast, so once her parents saw her, they would immediately know she was pregnant, anyway. Since she did not own a car, Essie said she "just stayed around the house." When someone stopped by to visit, Essie's mother told her to go upstairs to her room and to stay until the visitor was gone. If the visitor asked about Essie, her parents simply told them their daughter "wasn't home." Very few people, Essie recalled, ever knew she was pregnant.

As Essie's due date drew closer, her father became more concerned about his daughter's future and the future of her unborn child. When he called the North Carolina Children's Home Society to see if they would accept Essie and help place her baby for adoption, he was told there was no available room. He also learned that if a room had been available, he could not have afforded to pay the cost of Essie's room and board. Still determined to help his daughter, Essie's father met privately with the pastor of the local Presbyterian Church he attended. During the meeting, he told his pastor that he and his wife could not afford to support another child and asked for advice about his daughter's pregnancy. Although she does not know for certain, Essie believes the pastor recommended that her father send her to Homestead Maternity Home in Fort Worth, Texas. After her father returned home from the meeting with his pastor, he and Essie's mother told her she would be going to Homestead or she would not have a place to live. The pastor stopped by later and explained to Essie that he believed adoption was the best choice for her and for her baby, especially since neither of her parents thought she was capable of "settling down" enough to take care of herself and a child, too.

According to Essie, Homestead told Essie's father they preferred to admit women who were at least four to five months pregnant, so she had to wait another month after the pastor's visit before she could leave North Carolina. She explained the delay meant she had to remain at her parents' home and to "stay out of sight." Essie recalled the day her father walked to the post office and returned with a one-way ticket to Fort Worth. Although she never asked him for details, and he offered none himself, Essie believes Homestead sent the bus ticket for her trip to Fort Worth to her father's post office box. She said the one-way ticket was very troubling for her, since she was unsure when she left North Carolina if she would be allowed to return home after her baby's birth. "I didn't ask questions," Essie recalled, "because I was afraid of the answers." Before Essie left North Carolina for Fort Worth, her father explained that his pastor had arranged for her to live at Homestead without paying room and board, and in return, her baby would be placed for adoption as soon as possible after its birth. "To this day, very few people ever knew I went away," Essie added, "and my parents told anyone who asked about me that I was away visiting relatives."

Essie recalled how "very scared" she was when she got off the bus at the station in Fort Worth. Her father told her someone from Homestead would be waiting at the bus station to drive her to the maternity home. According to Essie, that individual was Mrs. Madge Hoskins, a "short, little prissy woman with snow-white hair," who was "friendly and helped ease some of my fears." Soon after they met, Essie learned that Mrs. Hoskins was Homestead's housemother and lived in an apartment on the maternity home's first floor. She recalled how much she grew to like Mrs. Hoskins and said the older woman had a "strong maternal side." Another older "stern-faced woman named Mrs. Gray" worked in one of Homestead's offices and lived in an apartment on the second floor. Essie described this woman as "big, tall, and wide," and added that she never smiled. "Mrs. Gray," Essie laughingly added, "acted as the bouncer" at the maternity home, and she and some of the other girls were "very afraid of her."

While she lived at Homestead, Essie said she had "plenty of food," and "saw the doctor regularly." On one occasion, Essie recalled, she developed a toothache and went to see a dentist. As far as she knew, Homestead paid for the dentist, since she had no money of her own. When asked about her daily life at Homestead, Essie said she preferred to "stay in the room most of the time," and added that "I read a little and slept as much as I could to make the time pass by faster." On Sundays, she and other Homestead girls attended a "chapel service" that Dr. Durham held in "the big room on the first floor" of the Homestead building. Neither of Essie's parents wrote to her while she lived at Homestead, but they did call her once a week. Their calls came in on Mrs. Gray's office phone, and Essie said the old woman "sat in the office and listened to my calls." One of Essie's good memories of Homestead was a Christmas party for Homestead residents, hosted by Dr. Durham and his wife. She especially enjoyed the food, festivities, and the personal gifts provided by local merchants.

Less than a week after Christmas of 1963, and about six weeks before her due date in February of 1964, Essie discovered a bloody discharge during a regular trip to the bathroom. According to Homestead procedures, Essie informed Mrs. Gray about what she believed must be a serious problem. Instead of trying to comfort Essie, Mrs. Gray began to scream loudly and accused the young woman of having done something to endanger her baby. The older woman loudly ordered Essie into a vacant room down the hall, and told her to lie on the bed. In a not-so-nice voice, Mrs. Gray said, "don't move." Essie was scared and was crying so hard that she said she couldn't see, but Mrs. Gray continued to yell at her and said "I can't believe you would do something like this when people have paid out a lot of money on you and that baby." A minute or two later, Mrs. Gray left the room and returned with a cup of water that she ordered Essie to drink. Although Essie doesn't remember taking a pill or the water tasting "funny," she believes Mrs. Gray must have given her something to "knock me out."

The next thing Essie remembered was waking up with her hands on her flat stomach and thinking that she must have given birth to her baby. She was confused, however, since she was lying in the same bed in the same room at Homestead where Mrs. Gray had sent her when the bleeding began. Although Essie said no one ever told her the date and the time her baby was born, or the baby's weight, Mrs. Gray did tell her she had a baby girl. Essie does not remember anyone giving her a pill or a shot after she first woke up. The next thing she does remember was getting out of a taxi at the Fort Worth bus station and someone handing her a one-way ticket back to her hometown in North Carolina. She remembers very little about the bus trip back home. In hindsight, Essie believes she must have delivered her baby in the room at Homestead and was never admitted to a hospital. She has no idea how long she remained in the room where she apparently gave birth to her daughter, nor does she recall signing a paper that relinquished her rights to the baby girl she never saw or touched.

Essie's father was waiting for her at the bus station when she arrived in her home town. After the two exchanged hellos, Essie said her father hugged her, and with tears in his eyes, he told her that she had "broken his heart." Neither he nor Essie mentioned her delivery or the baby she had delivered in Fort Worth. When she and her father walked into the house, Essie said her mother seemed happy to see her, but she never mentioned the baby to Essie, either then or later. Sadly, Essie said she would always remember the words her father said to her at the bus station, because he died of a serious heart condition only five months later. She added, "I've had to keep this inside me for fifty-three years. The only people I've ever told are my husband and two or three longtime friends I trust."

A few years after returning to North Carolina, Essie married, but after thirteen years, she and her husband divorced. They had no children, she said. Sometime later, Essie married again, and she volunteered that she and her husband are still happily married. "I've felt left out and bad over the years when I've had to listen to friends talk about their children. I didn't feel like I could talk about the baby girl I gave up." She explained that she could never have another baby and wondered aloud if maybe Homestead "did something to me" when she gave birth to her daughter years ago. When asked if she had talked to a doctor about her inability to become pregnant, Essie said she had not. She added, "I was afraid that I would have to tell the doctor the story about being pregnant and giving up my baby at Homestead."

A few weeks before Essie shared her story for this book, her birth daughter petitioned the court in Fort Worth, Texas, to open her adoption file. A Tarrant County judge granted the petition and turned over the file to a court-appointed intermediary, who reviewed the file's contents. Within weeks, the intermediary had located Essie, the adoptee's birth mother. Essie said her daughter wrote her a letter, and the intermediary mailed it. After Essie had time to receive the letter, the intermediary contacted her to see if she wanted to communicate with her daughter. Essie said she was overjoyed to have been "found," and she immediately answered "yes" to the intermediary's question. Just days before Essie was interviewed for this book, the intermediary phoned to say her daughter would be calling within the next few minutes. According to Essie, the phone reunion went very well, and her daughter, son-in-law, and granddaughter have shared numerous phone calls, cards, letters, and pictures. According to Essie, her daughter and family are planning a trip to North Carolina to meet her and her stepfather and other North Carolina family members. The sweetest part of the reunion, so far, Essie added, was the day her granddaughter called to ask what name she wanted to be called.

Janice

Raised in a military family, Janice said she lived "everywhere." When she became pregnant at fifteen, her family was living in Mineral Wells, Texas, where she attended high school. When Janice's parents eventually learned she was pregnant, they made a decision to send their daughter to Homestead Maternity Home in Fort Worth. They chose Homestead over Edna Gladney, Janice explained, because the room and board at Homestead was less. Janice said she had "no say at all" about where she would go or how long she would stay at the maternity home. Also, it was "understood" the baby she was carrying would be placed for adoption soon after she gave birth. Janice's sister, about a year older, knew about her pregnancy and understood she would be "going away." Her eleven year old brother, however, "knew nothing," Janice added. Since her high school would not allow pregnant girls to attend classes, Janice's mother ordered a correspondence course for her to study at home until she could be admitted to Homestead when she was about four months pregnant.

Janice remembers the drive from Mineral Wells to Fort Worth, and when her parents left her at Homestead Maternity Home, she felt very afraid and all alone. She remembers thinking "Dear God, No!" as she walked upstairs to the room she was assigned. "I thought I was going straight to Hell," Janice added. At Homestead, she worked in the kitchen and communal dining area in the facility's basement, trying to stay busy while she waited to give birth. Janice said Dr. Parchman was her doctor, and she and several other girls walked to their prenatal visits at his office near the maternity home. Once or twice a week, Janice's mother drove to Fort Worth, and they visited over a meal in a local restaurant. "Dad did not come to see me at Homestead," she added. On Sundays, she and some of the other Homestead girls went to church with Dr. Durham and his wife, and on several occasions, the Baptist minister and Homestead director invited the girls to his home for a Sunday meal after church. On other occasions, Janice went home with "Kathy," a Homestead resident whose family lived in Fort Worth. She still recalls how welcome her friend's family made her feel during these visits to their home.

A week or so before her due date in the spring of 1966, Janice said her water broke while she was walking with several other Homestead girls to Dr. Parchman's office. She does not remember how she got back to Homestead, but within a short time, Dr. Parchman arrived in his car and drove her to St. Joseph's Hospital. Janice said, "They must have knocked me out before the baby was born. The next thing I remember is someone taking a mask off my face and grabbing my arms and hands, because I was trying to take the baby away from the nurses. I was crying and screaming and struggling to keep them from taking my baby away. But they took him away anyway. Seeing them take my baby away was the saddest, most horrible, tragic thing that ever happened to me." Janice said she never saw Dr. Parchman or anyone from Homestead after she gave birth.

The day after she delivered the baby, a social worker visited Janice in her hospital room and brought the relinquishment form for her to sign.

Janice recalled thinking the social worker was totally heartless when she forced her to read the words out loud before she signed the document. Janice's parents also visited her the day after she gave birth, and she thinks she may have remained in the hospital for two more nights. When the hospital discharged her, Janice did not return to Homestead. Instead, her mother drove to St. Joseph Hospital and took Janice back home to Mineral Wells. After she returned home, Janice said her parents tried to "do things right," and moved the family to Weatherford where she enrolled the following fall in a different high school. The next year, Janice's father was discharged from the military and accepted a new job in the Dallas area, where the family moved and Janice graduated from high school. Soon after graduation, Janice married a young man she had met several years earlier in Killeen, and the couple had a daughter together about three years later. The marriage lasted about seven years, Janice said, before it ended in divorce. Over the years, Janice said she remarried and divorced a total of five times, but she never had other children.

During her interview, Janice expressed hope the son she gave up in Fort Worth in 1966 will find her one day. Although she has considered searching for him for many years, Janice feared that finding her son might disrupt his life. At the time she was interviewed, Janice said she was considering several options, including DNA testing and posting information on the state's adoption registry to make it easier for her son to connect with her.

> *Update:* A few months after Janice's interview, a Search Angel located Janice's son, and in early 2017, she and her son first met each other during a phone conversation, and they have remained in touch. Shortly before this book went to print, Janice learned her son and his family will be traveling to Texas in a few months to meet her in person. She is elated beyond words.

Karen Richards Rhoads

When she became pregnant at sixteen, Karen was living with her divorced mother, a nurse, and siblings in San Angelo, Texas. Karen said the father of her baby was a young man from Colorado, who was twenty-three years old when he was introduced to her by some friends. Although her mother was a nurse, Karen said she was young and naïve and knew little about her body or about sex and pregnancy when she "went all the way" with her boyfriend. She said he told her she would not get pregnant, because he "knew what he was doing," and she believed him. In hindsight, Karen said, "I had very little self-esteem, and he showed me a lot of attention." A few weeks later, when Karen believed she might be pregnant and shared the information with her boyfriend, he immediately responded, "Well, you'll just have to get an abortion." Karen emphatically replied "No," and that ended the relationship, she said. Several weeks later, Karen became sick and confided in her neighbor's older sister, who told her she might be pregnant. About four months into her pregnancy, Karen's mother "cornered her," and asked, "Are you pregnant?" Karen said, "I was forced to tell her the truth." Within a short time, Karen's mother took her to a doctor she knew in San Angelo, and he confirmed her daughter's pregnancy. When Karen's mother explained to the doctor that she was divorced and had other children and could not afford a baby, he suggested the baby be placed for adoption and gave her the number for Homestead Maternity Home in Fort Worth.

Karen knows nothing about the financial arrangement her mother made for her to go to Homestead, nor does she remember how she got to Fort Worth. She does recall walking upstairs to the third-floor room she was assigned and how she felt "very alone." The first person she met was Homestead's housemother, Mrs. Gray, who Karen described as "one step above the wicked stepmother in Cinderella." Soon after she was admitted to Homestead, Karen was examined by Dr. Jack Turner, a Fort Worth obstetrician who provided pre-natal care to Homestead mothers, and the doctor who later delivered her baby. She recalled walking with several other residents to prenatal checkup appointments at Dr. Turner's office a few blocks from the maternity home. During Karen's stay at Homestead, she helped prepare meals and shared kitchen duties with other residents. Personal chores included changing her own bed linens weekly, a Homestead requirement, and doing her own laundry. There were no prenatal classes at Homestead, nor was individual or group counseling offered. Karen recalled a clothes closet near the laundry area, where pre-worn, outgrown maternity clothes were stored for use by other residents. Although her mother did not visit her at all while she lived at Homestead, Karen said her father, who lived in Dallas, drove over to Fort Worth once or twice and took her and another girl who lived at Homestead back to his house for an overnight visit. Karen explained that her mother did not visit her at Homestead, because she told her that she had "disgraced the family."

When Karen went into labor at Homestead, she believes Mrs. Gray called a taxi to take her to the hospital, but she doesn't remember anything beyond walking down the back steps to get into the taxi. When asked if someone gave her a pain pill before she left for the hospital, Karen said she does not know. She remembers nothing at all about the taxi ride, getting out of the vehicle, or going inside the hospital. The next thing Karen said she remembers was waking in a hospital room at All Saints Hospital when one of the nurses brought a box with the perineal light into her room. Although the nurse told Karen she had given birth to a baby girl, she never saw or touched the infant. Before the nurse left the room, she warned Karen that she was not allowed to "leave the room." The next day, two women, including one who carried some papers in her hand, came into Karen's hospital room. The woman with the papers approached her bed, but the other "stood back, just inside the door." Karen said the woman told her, "You have to sign these papers," and she asked "What's the paper for?" The woman told her the papers were for the adoption, and Karen quickly responded, "But I don't want to give my baby up." The woman beside the bed, who Karen believes was a social worker, sternly said to her, "You have to give up the baby. What kind of life would you give it? You don't have a job. You're not out of school. How are you going to support it?" Before she finished saying the words, Karen began crying, and she continued to cry as she signed the papers. The two women left, and a few minutes later, the nurse came back into Karen's room and gave her something to help her "settle down."

To the best of her recollection, Karen remained in the hospital for several days. During that time, her mother called to tell her she needed to be home before June 1st, because her aunt and uncle from Ohio would be arriving in San Angelo. Since none of Karen's extended family knew about the baby, her mother wanted Karen to be at home when the relatives arrived to avoid answering questions about her absence. Apparently, Karen's mother had arranged for Homestead to drive Karen to the airport, where she flew back to San Angelo on Trans-Texas Airlines. Her mother was waiting at the airport, and she and Karen drove to the new house her mother had moved into while Karen was living at Homestead. On the trip home, Karen said her mother told her, "Don't tell anybody, including your aunt and uncle, where you've been." And that was the last reference she ever made to Karen's pregnancy, experiences at Homestead, or the baby she gave up for adoption in Fort Worth. Although Karen returned to high school, she was not allowed to continue her education after her marriage in 1966 to a local young man who had recently returned from Vietnam. Within a very short time, Karen became pregnant and eight months later, she gave birth to a baby boy, who only lived twenty-six hours. The marriage lasted about three years before the couple divorced. In 1970, Karen remarried, and two years later, she gave birth to another baby boy, her only other child. She and her second husband divorced after almost four years of marriage, and Karen later married three more times.

In 1990, Karen read an advertisement in her local newspaper about an adoption search group that met in Fort Worth. She attended the meeting and met a birth mother who worked as an intermediary and who assisted her in the search for her daughter. Their initial search efforts included a review of Texas birth records where the two women determined eight baby girls were born in Fort Worth on Karen's daughter's birth date. Next, the women traveled to Austin, Texas, and examined the state birth books to learn the adopted names of the eight babies born in May of 1965. Karen said the other birth mother helped her search for the women and initiated phone calls to them on her behalf. Fairly early in the process, the other birth mother connected with Karen's daughter and arranged for the two women to talk on the phone. About a week later, Karen traveled to an adjacent state to meet her daughter in person.

Although she was filled with anxiety before the meeting that something might go wrong, or that her daughter would not "like" her, Karen said the actual meeting was "awesome." She discovered her daughter was a beautiful woman who resembled Karen's own sister, and her son-in-law, who accompanied his wife to the meeting, seemed "awestruck" by the two women's similar expressions and body mannerisms. In the weeks and months that followed the meeting, Karen and her daughter met again in person and communicated in letters. In one of the two letters, Karen's daughter shared a concern that her adoptive mother might not be happy to learn she had met her birth mother. She also added that she did not think her adoptive mother would be receptive to meeting Karen. Since 1993, Karen's only contact with her daughter has been a Christmas card she sent to the only address she knew. According to Karen, "My daughter just stopped communicating, and I don't know why." Karen recently learned that her daughter's adoptive mother now lives with her, and she wonders if maintaining a relationship with her birth mother and her adoptive mother might have been just too difficult for her. And although more than a decade with no contact has gone by, Karen still wants to be in touch and hopes her daughter will reach out to her at some point in the future.

Margie Davis

An almost lifelong resident of Tarrant County, Margie grew up in south Fort Worth where she lived with her mother and stepfather and attended school. By the time she was twenty-one years old, Margie had married and divorced twice. She also had given birth to two sons during her second marriage. In early 1970, Margie discovered she was pregnant by a young man she had known since childhood and who she had dated briefly after her divorce. Although Margie had lived for a time in Corpus Christi where her boyfriend worked, she was living back in Fort Worth with her mother when she learned she was pregnant. After Margie told her mother she was pregnant, her mother contacted the Volunteers of America (VOA) office located a few blocks from her home. Although Margie was not present when the arrangements were made with VOA, her mother explained to her that she would continue to live at home until she gave birth and her baby could be placed for adoption. According to Margie, she never heard the word "Homestead" mentioned, nor did she know that anyone other than VOA, Dr. Hugh Parchman, the obstetrician whom she saw for prenatal visits, and All-Saints Hospital, were involved in her baby's adoption. Margie said she learned from hospital staff that she could not see her baby after its birth and she would not be told the child's sex. Although her baby's father was not involved during her pregnancy, Margie said the two of them renewed their relationship after she gave birth and were married for a short time.

Margie does not remember many details associated with her labor and delivery, and she attributes her lack of memory to the fact that she was heavily medicated before and possibly after she gave birth. She does remember asking an All Saints nurse whether her baby was a boy or a girl, and the nurse refused to answer. Later that same day, Margie asked a hospital volunteer, a "Candy Striper," if she would tell her the sex of her baby, and the young girl told her she had given birth to a baby girl. Although Margie has seen her signature on her daughter's original birth certificate, she does not remember signing that document or any paperwork relating to the relinquishment of her baby. When asked if a minister or social worker visited her in the hospital, Margie said she does not recall either individual visiting her room. After staying in the hospital for a couple of days, Margie returned to her mother's household. She especially remembers her mother refusing to talk about her pregnancy or the baby she gave up for adoption. Margie added that this sort of behavior was not unusual with family members who were her mother's age, since they believed uncomfortable subjects should not be discussed at all.

Over a decade ago, Margie contacted TX Care, an adoption support group located in Dallas, where she met Nancy Schafers, a search helper. At her suggestion, Margie submitted her name and contact information to the Central Adoption Registry in Austin, and she believed at one point that she might have located her daughter. Neither of the individuals, however, confirmed a possible relationship with the other. Margie explained that she remained on the registry and continued to wait with hope that her daughter would find her. In early 2016, Margie's long years of patiently waiting ended when she received a call from someone who said she was working with a Homestead adoptee whose DNA matches indicated a strong possibility that Margie was her birth mother. Margie says she will always remember that phone call and the many others that followed with her daughter. Very soon, Margie learned through conversations and exchanging photos that she and her daughter strongly resembled each other, and that her daughter's laugh reminded her of an aunt's laugh. After a period of getting to know each other through phone calls and other types of communication, Margie and her daughter met in person and spent a few weeks getting to know each other. The reunion, Margie said, was very special, and that meeting and getting to know her daughter has made her feel complete.

Although Margie said she had no involvement with Homestead staff members and never knew any of their names, her daughter has shown her documents that verify her adoption was processed through Homestead's child placement agency in Fort Worth. One of the documents was a non-id information sheet, which Margie said contains several inaccuracies, including educational background information about her and her daughter's birth father. In addition, her daughter's original birth certificate filed in Austin shortly after she was born shows her surname was Margie's married name. Margie said the inaccurate information, whether intentional or just a bad mistake, could have prevented her daughter from ever locating her original birth certificate.

Mary Lynn Calicoat Parrish

For years, Mary Lynn told no one that she had given up a baby for adoption. Her best friends nor her minister knew the story, and her four children knew nothing about their mother's early pregnancy or the half-sibling they shared. As an adult, a wife, and a mother, only Mary Lynn's long-time husband, Abby, knew the secret she had kept closely guarded for years. Mary Lynn's story began in Carlsbad, New Mexico, where she lived with her parents and attended high school. At the age of sixteen, she became pregnant by her high school boyfriend. Her parents did not offer to help her with the baby, Mary Lynn said, but instead, told her she would be staying at a maternity home in Fort Worth until she gave birth. Although she does not know how her parents heard about Homestead Maternity Home, Mary Lynn said she believes they may have been referred by a Baptist minister in Carlsbad or by her aunt who worked as a pharmacist in Austin, Texas. Mary Lynn said she understood from the beginning that her baby would be adopted at birth.

Mary Lynn's parents drove her to Fort Worth, where they spent the night in a hotel before driving across town the next morning to admit her to Homestead. Her parents accompanied Mary Lynn inside the maternity home and spoke with Mary Jo Maruda, a social worker, about the cost of their daughter's room and board. Although Mary Lynn was not actively involved in the conversation with her parents and Ms. Maruda, she did hear them say her room and board would be fifty dollar per month. According to Mary Lynn, she entered Homestead on June 5, 1967. When her parents left to return home, Mary Lynn met Homestead's housemother, Mrs. Gray, who assigned her to an "upstairs" room and introduced her to her roommate, a girl from Weatherford, Texas, named "Cherry." Mary Lynn described Mrs. Gray as a nice, kind woman, who was a "Godsend" during her stay at Homestead, and added that she will always remember the nice letter Mrs. Gray wrote to her after she returned home to New Mexico.

Mary Lynn's daily life at Homestead involved making her bed and keeping her portion of the room tidy. Each of the girls did their own laundry, which included changing their beds, washing the linens, and ironing their clothes. Although Homestead had a cook who prepared meals in the basement kitchen, each of the girls were assigned simple chores, such as making salads or setting the table. On one occasion, Mary Lynn recalled cleaning out a closet containing a large number of books left behind by girls when they left the facility. That chore was an uncomfortably hot job, she recalled, since Homestead had no air-conditioning. Mary Lynn said she and the other girls attempted to stay cool by leaving their windows open and using fans. Homestead residents, Mary Lynn recalled, were allowed to walk to Shockley's Grocery, a nearby convenience store, where they purchased cigarettes and snacks. They also walked in groups to Dr. Turner's office on 8th Avenue, for their prenatal checkups. The girls at Homestead were allowed to receive limited phone calls, and during the time Mary Lynn lived at the maternity home, her boyfriend from high school, the father of her baby, called her several times. She explained that he knew she was pregnant before she left Carlsbad and wanted to marry her before her parents decided to send her away. He called her a few times while she lived at the maternity home and continued to ask her if she would marry him. "I knew my parents wouldn't approve, because I was only sixteen," Mary Lynn recalled, "and to further complicate matters, he and his family had recently moved to Colorado."

Although Dr. Turner provided prenatal care to Mary Lynn, Dr. Hugh Parchman delivered her baby. Her mother had asked the doctor to induce her daughter's labor, Mary Lynn explained, since she wanted her daughter to return to high school when classes began in September. The doctor agreed to induce Mary Lynn's labor, and on August 22, 1967, she gave birth at All Saints Hospital. Mary Lynn remained in the hospital for three days before she returned to Homestead, and stayed there for three more days before the doctor released her to return home. Although Mary Lynn's parents had driven her to Fort Worth, they did not return to drive her back home. Using money her mother had sent her, Mary Lynn bought a ticket on a bus bound for New Mexico. The bus trip from Fort Worth to Carlsbad, New Mexico went through Pecos, Texas, and it took an entire day. She still remembers how uncomfortable she was on the bus and recalled that she sat behind the driver in order to leave the bus first and get to the terminal's restroom before other female passengers. She was also hungry and thirsty, but the cost of the bus ticket, Mary Lynn explained, left her with no money to buy food or drinks on the trip.

When Mary Lynn arrived at the bus station in Carlsbad, her mother was waiting to drive her home. Although the two women said hello, and her mother did tell Mary Lynn she was "glad to see her," she didn't hug her daughter or express any sort of affection. Later that afternoon, when Mary Lynn's Dad came home from work, she recalled he never even said hello. "He was never a lovey, dovey person," Mary Lynn explained, "so I wasn't really expecting any expression of physical affection from him." On the second night home, Mary Lynn's Dad finally approached her, and as he "rocked up and down on his heels," something Mary Lynn said he often did to emphasize a profound statement, he said something that Mary Lynn will never forget. As he looked directly at her, he said, "I sure hope you know that after this, no decent man will want you." Mary Lynn admitted that going back to high school was not easy, either, since Carlsbad was "a small town where everybody knew everybody." Although her parents told their friends and neighbors that Mary Lynn had spent the summer in Fort Worth helping an aunt, she felt as if the other students knew the truth and talked about her behind her back. At some point after she returned to school, Mary Lynn recalled seeing her old boyfriend while he was in town for a visit. "Things were different by then," she explained, "and I knew that getting married at sixteen was not the thing to do. And it wouldn't have worked out anyway."

Abby Parrish, Mary Lynn's husband of forty-seven years, was present during her entire interview and explained how he had located his wife's daughter. Initially, he began searching for Mary Lynn's baby in the summer of 2003, but it was about six months before he told his wife that he was searching. First, he posted Mary Lynn's information on an adoption registry, and he talked on numerous occasions with Pat Molina, who worked at Texas vital records in Austin. Over a period of time, Abby said Molina told him to "ask me questions," and in response to his questions, Molina gave him "clues about the adoption." As Abby gathered more information about Mary Lynn's first child, he posted details that he had learned on other adoption registries and websites. Within a reasonably short time, an adoption search angel called Abby to give him some information and to offer further assistance. Abby agreed, and the search angel continued her research. About that time, Abby decided to tell his wife that he was searching for the baby she gave up in Fort Worth. Very soon, the search angel contacted Mary Lynn and told her she had found her daughter and offered to make the initial contact with the young woman. Abby said he and Mary Lynn told her to "proceed, and we will stay out of it." When the search angel initially called Mary Lynn's daughter, Heather, there was no answer, and she left a message. Several days passed before Heather returned the call, and during the phone conversation, Heather confirmed her birth date and told the search angel she had been adopted through Homestead's child placement agency. But she also told the search angel she wanted nothing to do with her mother.

Heather's pronouncement to the search angel was firm, but she conveyed the message to Abby and Mary Lynn, who were both sad and disappointed. But Mary Lynn's determination to meet Heather was strong enough at that point to cause her to write her newly-discovered daughter a long letter. According to Abby, the letter was eleven pages long, and it took Mary Lynn about three months to write it. When the letter was complete, Mary Lynn asked the search angel if she would mail the letter to Heather so she would receive it on or about her birthday in August of 2005. The search angel did as she was asked, and Mary Lynn and Abby patiently waited for a response.

In October of 2005, Heather emailed Abby directly and told him she was "not ready" to meet her mother, but she wanted to "start slow" and begin communicating with him in order to get to know her birth mother. Abby said he and Heather became acquainted during this period of time, and he answered Heather's questions about Mary Lynn. Things went so well, Abby recalled, that Heather called her mother in February of 2006, and the mother and daughter heard each other's voices for the first time ever. During their conversation, Mary Lynn asked Heather to send a photo of herself. Laughingly, Heather responded, "Just go look in the mirror, because I look just like you!" On April 22, 2006, Mary Lynn and Abby, accompanied by Mary Lynn's sister and her husband, met Heather and her husband at a Fort Worth restaurant. The meeting was a very special one, Abby said, and he explained how Heather made it even more memorable by presenting her birth mother with a scrapbook that told her life story in pictures. When Heather handed her mother the scrapbook, she said "I've been waiting all of my life to do this." According to Abby and Mary Lynn, their reunion in Fort Worth began a wonderful relationship with Heather and her husband, and since then, they have enjoyed many memorable family moments together.

Mary Schwitters Knudsen, in her own words

"In the 60s, being unmarried and pregnant was a shame worse than death. 'Nice' girls were supposed to be virgins and able to wear white on their wedding day. Some of us fell in love and 'slipped up.' Or as society said, 'we got in trouble.' For some reason, it was always the girl's fault, and she paid the price. You had two choices: either get married (and give birth to a premature baby!) or get sent away where you were hidden (and nobody in your hometown would know) and give your baby up for adoption. Of course, in any case, you were not really fooling anybody.

Many parents had their daughters literally hide in the closet when someone came to their home before their girls were sent away. The guilt and shame that we felt is indescribable. Not only did we have to deal with the rejection of the young man we had loved, but we also had to now deal with the alienation of all that we were used to. Of course, we were not given the opportunity to talk about what was happening to us or have any real counseling. We were told 'if not directly then' but by society that we were not worthy or good enough to be a mother to our child. We were damaged goods and no one would ever want us.

I was one of the more fortunate ones. My parents never said to me 'how could you?' Or 'what will the neighbors think?' Or any of the other things many girls heard. I was a junior in college and when I wrote to my father (and asked him to tell my mother) to tell them that I was pregnant, I also told them that I would not be getting married. So they set out to do what they felt they had to do. My mother got a post office box and did a lot of research in the library. She sent away for information, and after studying it all, they decided that I would go to Homestead Maternity Home in Fort Worth. This was 900 miles away from my home in Iowa. There were several reasons they picked this home over others. First and foremost, they did not know anyone in Fort Worth. My father at that time was President of the National Farm Equipment Dealers Assoc., and people all over the country knew him and had seen me at conventions. The other main reason they picked Homestead was because all girls living at Homestead were giving up their babies. This decision had to be made before you were allowed to live there.

My mother drove me to Homestead, and I arrived in the middle of March 1965. I left my three sisters behind, none of whom knew what was really happening. They were told that I just couldn't decide what to major in (I was on my third major!) and needed to take some time off to figure things out and to work. She dropped me off and returned to Iowa. Every Sunday my Mom would go to my Dad's store and call me. She told my sisters the store had a special line that was cheaper for long distance. I would write letters to my parents at the post office box. Occasionally, I would write letters to the whole family at home – these were pretend letters full of lies about things I was doing. This is just the way things were. Now I look back and wonder how I could have gotten through that, but I did what I had to do to protect my family and me from the shame of my situation. As I look back on it now, the shame never really had anything to do with being pregnant or having my child, but was for what I had done to create the situation in the first place.

Homestead was a decent place to be. We were never treated like second-class citizens or made to feel ashamed. Dr. Durham was a retired Baptist minister, and he ran the home and the child placement agency. In 1965, Homestead was located on the corner of W. Rosedale and 5th Avenue. It was a building that was the original Harris Hospital and most recently, was a nurses' residence. It was not fancy but was clean; we had decent food, and excellent medical care. Mrs. Corrine Gray was our housemother. It really was not too different from the sorority house I had lived in before going there – except it wasn't as fancy, and we all had big bellies. Dr. Jack Turner was our obstetrician, and his office was located on 8th Ave. On Wednesdays, we would have a light lunch at noon, and then those that were scheduled to see the doctor would walk there in a group. On Wednesday nights, we had the best meal of the week! Often, it was roast beef with all the trimmings. We could eat well, because no one had to weigh in before the next Wednesday.

Until our last month of pregnancy, we all had chores to do, such as help cook dinner or do dishes (no dishwasher!), or mop the floors, or whatever we were assigned to do for the week. We were not overworked. We did keep up our own rooms, did our own laundry, etc. We had plenty of free time. We would walk to the Fort Worth Zoo or to the Episcopal hospital to see our friends. In 1965, our babies were delivered at All Saints Hospital. Previous to that, the babies were born at Harris Hospital. I am not sure if other hospitals were ever used. If one of our friends had a car, then we could go further for shopping or whatever. We always told Mrs. Gray where we were going, but I don't remember ever not being allowed to go where we wanted to.

Each week my Mom would send me five dollars a week for spending money. There was a little open air market (like an early Stop 'N Go) called Shockley's that was a block away. The building is an insurance office now. Every week I would go there with my money and buy my weeks' supply of fresh fruit, Pepsi, and cigarettes. On Sunday nights, a group of us would go to the store and buy a box of Chef-Boy-R-Dee pizza mix and a package of Mozzarella cheese, and we would cook a pizza for supper. In those days, there was no such thing as frozen pizza. And we couldn't afford to order pizza. There was a wonderful hamburger stand across the street, and they made the most heavenly French Fries with the skins on. Once in a while, we would get those.

There were two TV rooms, one large and one small, and both were air-conditioned, but the rest of the home was not. On the 5th Ave. end of the building, the Homestead Child Placement Agency was located. All the offices were there. I think those offices were air-conditioned. I did some work in the library organizing the books. I think I must have done that because it was cooler in there! On Sunday at 4 o'clock, Dr. Durham would come and have a church service for those of us who wanted to attend. I'm sure that someone took the girls who were Roman Catholic to Mass.

Though we did talk about what was happening to us physically, I cannot remember anyone talking about or dealing with the emotional aspect of what we were going through. We had no counseling of any kind. We were told that we were doing the right thing for our babies, and that we would go on with our lives and forget the whole experience. We were also told that we never needed to tell anyone that we had had a baby. Now, mind you, I am (or was!) a very slim, very blonde, young woman who gave birth to an eight pound, two ounce baby. And I could hide those stretch marks from my husband (if I were ever able to marry??? Get real!!!)

I gave birth to a son on August 28, 1965. During delivery we were put to sleep. Last year, I received my hospital records and discovered that I was also given scopolamine, which is a drug used so we would not remember what went on. We were not allowed to see our babies or to hold them or to tell them we would always love them. Again, we had no counseling or legal representation of any sort. A social worker and a notary came to our hospital room two days after delivery for me to sign away my paternal rights. They would not allow my son's birth father's name on the original birth certificate, because we were not married. That was the law until about 1970. It is now law that a birth mother cannot sign papers relinquishing her child until forty-eight hours after delivery. That was not the law in those days but the policy of Homestead. At some places, girls were given those papers to sign in the delivery room immediately after delivery, even while still drugged.

I spent a week or so at Homestead after delivery before I flew back to Iowa and the life I had left behind six months before. But life was never to be the same again. I had lost a part of my soul in that hospital room when I signed away my baby. It was part of me that I was never able to regain.

For thirty-one years, my son was rarely spoken of by me or by anyone else. Very few people knew he existed. As the years went by, I did tell two of my sisters of his existence. My husband knew from the first, though we didn't talk about it much. My parents never told one person until after my son and I were re-united. During the winter of 1996-97, I searched for my son. I eventually hired a searcher as I felt time was of the essence – my Dad was suffering from congestive heart failure. On February 14, 1997, I called a young man in Corpus Christi and told him that I was his birth mother. And his response was to thank me for giving him a wonderful life. It has been a dream come true for him to have accepted me into his life. He is a fine young man with a wonderful wife, two teenage stepsons, and one son born April 13, 1998, on my Father's 84th birthday. His adoptive father passed away a few years earlier, so I was never privileged to meet him. His adoptive mother is a wonderful woman, and I am very grateful she was his mother when I was not able to be. She is still his mother. I am not. I live out-of-state, so we are able to see each other when time permits. He has been to Iowa to meet my family and his birth father's family. In June of 1998, my parents were able to meet their only great-grandchild. In August, Ted and I flew up for my parents' sixtieth anniversary celebration, and he was able to meet many relatives who did not know of his existence.

All this has been a big part of my healing. Just to let go of all the secrets and lies that were inflicted on us by society has helped tremendously. I continue to actively work to change adoption laws to eliminate the secrets and lies that are still perpetrated on those who are adopted and on those who gave them life."

Pattie

When Pattie became pregnant, she was working and still lived at home with her parents in Indiana. As soon as she suspected she was pregnant, Pattie visited a local doctor who confirmed her pregnancy. During the visit, the doctor asked Pattie what she planned to do about the baby, and when Pattie told him she really didn't know, he suggested she contact

Homestead Maternity Home in Fort Worth, Texas, and gave her a number to call. Since Pattie was working and had money saved, she made her own arrangements with Homestead and traveled alone to Fort Worth. She remembered telling her employer that she needed to be away for a few months to complete a college course that would help her to better perform her job. Fortunately, she said, her employer believed the story and placed her on an unpaid leave of absence.

While Pattie was willing to be interviewed for the book, she preferred to retain as much privacy as possible by answering only a few questions about her stay at Homestead. The first memory Pattie recalled about her stay at the maternity home was from the day she was admitted. She explained that a Homestead staff member offered her a choice of "fake" names she could use during her stay at the facility. Although Pattie decided to use her own name, she said a majority of the maternity home's residents did use the "fake" names suggested by Homestead staff. According to Pattie, Homestead had no official rules in place that governed the girls' "coming and going in the daytime," although an evening curfew required residents to be inside the building no later than 7:30 p.m. Besides the evening curfew, Pattie did not remember any other restrictions or anyone who ever "told me what to do." Mrs. Gray, Homestead's housemother, Pattie added, was "nice to her," but some of the other girls didn't like the older woman because she was very stern. Pattie fondly remembered that after she gave birth and had returned home, Mrs. Gray sent her a "card with a handwritten note inside" saying she hoped everything was going well for her. Pattie explained that she had a large, comfortable room and was content to stay in her room and read or to walk to the store for exercise. In addition to the girls' sleeping rooms, the facility included a "big room with a TV where some of the girls played cards and board games." Since she and a number of other young women were not paying room and board to Homestead, Pattie "always felt the adoptive parents must have been subsidizing our room and board." But she never asked questions.

Dr. Jack Turner was the Fort Worth obstetrician whose office Pattie visited for periodic prenatal checkups and who later delivered her baby.

Pattie and several other Homestead residents walked to the doctor's office, located several blocks away from Homestead. Her visits with the doctor were scheduled on Wednesday afternoons, when it seemed the obstetrician's office was closed to everyone except "Homestead girls." Dr. Turner's nurse, a short, slender auburn-haired woman, whose name she does not recall, was always present during these office visits. Pattie remembered Dr. Turner as a shorter, dark-haired man with a pleasant personality and a kind demeanor. He asked her questions, and at the end of each visit, Pattie said the doctor asked her if she had any questions for him.

Pattie added that she was never sad or unhappy during her stay at Homestead, and she doesn't recall being depressed. Her goal, she said, was "to deliver my baby," and "to go back to work in Indiana." But after she had given birth, someone at Homestead offered Pattie the opportunity to see a psychologist, whom she recalled seeing "only once." During the visit, the clinician specifically told Pattie, "Now I want you to never think about this place. And I don't want you to talk about it to anyone. This is a new chapter in your life, a new beginning." And Pattie said, "I bought it hook, line, and sinker." She added, "I knew I had to go back home, but I felt as if I wasn't the same girl anymore. And I don't think I've ever been that girl again. I left ME behind." After Pattie returned home, she said her parents "never mentioned what happened to me at any point – never."

After some time, Pattie married and had another child, a son, but she never mentioned her first child to either her husband or her son when he was old enough to understand. Her life changed, she said, when her son was thirty-one years old, and she received a phone call from the daughter she had placed for adoption years before. Pattie recalled that she was "very surprised." Since she had kept the information about her first child a secret from her husband and her son, Pattie soon found herself telling them the story of her pregnancy and the baby's adoption in Fort Worth. Pattie remembers well the day her daughter contacted her, and she also remembers vividly how full of "guilt and shame" she felt when she broke the news to her husband and son. Her greatest fear, she said was that neither her husband nor her son would ever feel the same about her.

Although Pattie and her daughter, who grew up as an only child, lived in the same state, it took some time for them to meet. During their initial conversation, Pattie's daughter revealed that she had located her birth mother with the assistance of an attorney and a private investigator. And as the two women continued to talk, Pattie shared her own family history and heritage with her daughter. Eventually their two families met, and Pattie said that over time, she and her daughter have developed a very close relationship and visit each other as often as they can.

Polly King Speed

Polly met the father of her baby while she was living in San Angelo, Texas, where her dad was stationed at Goodfellow Air Force Base. Initially, Polly did not tell her mother she thought she was pregnant, but early morning sickness made it impossible to conceal her condition for very long. According to Polly, her mother did not want anyone to know her daughter was pregnant, especially her two younger sisters. Polly said her mother visited the local welfare office and "found out about Homestead [Maternity Home.]" Both of her parents "made me feel so ashamed," Polly remembers, and she stayed in her bedroom at home as much as she could until it was time to leave for Homestead. When Polly told her two younger sisters goodbye, the two girls believed she was going to work in Fort Worth. Polly said her parents drove her to Homestead, and the one thing she remembers about the road trip between San Angelo and Fort Worth was "ducking into the back seat, hiding my head, and crying." She said her Dad was a Master Sergeant in the Air Force and was "very stern" and often treated his daughters like "his troops." Although she was reluctant to admit it, Polly said she considered it "a blessing to get out of his household."

When Polly and her parents arrived at Homestead, they met with Dr. Durham, the director, who told Polly's father he would be charged thirty dollars per month for his daughter's room and board. Polly does not recall seeing her parents read or sign any paperwork or documents on the day she was admitted, nor does she remember reading or signing any documents herself. When asked what it was like to live at Homestead, Polly replied, "For the most part, I was treated well during my stay. Most of us had our own rooms, and there were a few rules like turning out the lights at a certain time." Polly described the Homestead facility as a three-story brick structure, and during her stay, "most of our rooms were on the second floor." In the evenings, Dr. Durham's wife, a "mean, old woman named Hassie," stayed overnight at Homestead with the girls. Polly explained that Mrs. Durham was "nice in front of my parents when they met her, but she didn't much like me, although I don't know why." Once Polly got settled in, she was sent to Dr. Parchman's office on 5th Avenue, which was within walking distance of the maternity home. She said Dr. Parchman examined her and gave her a delivery due date of October 27, 1969. When she was about a week overdue, Dr. Parchman decided to induce her labor on the morning of November 5, 1969.

Dr. Durham drove her to All Saints Hospital, and explained to her that girls who went into labor during the night usually went to the hospital in an ambulance or a taxi, depending on the stage of labor. At the hospital, Polly was surprised to learn she would be "prepped for delivery," and the process included "giving me an enema." She remembers feeling "really scared." After the delivery prep was complete, Polly recalled "someone gave me a pill that tasted like coffee, and the drug must have knocked me out. The next thing I remember was being slightly awake and touching my baby's head. I also remember someone telling me I had a baby girl." Polly remarked that what she remembers most after giving birth to her daughter was "crying a lot. I was all alone in the hospital room, and no one attempted to console me. The day after my baby was born, a caseworker came in with some paperwork. I cried while I was signing the papers, and I don't really remember her explaining anything about the papers, because I was just crying too much." Polly said Dr. Durham was the only other person who visited her during her stay at All Saints Hospital. The elderly Baptist minister, she recalled, came to her room for about five minutes each morning and talked to her and prayed, but she does not remember anything he said to her, and she doesn't recall talking to him at all. Polly said she returned to

Homestead after spending three nights in the hospital, and she remembers visiting with some of the other girls who recently had given birth. She said, "Most of the girls were just as depressed as I was, and they cried a lot, too." According to Polly, Homestead staff did not offer counseling to her or to the other girls she knew who were depressed after giving birth and giving up their babies.

Within a few days, Polly's parents drove to Fort Worth and took her back home to San Angelo, where she tried to "get myself back to normal." In December, Polly's family drove to Columbus, Mississippi and visited relatives over the Christmas holidays. When the holiday visit ended, and her parents and sisters returned to Texas, Polly stayed in Columbus. Before her father left, he helped Polly rent a room for a month from an elderly lady who owned a house near downtown Columbus. She said he also gave her money for food. By mid-January, Polly proudly recalled that she had found a job at General Tire, a local tire manufacturing plant, where she continued to work for about seven years. While she was working in Columbus, Polly "met up with an old high school friend," got married, and had two children. She said her husband was in the military, and she traveled with him to several duty stations, including Hawaii, but she waited a few years to tell him she had given up a baby for adoption. It turned out to be a mistake, she said, since he frequently used the unwed pregnancy and adoption against her each time they argued. Eventually, Polly returned to Mississippi with her two children, and the couple divorced. Later, in 1985, Polly remarried and had one son with her present husband. But she failed to tell him about the baby she gave up for adoption years before they married.

Polly says she never forgot her baby, and in 1997, when the internet was still fairly young, she began searching online for her daughter. Within a very short time, she discovered an adoption support group and joined other birth mothers, adoptees, and siblings who were searching for their family members. Polly remembers that someone in the support group suggested she tell her husband, and she took the advice. Her husband's response was "very sweet," Polly said, and he told his wife to "find her, just find her." Laughingly, Polly remembers her husband saying he actually was relieved to hear the news about her daughter. She explained that he had been concerned about the amount of time she was spending on the internet, and he had become concerned that she might have been having an affair.

With her husband's help and the assistance of other Homestead birth mothers in the support group, Polly searched the Texas birth index for her daughter. She also searched the entire list of registered voters in the State of Texas in an attempt to locate her child. Eventually, Polly mailed out over five hundred letters to names on the list, telling each one of the addressees she was searching for her daughter. In the letters, Polly purposefully omitted any information about Homestead Maternity Home, since she knew her daughter was the only Homestead baby born in Fort Worth on that day in November 1969. The response to Polly's letters was magnanimous, and eventually she located her daughter. Meeting her oldest child, Polly recalled, was bittersweet, especially when she saw how the young woman looked like her own younger sisters, her daughter's maternal aunts. Polly soon discovered her daughter had been adopted by a Tarrant County couple who still lived in the area and that she had a younger brother who also had been adopted through Homestead's agency. Although Polly has developed a good relationship with her daughter and her grandson during several visits she has made to Texas, her daughter still remains unwilling to tell her adoptive parents she has met her birth mother. Polly said she will continue to travel to Texas as often as she can, and she enjoys the time she and her daughter and grandson spend together.

Rene West

When Rene became pregnant in 1965, she was a nineteen year old college student in Durant, Oklahoma. Rene explained she had been dating a young man she had "met at school," who was a couple of years older. She added, "I was pretty crazy about him." Shortly after the school year ended, Rene believed she might be pregnant. Her boyfriend already had left town for the summer, so she did not tell him. When Rene returned home after the semester ended, she also was afraid to tell her mother she might be pregnant. Although her mother did not say anything for some time, Rene knew her sudden weight gain must have been noticeable to her mother. But the two women still did not talk. Very soon, Rene overheard her mother and her dad discussing their daughter's possible pregnancy, and she clearly remembered hearing her mother say she was "hurting" to think her daughter was pregnant, and she didn't know what to do. This was the first time in her life, Rene said, that she realized her mother really loved her.

The next day, Rene's mother called her aside and said "I'm taking you to the doctor." Since she and her parents lived near Ada, Oklahoma, Rene said her mother made an appointment for her with a doctor in that town. This was Rene's first gynecological exam, she said, and she remembered it well, because the doctor was an older man and was "sort of grumpy." During the physical exam, the doctor told Rene she was about four to five months pregnant, and after a discussion with Rene and her mother, he referred Rene to Homestead Maternity Home in Fort Worth, Texas. On the way home, she and her mother shopped for maternity clothes, and within a week, Rene said, "I was in a car with my parents headed for Fort Worth." While she was away, Rene's parents told anyone who asked about her that she was visiting her grandparents in Arkansas.

When Rene and her parents arrived at Homestead Maternity Home in Fort Worth, they went directly to Dr. Durham's office, where the Baptist minister who was Homestead's Executive Director "talked to all of us." Rene said she doesn't remember anything said during the short meeting. After she and her parents said goodbye, Dr. Durham sent Rene to see Mrs. Gray, the housemother, who worked in a small office at the end of the residential hall. During her brief visit with Mrs. Gray, Rene said the older woman assigned her a name she was told to use at Homestead. The name, Rene explained, consisted of her middle name and a fictitious last name that began with the first letter of her legal surname. When asked for details about her stay at Homestead, Rene said she "shared a room with a woman named Cheryl from somewhere in Texas." The two women shared a "communal bath and shower, located just outside their door, with other residents on the floor." They communicated well, and "got along," she added. One of the situations at Homestead that Rene remembers most involved another resident who was "only sixteen years old and at Homestead for the third time." The young Louisiana woman's second pregnancy had ended in miscarriage, and Rene heard from other residents that the father of all three babies was an older man.

Rene's daily life at Homestead consisted of doing prep work for meals prepared in the basement kitchen, making salads, setting the tables in the main dining room, which was also in the basement, and helping wash dishes. She said she also cleaned her room. About every three or four weeks, her parents drove to Fort Worth to visit her, and she was allowed to stay overnight with them at a local motel. Ironically, it was during one of these visits with her parents that Rene went into labor, and they drove her to the hospital. She explained that she was given "lots of anesthesia" and was "out of my mind" during her entire labor and delivery. Rene added that she must have been "knocked out completely before the actual birth" and "woke up in the recovery area in a cubicle with my parents beside the bed." Although Rene remembered very little about the rest of the day after she gave birth, she knows that neither she nor her parents ever saw her baby. The doctor had told her during visits to his office for checkups that "it was for the best," that she should not see the baby after it was born. She doesn't remember how long her parents actually stayed at the hospital, but she believes they left for home later that same day.

Rene remained in the hospital for five days, although she never understood why her confinement was longer than most of the other Homestead girls she had known. She always wondered if it was because she "cried a lot," when a man and woman she believed to be Homestead board members brought the "relinquishment paper" to her room several days after she gave birth. The two people were "very stern, strict, and business-like," she said, and she was so emotional that she "just signed them so they would go away." She doesn't remember much that was said during the visit, because she was "crying so hard." Rene believes, however, that she would have remembered if either of these people had told her she could change her mind about giving up her baby for adoption. After her discharge from the hospital, Rene returned to Homestead where she remained for a few days before her parents arrived to drive her home to Oklahoma. She remembers some "general talking" with her parents in the car after they left Homestead, but she does not remember any conversation with her parents about her labor, delivery, and giving up her baby for adoption. Rene said "life as usual" continued once she was home, but neither she nor her parents ever discussed her pregnancy or the baby she delivered. In fact, Rene added, she never talked about the experience at all until she "was married and had three kids."

Over a decade ago, Rene received a package from an "adoption search consultant" in Fort Worth, and she was very surprised to discover the package contained a letter from her daughter. She showed the letter to her husband, and he said "Open the Letter!" After reading the letter, Rene said she was "elated," but she was also fearful, because she did not know how her daughter would feel about her. When she became calm enough to do so, Rene said she signed the "confidentiality statement for mother and daughter" included in the package, allowing her daughter to initiate contact with her. Minutes later, Rene answered a phone call from her daughter, and told her "I've been expecting this call for a very long time." She and her daughter talked for hours, and Rene was both pleased and relieved to learn the baby girl she never saw or held wanted to establish a relationship with her.

Sandra Leigh Cawthorn

At the time she became pregnant, Sandra lived in Metairie, Louisiana, and worked in downtown New Orleans. She explained that her pregnancy resulted from an attack and rape in her apartment parking lot one night as she got out of her car after arriving home from work. Other residents of the apartment complex found Sandra in the parking lot and helped her get her into her apartment, where her roommates cared for her. She never reported the rape to the police, since the parking lot was dark, and she would not have been able to identify her attacker. When Sandra learned she was pregnant, she told her mother and father who lived nearby. Very soon, her parents contacted Homestead Maternity Home in Fort Worth and arranged for her to board there until she gave birth. When asked how her parents knew about Homestead, Sandra said she never asked, and her parents did not tell her. She said all she knew was they "got me the hell out of town as fast as they could."

Sandra arrived at Homestead in April of 1969 when she was about six months pregnant. A maternity home staff member, whose name she does not recall, took her to Homestead's obstetrician "right away." She does not remember the doctor's name, but she said he was "always very nice." Sandra remembers that she was "treated very well at Homestead," and she developed a friendly, personal relationship with Dr. Durham, a Baptist minister and Homestead's director, and his wife, Hassie Durham. According to Sandra, Dr. and Mrs. Durham lived at the maternity home, and she recalled visiting them in their apartment. "I was their favorite," Sandra added. During one of her early visits with the couple, Sandra said Dr. Durham assured her that he already had parents waiting for her baby. She also attended weekly church services held by Dr. Durham in "the large room" at Homestead, and frequently, she accompanied the minister to Sunday services at Arlington Heights Baptist Church in Fort Worth.

As her July due date quickly approached, Sandra asked her doctor what she should expect when she went into labor and when she gave birth. He explained to Sandra that he would put her to sleep and when she woke up, it would "all be over." When Sandra finally went into labor, she said she was "hysterical," and Dr. Durham allowed her to call her mother before he drove her to the hospital. After she gave birth, Sandra remembers Dr. Durham visiting her in the hospital room, but she recalls very little about the visit or about her labor and delivery. Since the minister and his wife, the obstetrician, and her parents had convinced her that she should not see or hold her baby, Sandra did not ask if her baby was a boy or a girl.

In early 2016, Sandra learned the baby she had given up for adoption in Fort Worth in 1969 was searching for her. According to Sandra, individuals assisting her daughter initially contacted other family members who did not know anything about her pregnancy or that she gave up a baby for adoption. "That did not set very well with me," she recalled. A short time later, Sandra and her daughter, who lives in another state, met in person for the very first time. She added that everything is "all worked out now." When she was interviewed for this book, Sandra explained that her daughter's birthday was the next day, and she remarked how excited she was about wishing her "Happy Birthday" for the first time ever.

"Sandy"

She was an unmarried nineteen year old when she became pregnant in Colorado. At the time Sandy became pregnant, she lived with her divorced mother and worked as a receptionist and sales clerk for a small, locally-owned company. Her pregnancy, Sandy reluctantly told me, resulted from "sexual harassment at work that ended in rape." When she admitted to her mother that she was pregnant and told her how the pregnancy occurred, Sandy said her mother was furious and called her a "slut," a "tramp," and a "whore." Sandy explained that her relationship with her mother had never been a good one, but it became worse when her mother learned she was pregnant. Sandy further explained that when she was only six months old, her mother left her with her father's mother, since her own mother had died while she was pregnant with Sandy. She referred to her paternal grandmother who cared for her as an "angel," and sadly recalled that her paternal grandfather died in her presence when she was only four years old. When Sandy was about ten, her mother "came into my life again," and she had been living with her mother since that time. Her father, Sandy explained, worked in the oil fields in Oklahoma, and she rarely saw him.

When asked how she or her mother learned about Homestead Maternity Home in Fort Worth, Sandy said her mother worked for a "well-respected doctor" whose office was in their Colorado neighborhood, and she believes the doctor must have told her mother about Homestead. Sandy still remembers her mother's misplaced concern that a pregnant and unwed daughter would adversely affect her "image at work and her standing in the community." Sandy's mother drove her to Fort Worth and went inside Homestead "just long enough to sign some papers." Although Sandy was never sure what type of papers her mother actually signed, she later learned from her Dad that she had agreed to pay her daughter's room and board amounting to $35 per week. Sandy's Dad also told her that her mother had called him and demanded that he pay the room and board expenses. Although Sandy said she recalls very little about the day she entered Homestead, she clearly remembers the absence of a tearful goodbye when her mother left her and returned to Colorado.

Sandy chose to use her actual name during her stay at Homestead and said she does remember providing family details for an information sheet requested by a staff member. The sheet asked for "hair and eye color for me and for my baby's father, for each parent's family history information, and for my occupation and the father's," Sandy said. When asked about her daily life at Homestead, Sandy said she and the other girls "helped cook and serve meals," although a "grandmotherly figure" had primary responsibility for preparing the food. She fondly remembers how this woman made "the best cinnamon rolls in the world" and "made sure all her girls got their meals each day." Although she ate healthy meals, Sandy said "the iron in my blood was low, and the doctor gave me iron shots." Sandy recalled the kitchen and dining room were located in the basement of the Homestead building, and the girls ate their meals there. In addition to the basement, the old red brick building contained three floors, and Sandy said she occupied a room on the second floor. Although each room contained two single beds, Sandy never shared her room with anyone else. The third floor was used as an "activity center" where the girls played board games or cards, but no one "roomed" on that floor. According to Sandy, Homestead girls had few restrictions, except they were not allowed to go out alone and were required to obey an evening curfew. Sandy and the other girls "walked in groups down the street to a convenience store," but they "weren't allowed out after dark." Periodically, she and a few other girls walked as a group to Dr. Turner's office on 8th Avenue where they received prenatal checkups. She remembered the obstetrician as "business like," but she did not think he was "concerned about our emotional health."

During her stay at Homestead, the highlight of Sandy's week was dinner with an aunt, one of her father's sisters who worked in Fort Worth. Sandy said her aunt stopped by Homestead after work on Friday nights, and they went out to dinner. She also made friends with one of the other residents, a young woman from New Orleans, but the two of them lost contact after they gave birth and returned to their respective homes. Although her mother did not write or call during the four and a half months she lived at Homestead, Sandy said she was allowed to call her mother collect once each month. The phone calls home, Sandy recalled, primarily involved listening to her mother talk about her sister and her brother's wife, who each had babies during the months she lived at Homestead. Her mother never asked how she was doing, and when Sandy attempted to say anything about herself, her mother ignored her and resumed talking about her siblings and the new grandbabies. Wistfully, Sandy said she wanted to keep her baby, but she knew from the very beginning that "everything was stacked against me."

According to Sandy, her mother asked the doctor to induce her daughter's labor. Although she knew her baby was born at All Saints Hospital in Fort Worth, Sandy remembers nothing at all about giving birth. She attributes her loss of memory to anesthesia she was given that totally "knocked me out." Sandy does remember one of the nurses telling her after the delivery, when she was in a semi-awake state, that she had given birth to a baby boy. She was quite surprised the nurse gave her that information, since she and other Homestead girls were told they would not know the sex of their babies. After Sandy left the hospital and returned to Homestead, she experienced excessive post-partum bleeding and developed a fever. The fever persisted, and Dr. Turner told Homestead staff she should be readmitted to the hospital. When Sandy's mother called Homestead to find out when her daughter could leave the facility, a Homestead staff member told her that Sandy had fever, and the doctor intended to send her back to the hospital. Sandy's mother became very upset and told the Homestead official she was leaving Colorado immediately to drive to Fort Worth and would be taking her daughter home. According to Sandy's recollection, Dr. Turner and the Homestead staff member disagreed with her mother's decision to take her home and harsh words were exchanged over the phone. When Sandy's mother arrived at Homestead, Dr. Durham told her the obstetrician wanted to send her daughter back to the hospital, but her mother refused, and she and Dr. Durham argued. The argument ended when Sandy's mother agreed to sign a document releasing Dr. Turner and Homestead from liability for any medical issues that might result from refusing to follow the doctor's recommendation to send Sandy back to the hospital. Sandy had tears in her voice when she repeated the painful words her mother said as she ordered her into the backseat of the car for the drive back to Colorado: "Keep quiet, and I hope you die on the way home."

Several years after Sandy returned to Colorado, she married and had two children, but the relationship ended in divorce almost eighteen years later. Sandy married again, and she and her husband are still together. Several months ago, Sandy and her son met for the first time, and she was very surprised to learn they had lived only two hours away for more than two decades. "I was happy to learn he had a good life," Sandy said, "and I'm grateful for that." Although her son's adoptive mother was already deceased when he and Sandy met, his adoptive father is still living. She hopes to meet her son's adoptive father at some point in the future, because she wants to thank him for "raising my son." At the time Sandy was interviewed for this book, she and her son continue to see each other as often as possible.

"Scottie" as told by her daughter, Sharon

Born in Scotland, Scottie traveled to the United States to work as an *au pair.* Later, the young woman worked at a restaurant in Louisiana, where she met an Asian man who was ten years older. He and Scottie began dating, and eventually the couple fell in love. The relationship blossomed, and in early 1965, Scottie became pregnant. The couple were faced with a decision that involved two issues in relation to keeping their baby. They were from different cultures, and unwed pregnancy was unacceptable in mid-century America. Exactly why the two young people chose Homestead Maternity Home and Child Placement Agency in Fort Worth remains unclear, but Sharon does know that her mother went to Homestead knowing she would be leaving without her baby. After giving birth at All Saints Hospital, Scottie signed relinquishment papers that set her baby girl's adoption process in motion.

When *"Baby Girl Barclay"* was about nine months old, she was adopted by an older couple from San Antonio who raised her as an only child. Sharon explained that most of her adopted relatives were older, and she lost her parents when she was still a young woman. In 1999, after each of her adoptive parents had passed away, Sharon began searching for her birth mother. With the help of another birth mother who had shared a room at Homestead Maternity Home with Sharon's birth mother, she learned the young woman was nicknamed "Scottie" while she lived at the maternity home. During this same time period, Sharon discovered that Teri Davidson, who fostered several dozen Homestead babies, also was her foster mother before she was adopted. And through conversations with Teri, Sharon learned she had been adopted twice before her adoptive parents who raised her took her home. According to Teri, each of the two couples returned "Baby Girl Barclay" to her foster home because their relatives and friends were unaccepting of their Asian baby. In 1999, Sharon and her husband hired a professional adoption search group to identify and locate her birth mother. When she received the search results, Sharon discovered her birth parents were still living and had married each other a few years after she was born. In addition, the search results established the couple had three sons together. Sadly, Sharon later learned from her birth mother the youngest of these sons died from what she referred to as "crib death." As soon as Sharon received her parents' contact information, she called her birth mother. The two women talked on the phone for about four hours, and two weeks later, they met for the first time in person at Sharon's home. During the visit, Scottie also became acquainted with her daughter's husband and the couple's twin boys. During their reunion, Scottie told Sharon all about her family, her birth father and his family in China, and Sharon's two brothers. Sharon said she always wanted siblings and a large family, and finally, her wish has come true.

Sue Dennis Gwathney

When Sue was born, she and her mother were living with Sue's maternal grandmother in Henderson, Texas. According to Sue, her mother had received a scholarship to Rice University in Houston, where she was living when she met and married Sue's father. Although Sue's grandmother did not know it until later, her daughter had not been attending classes and had dropped out of Rice when she became pregnant. Apparently the young couple's relationship was not going well, and Sue's mother came home to give birth. Based on the story her grandmother told Sue, her mother left her when she was five days old, allegedly to "go buy cigarettes," and did not return until several years later when she wanted Sue's step-grandfather to pay her in exchange for adopting her daughter. He refused, and Sue's grandmother and step-grandfather cared for her until her grandmother developed gallbladder cancer while Sue was still in elementary school. When her grandmother became unable to care for Sue, she and her husband drove her to San Antonio to live with her mother.

Sue remembered life with her mother meant they were always on the move, living in San Antonio, Houston, and Dallas, and back and forth between the three cities. During the brief period Sue lived with her mother, she remembers attending twenty-seven schools. She vividly recalled her thirteenth birthday when she was living with her mother and attending school near downtown Dallas. According to Sue, her mother called the school's office and told the principal to check Sue out of school since she was going to "live with her father." Sue told the school official she didn't even know her father and asked the individual to call her grandmother. At the time, the school official couldn't reach Sue's grandmother and decided to send a "visiting teacher" home with her. She and the teacher had to "wait outside," Sue recalled, until her mother came home, since the thirteen year old was not allowed to have a key to the house. When the young teenager's mother got home and saw the teacher, Sue explained her mother "went ballistic" and told the teacher to "take her [Sue] back with you." The teacher left with Sue and explained that she was taking her to the Dallas County Juvenile Services office for further help, since she could not take her back to school or to her own home. After the county juvenile office evaluated Sue's circumstances, officials assigned Sue to the Sunshine Home on South Ewing Street in Dallas. During those years, Sue begged to be sent to live with her grandmother, but the counselors kept putting her off. When she turned sixteen, Sue said, "I finally decided to run away. Since I didn't have anywhere to run to, I walked to the downtown police station and told the officers on duty I wanted to go live with my grandmother." Much to Sue's dismay, someone from the police station took her back to the juvenile home, where she remained about three days until someone finally gave her a bus ticket to Cooper, Texas, where her grandmother lived.

Seeing her grandmother again was a bittersweet moment for Sue. As she became reacquainted with the older woman, Sue discovered her grandmother had failed to answer the phone when the school called her three years before, because her grandmother had been killed in an accident that same day. Her grandmother since had remarried, and once Sue became acquainted with her new step-grandfather, they learned to "tolerate each other." The living arrangement worked out well for her, and she attended high school and worked part-time. At seventeen, Sue wanted to marry a young man she met in Cooper, but her grandmother agreed to allow Sue to marry only if she promised to complete high school. Sue kept that promise and graduated from Cooper High School in May 1959. But the marriage lasted only nine months.

Single again and with a diploma in hand, Sue moved to Dallas where she went to work for Continental Trailways as a telephone information clerk and dispatcher. In late summer of 1962, a young man named

James Allen Dennis, who had been Sue's boyfriend when she lived at the Sunshine Home, came through the bus station after he arrived in Dallas on leave from the U.S. Navy. Sue said she was very happy to see someone she knew, and James seemed thrilled to meet up with her again, too. In the days and weeks that followed, the young couple saw each other almost every day, and they decided to get married before he was scheduled to ship out to Japan in early October of 1962. Shortly after their marriage James left for San Diego where he boarded a ship for Japan. Days before James arrived in port, Sue received a letter from her new husband explaining that he wanted out of the marriage. By the time his letter arrived, Sue already knew she was pregnant with James's baby. Ironically, Sue said, she had dated and been married to her baby's father for less than forty-five days when she received the letter. At first, Sue said, she didn't know what to do, but after some serious thinking, she decided not to tell James that she was pregnant. Once she made that decision, Sue said, she carefully thought about what she should do next. "I couldn't see bringing a baby into the world since I was working," she said. And she admitted that she was not certain she even wanted kids, especially because of "the way I grew up."

A short time later, while she was sitting in the coffee shop on a break from work, Sue saw an advertisement in the Dallas newspaper for Homestead Maternity Home in Fort Worth. As soon as she could arrange a day off, Sue recalled, "I went over to Fort Worth to visit the maternity home. I told Homestead the truth about being married and that my baby's father was in the Navy in Japan. I also told them that I had no plans to continue my marriage." As soon as she learned that Homestead had approved her admission to the maternity home, Sue resigned from her job at the bus company and entered Homestead in February of 1963.

Although she does not remember all the details of her stay at Homestead, Sue said, "I was comfortable, and I was treated well." While Sue lived at the maternity home, she continued to receive her Navy allotment check since she and James were still married, but the maternity home did not charge her for room and board. She and the other girls helped with cooking and cleaning up after meals, and they kept their rooms clean. After she completed her chores each day, Sue said she passed the time by reading magazines purchased during trips to the store with other girls to buy cigarettes. Her roommate was from Arkansas, Sue said, and another girl she met lived in Fort Worth. Although she could not remember the name of the doctor she visited for prenatal exams, Sue did recall walking with other Homestead girls to his office located in a "converted garage at his house, around the corner from the maternity home. Sue does not recall much about going into labor and delivering her baby, but one of the nurses at Harris Hospital told her she had given birth to a baby girl. The last thing Sue remembers before checking out of the hospital was something one of the doctors said to her: "Go back to work, get your divorce, and go on with your life." After she was discharged from the hospital, Sue remained at Homestead for a few days. The only memory she has of those days, she recalled, was going to see an Ann-Margaret movie with her roommate the day before she left the home.

After Sue left Homestead, she applied for work at Greyhound Bus Lines and was hired to work "swing shifts" as a "fill-in" employee. She explained her plan was to "leave Dallas, but I never left. I didn't like change because of what I went through with my mother." Her divorce was final in November of 1963, and in March of 1964, she married the brother of a friend. Late that same year, Sue gave birth to another daughter, who she said is her only other child. The marriage lasted until 1978, when the couple divorced. Sue admitted to "over spoiling" her daughter and said she did so to make up for the fact she had given up her first child for adoption. For almost two decades, Sue raised her daughter and developed a large commercial business in the Dallas-Fort Worth area. But she has spent endless hours searching for the baby girl she gave birth to in 1964. In addition to DNA testing, Sue has searched over the years for her daughter in *Gray's People Finder*, on numerous websites, and on dozens of adoption message boards. But she has never lost hope that her daughter is searching for her, too. At the time Sue was interviewed for this book, her years of patience and persistence in searching may have paid off. Although she had not made contact at the time, Sue happily explained she believes she may have located her daughter.

Chapter 9

Homestead Adoptees

"In all of us there is a hunger, marrow deep, to know our heritage, to know who we are, and where we have come from. Without this enriching knowledge, there is a hollow yearning, no matter what our attainments in life, there is a most disquieting loneliness."

-Alex Haley

No one knows exactly how many babies were adopted through Homestead's child placement services. But if one uses the "baby #" designations on Homestead-prepared non-id information sheets given to adoptive parents during the 1960's as consecutive indicators, the total number of babies adopted during the years the facility operated could be more than fifteen thousand. Although the number of adoptees interviewed for this book amounts to less than one percent of the possible total, information provided by the adoptees about their parents' backgrounds, the circumstances of their adoptions, and their years growing up, likely mirrors the stories of thousands of other Homestead adoptees.

During the course of writing this book, over one hundred Homestead adoptees were interviewed. Each individual who agreed to be interviewed was adopted in Texas, where many still live, often very near where they grew into adulthood. Other adoptees currently live in various states throughout the country, including Hawaii, for reasons that primarily involve their own employment or that of their spouses, if they are married. A small percentage moved to other states when they were growing up, most often because their adoptive parents were transferred in their jobs or were relocated with the military. One particular adoptee, a triplet, whose story appears in this chapter, was taken by their parents, along with her two sisters, shortly after they were adopted to live in Saudi Arabia, where their father practiced medicine. Before they were eighteen, the triplets had become world travelers.

Homestead adoptees whose names appear in this chapter represent a variety of childhood experiences, educational backgrounds and occupations. While some adoptees interviewed have experienced successful reunions with one or both parents, others have not, and much like the majority of all Homestead adoptees, many have searched in vain for decades. Each search is unique and with very different circumstances, just like the adoptees themselves. But a common thread exists among all Homestead adoptees interviewed, with only a few exceptions - they loved and were very much loved by their adoptive parents.

Alison

One of triplets, Alison and her two sisters, Michelle, and Kristen, were adopted through Homestead's Child Placement Agency by a forty-year-old ARAMCO physician and his thirty-two year old wife. According to Alison, she and her sister were delivered by Dr. Jack Turner at All Saints Hospital in late spring of 1968. Her adoptive parents learned about the agency from other ARAMCO employees who had adopted babies born to mothers who lived at Homestead Maternity Home. Initially, Alison's parents wanted to adopt a boy and a girl, but when they learned that triplets were available, the couple "thought about it for half a day" and decided to adopt the three babies. Alison's adoptive parents were not religious, she said, but before Homestead would approve their adoption, the physician and his wife were asked to join a church of their choice. Alison said her parents really wanted to adopt the babies, so they complied with Homestead's request and joined the Unity Church. According to Alison's knowledge of Homestead's practices, her parents were interviewed and subjected to a "vetting process" that "catered to wealthy parents." Alison said she learned later that Homestead birth mothers were "very young" and "came from all over the United States." When she was asked how much her parents paid for her and her two sisters, Alison said, "The story goes that we cost $10,000 apiece."

Alison's adoptive parents picked up the triplets in Fort Worth and took them home to San Antonio, where they lived for a time before going overseas. Until they were twenty-one years old, the triplets lived with their adoptive parents in various countries, including Scotland, France, and in Saudi Arabia, where their father was the physician to the royal family. In Europe and in the Middle East, Alison said triplets were quite unusual, and she and her sisters always were considered unique. Growing up overseas, Alison and her sisters did not have access to resources available in the United States, so they knew very little about adoption or searching for their birth parents. In hindsight, Alison believes her adoptive parents felt this was the best way to raise their young daughters. She considers herself very fortunate to have had every opportunity growing up, have college costs paid by her adoptive parents, and overall, to have parents who provided everything she and her sisters needed. "But I always had a lurking feeling," Alison added, "and I wanted to learn about my medical history. The biggest reason to search, at least for me, was to learn about my roots and to satisfy a need to belong."

From the beginning to the end, Alison said the search for her birth mother took fifteen years. Initially, she hired a private investigator, who "did nothing," Alison recalled. But early in the search Alison was able to obtain a copy of All Saints hospital records that identified her birth mother as Donna Duncan. "The next thing that happened," Alison said, "was that

I discovered Donna had passed away in 1991." Alison's memory of 1991 was that it was a "very bad year. I was so close, but I had nothing else to go on." In the mid-1990's, Alison's sister, Michelle, hired a Texas intermediary named Pat Palmer to help the girls search for their birth mother, but the non-id information sheet Pat obtained through a Tarrant County court, Alison said, was the only adoption paperwork they had. And she added, "The next six years continued to produce nothing at all."

In the late 1990's, Alison attended a reunion of birth mothers, adoptees, and adoptive parents. At the reunion, she met and talked with her foster parents, Teri and John Davidson, who informed her they had a list of all Homestead babies who had been in their care. Teri said she added each foster baby to her list after the infant was baptized at their church in Fort Worth, Castleberry Baptist Church. According to Teri, Alison and her two sisters, weighing less than four pounds each and born within a ten minute span, were kept in incubators for the first few weeks of their lives. Alison also met and talked to several birth mothers at the Homestead reunion who were actively assisting other birth mothers and adoptees as they searched for their babies and their birth families. After the reunion, Alison said she was determined to learn more about her birth mother and her life and wrote a letter to Dr. Jack Turner in 2003. In his reply to Alison, the long-time Fort Worth obstetrician offered insight into the processes of Homestead.

> 12/04/03
> Dear Allison,
>
> This will acknowledge receipt of your letter of October 20, 2003. I have been away; hence my tardiness in replying. I greatly appreciate your bringing me up to date in the happenings in your lives. I delivered 1500 babies in ten years for the Homestead. Yours was the only set of triplets, plus numerous sets of twins. Dr. T. E. Durham, our director, and the board of trustees were wonderful gentlemen. The "girls" came to the office as private patients, and we delivered them in a private hospital *(illegible.)* Babies were

placed with utmost concern for the babies as your parents have *(illegible.)* I almost served in Saudia Arabia for Whitacre Corporation. Instead I flew on from Riyahd (sp) to Kabul Afghanistan to serve there two months a year for several years. If I could have served in Jeddha, Saudia Arabia, I would have served there probably for a year. As it was, I served *(illegible)* for many years in Afghanistan and Pakistan 1972-1991.The Homestead girls came from every state in the Union. I never knew their true names. After they delivered, I saw them ten days postpartum and then released them. Dr. Durham and the trustees closed the home as soon as the U.S. Supreme Court sanctioned abortions. Our entire staff was pro-life. Dr. Durham incinerated all Homestead records, so there are no records. In Texas, the infants adoption must be done by one year of age – can be done at six months.

After the adoption is finalized, a new birth certificate is issued with the adoptive parents *(illegible)* name on it. The original birth certificate is then destroyed. From that point on, there is no remaining record. Earlier *(illegible)* action I suppose you be happy with your life. Out of 1500 deliveries for Homestead, not more than six have ever contacted me about their birth parents. The placements have nearly all been perfect.

I enjoyed hearing from you. I am proud to hear about your life. Please accept the fact that no record of any Homestead delivery is in existence today.

Most sincerely,
Dr. J. Turner

About ten years ago, Alison located her maternal family members who lived in Kingman, Arizona, where her birth mother lived and is buried. After numerous phone calls and DNA testing, Alison and her sisters learned Guess Donna Duncan, their birth mother, was thirty-one years old when they were born, and she previously had given birth to two other children. Duncan relatives told Alison the two older children were adopted by Donna's mother, Sadie Pearl Young, who raised them as her own. Other family members who were willing to share information with the triplets about their birth mother and her life, said Donna was "very transient" and worked as a waitress in several places where she lived over the years. Alison and her sisters also discovered Donna and their birth father had divorced before they were born. According to the relatives, Alison said there were "lots of men" and possibly "lots of babies," before and after Donna gave birth to her and to her two sisters. After Donna's death, members of the Duncan family discovered three baby hospital bracelets in a jewelry box in her bedroom. Alison said the bracelets are validation to her that "our mother loved us and cared for us." Interestingly, the triplets' DNA tests show the two dark-haired sisters are twins, and the blonde triplet's DNA results prove she is a "close family match" to the twins.

Mary Jo Maria Liggins Allen

Allegedly born in the spring of 1967 at All Saints Hospital in Fort Worth, Texas, Mary Jo recalled she has never had an official birth certificate. She explained that her church baptismal record, made when she was five years old, is the document she has used in lieu of a birth certificate throughout her entire life. At eight months old, Mary Jo said she was adopted through Homestead's child placement agency in Fort Worth by Rev. Napoleon Lawrence Liggins, a thirty-eight year old Baptist minister in San Antonio, and his wife, Emma Lee Liggins, who was forty-five. Her adoptive parents, Mary Jo added, already had three children, two sons, thirteen and twenty years old, and a five year old daughter, when they adopted her.

According to Mary Jo, who grew up in several states as her father pastored various churches, she was teased by kids in the neighborhood and at school about being adopted. At the time, however, she had no idea that she actually had been adopted. The kids at school and in her neighborhood often called her "half-breed," since her skin was "fair," and her parents were "more brown-skinned." Mary Jo said she was a "very quiet kid," and accepted her light colored skin, primarily because her maternal grandmother was "fair-skinned too." She rarely told her parents about the taunting and teasing, because she "respected them" and didn't want to "hurt them."

In 1994, Mary Jo shared her concern about being adopted with her husband of five years. After their discussion, and with her husband's full support, Mary Jo talked to her adoptive mother, who lived with the couple at the time, over coffee the next morning. During their conversation, Mary Jo's mother gave her all the letters she and her husband had written to Homestead, as well as the letters Homestead sent to the couple in the months preceding Mary Jo's adoption. According to Mary Jo, there was a total of five letters. Her adoptive mother also gave Mary Jo a document showing her birth mother was eighteen years old and was "Caucasian with English and Dutch" ancestry. The document described Mary Jo's birth father as a nineteen year old college student who was a fair-skinned "Negro," with "English and Indian" ancestry. An additional note on the document indicated Mary Jo's paternal grandparents were "upper middle class," and of "good health and reputation." During this same conversation, Mary Jo's mother said "your Dad would not want you to know about being adopted." Soon after talking to her mother and reviewing the Homestead paperwork, Mary Jo hired a private investigator to help locate her birth parents. Unfortunately, the search was unsuccessful.

Mary Jo's adoptive mother passed away in 1998 after a yearlong illness. After a period of grieving the loss of her mother, Mary Jo signed up on an adoption registry and re-read the letters her mother had given her. For the first time, Mary Jo realized her adoptive parents had asked Homestead on more than one occasion to adopt an African American child, and each time, they were turned down. The fifth letter, typed on Homestead Child Placement Agency letterhead and signed by social worker Mary Jo Maruda, provided much insight into Mary Jo's adoption in 1967 when she was already eight months old. In her letter, Mary Jo Maruda asked Reverend and Mrs. Liggins if they would be interested in adopting a baby girl whose foster mother had named "Maria." Mary Jo's parents were thrilled, and they immediately contacted Maruda to tell her they were interested. According to Mary Jo, her name is a combination of the social worker's first and middle name, an honor her adoptive parents bestowed upon the Homestead employee for contacting them about their baby girl. Maria, her third name, Mary Jo explained, was the name given her by the foster mother who cared for her during the first several months of her life. According to Mary Jo's adoptive mother, the foster mother wrote a letter that she tucked into the baby's diaper bag. In the letter, the foster mother wrote that Baby Maria's preferred cold milk instead of warm, and that she preferred only a light blanket as cover while she slept.

As she ended the interview, Mary Jo mentioned that she is the mother of three girls, now adults, and "they all know Mom's story." With her adoptive parents both deceased, and the search for her birth parents still incomplete, Mary Jo lovingly admitted that she takes out the letter from her foster mother each year on her birthday and reads it. The letter, she said, brings comfort and joy to know that she was loved, first by her foster mother, and next, by her adoptive parents who raised her.

Carolyn Dow Allison

Born at All Saints Hospital in Fort Worth in late 1965, Carolyn is employed as a fourth grade school teacher in Midland, Texas, where her parents lived when they adopted her. Carolyn's adoptive parents, Anne Douglas Dow and Don Frank Dow, were in their early thirties when Anne learned she and her husband could not have a child. Her adoptive father's brother and his wife, Carolyn recalled, adopted a baby from Homestead in 1960 or 1961, and when Anne acted on their referral and contacted Homestead's adoption agency, she received an immediate reply. Although her adoptive mother died when Carolyn was only four years old, she said "I was raised by the most wonderful stepmother in the entire world. I always knew I was adopted, and I was as happy as a clam growing up with parents I adored." She remembers many happy times with her family throughout the years and still misses her parents who passed away in 2001 and in 2003.

Carolyn said she did not have an "impetus to search," until she was in her twenties and gave birth to her first child. After experiencing a difficult birth her doctor was unable to explain, she felt as if she needed to know her medical history. But Carolyn did not begin a full search until more than a decade later, when she was diagnosed with deep vein thrombosis, a condition the doctor said was caused by a "hereditary clotting factor issue." After learning she may have inherited the medical problem, Carolyn found herself at the Midland Library about to embark on a rather serious search for her birth mother. She recalled "digging through microfiche, searching for all baby girls born in Fort Worth on my birthday" and said she found seven names. "I sent letters to all seven women," she said, "including a woman named Linda Stephenson. Immediately I got three denials, including a phone call from a woman who told me she was touched by my story." The woman told Carolyn she had given birth to a baby before she was married, but she had kept her child. None of the seven women, however, identified themselves as Carolyn's birth mother.

A few years later, in 2009, Carolyn received a phone call from Linda Stephenson's sister who identified herself as Carolyn's biological aunt. Carolyn remembered the call was "warm and friendly," and she experienced "not one ounce of awkwardness" during the conversation. According to her aunt, Linda had passed away recently. She explained that Linda had called her after she opened Carolyn's letter, since she was one of the few people who knew anything about her sister's pregnancy. But she said her sister was still "so embarrassed and so upset because she had disappointed their parents," that she could not respond to Carolyn's letter. Carolyn's aunt did remember Linda telling her the name of her baby's biological father, but she remembered only the young man's surname. Later, Carolyn searched for the surname in the location where her birth mother lived when she became pregnant and discovered two brothers, very close in age, who shared that name. The father of the two young men, Carolyn learned, was an Air Force sergeant who was stationed in Texas during that same time period. At the time of her interview, Carolyn had participated in DNA testing in an effort to determine the identity of her birth father, but she said the DNA results had not been helpful.

Beck

This Texas resident acknowledged she was born in 1965 at All Saints Hospital in Fort Worth and is "one of the Homestead Kids." She "grew up with the adoption story" and knew her parents adopted her when she was two days old. Beck's adoptive father was thirty-three years old, and her adoptive mother was thirty when they adopted her, and at the time, her father was stationed at the air base in Amarillo, Texas. Later, her adoptive parents adopted two more children, including her youngest sibling, who was a foundling from Ohio.

According to Beck, her adoptive mother is still living and has shared several Homestead documents with her. Two of the letters are from Homestead, typed on the maternity home and child placement agency's letterhead. The first letter instructed her parents to meet with Homestead staff in Fort Worth for an interview the agency required before the couple could be approved to adopt. The second letter, also on Homestead stationery, notified Beck's adoptive parents of the date of a home inspection visit scheduled before they would be allowed to pick up their baby. In addition to these two letters, Beck described a third document as an itemized statement of expenses paid by her parents before they could take her home. A fourth document, Beck explained, was a "typewritten, one page information sheet," describing each of her birth parents as a nineteen-year old college student. Her birth parents' ethnicity, Beck added, was listed as "Irish." Based on conversations Beck had with her adoptive mother, the young woman who gave birth to Beck may have been "matched up" with her baby's adoptive parents while she was still pregnant. After Beck's parents picked her up at All Saints Hospital, they drove to the Homestead attorney's office, where he explained the adoption process and said the baby's adoption would be finalized six months later in Tarrant County court.

Beck has a medical condition that doctors have treated for most of her life. And she says it is important for her to learn her mother's identity and obtain medical history information that may help doctors treat her condition.

Lauryl Aimee Blossom

A longtime resident of Tarrant County, Texas, Lauryl was born in early 1965 at All Saints Hospital in Fort Worth and was delivered by Dr. Jack Turner. According to Lauryl, the name on her original birth certificate was "Baby Girl Sain." When Lauryl was six days old, her adoptive parents, Felton and Luan Phillips, took their baby home. According to Lauryl, "I knew I was adopted all of my life."

When Lauryl was about twenty, she began searching for her birth mother. Her parents knew she was searching, and she said they also wanted to know the identity of the woman who had given birth to the child they adopted and loved. First, Lauryl said, she wrote a letter to the Texas state adoption registry, but she received no responses during the time her name was on the registry. During the years that followed, Lauryl wrote letters to various Texas state offices advocating that adoptees should be allowed access to their original birth certificates. Although Lauryl did not remember the exact year, she was denied access to her "closed" adoption file after she petitioned the Tarrant County court to open it. She believes judges are "starting to come around" and are opening more and more adoption files. Lauryl also recalled that in the 1990s, during the time she was actively searching for her birth mother, she helped organize a meeting/reunion of Homestead adoptees, birth mothers, and adoptive parents. The meeting took place at a Luby's Cafeteria in Fort Worth, and approximately one hundred individuals, including Judge Harold Valderas, attended the event. When asked if Dr. Turner, the obstetrician who delivered her and thousands of other babies, attended the event, she said he did not.

During Lauryl's more recent search efforts, she discovered her mother's "termination of parental rights" order had not been "sealed." That apparent error allowed Lauryl to see her birth mother's name and further allowed her to use the name to search for her original Texas birth certificate. Not only did Lauryl find her original birth certificate, she found other documents, as well, including a copy of her final adoption decree signed by former Tarrant County Family Court Judge Eva Barnes months after Lauryl was born. "I finally had my birth mother's name," Lauryl said. Armed with more information than she ever expected, Lauryl set out to locate her birth mother and soon found that she lived in another state. She made contact with her birth mother, and Lauryl said that her adoptive mother later wrote a thank you note to the woman who gave birth to the daughter she had raised.

Lauryl explained that her birth mother was a nineteen year old freshman at an Oklahoma college when she became pregnant. Although she shared very few details with Lauryl about her pregnancy, why she chose Homestead Maternity Home, or what her stay at the facility was like, she did relate what happened after she left Fort Worth. According to Lauryl, her birth mother was a passenger on a bus headed out of town when she met a young man she later married. At the time Lauryl was interviewed for this book, her birth mother and stepfather had been married fifty-two years. Lauryl also discovered she has two half-sisters who were born during her mother's marriage to the man she met on the bus. She also told Lauryl the name of her birth father and the state where he lives. However, Lauryl's attempts to contact her birth father by letter, emails, and Facebook messages had been unsuccessful at the time of her interview.

Kathleen Bradley

Born in Fort Worth in 1965, Kathleen or "Kat" as she is known to her friends, was adopted through the Homestead Child Placement Agency in Fort Worth by Robert William Bradley and Jo Ann Hawley Bradley. Kat's adoptive parents learned she was available to adopt through a phone call from a Homestead staff member who said, "You already have two children. Do you want another one? We have a baby girl, if you're interested." Since her parents were on the way to a family wedding when Homestead called, they made arrangement to pick up the baby girl when they returned on August 30, 1965. Many years later, in 2009, hospital records obtained by Kat's birth mother from All Saints Hospital, where she was born, revealed Kat suffered from "failure to thrive" syndrome when she was an infant, and that she was also checked for diabetes. For two months, Kat remained in foster care because of her health issues, although Homestead did not inform her adoptive parents of those issues prior to their daughter's adoption, and instead, allowed her to be adopted with an alleged "clean bill of health."

Kat grew up with two older adopted siblings. Her adoptive mother's first husband, Nelson Ensor, tragically died in a military plane crash on May 25, 1955, before the couple could finalize the adoption of their first child, a son named Mark and a Homestead baby. Although Mark's adoption hearing was set for May 26, 1955, the military backdated the child's adoption to May 15, 1955, and allegedly barred Joann from entering into another marriage for two years after the adoption. In November of 1957, the young widow married Robert William Bradley, but since Mark had been legally adopted by his wife's first husband, Bradley never legally adopted his stepson. Kat recalled her adoptive father's rationale was that if he adopted his stepson, the child could lose any military-related survivor benefits for college for which he might later become eligible. In 1962, Joann and William Bradley adopted a second child, a baby girl, through Homestead's child placement agency. And in 1965, the couple adopted a third Homestead baby they named Kathleen. When Kathleen's adoptive parents took her home, the family was living in Roswell, New Mexico, but when the final adoption hearing was held six months later in Tarrant County, the family used a Midland, Texas address. Kat's adoptive father's job required him to relocate, and within a year after her adoption, the family moved to Abilene, Texas, where they lived until 1972 before moving again to Algiers, Louisiana. Two years later, in January 1974, Joann Hawley Bradley passed away and left a husband and three children. Kat's brother was eighteen, and her sister was a teenager, but Kat was only eight years old. On April 16, 1976, Bradley remarried, and Kat's new stepmother adopted her on April 24, 1976. During the years after her adoptive mother's death, Kat's family lived first in Houston, and in August 1976, they returned to Abilene, Texas.

At some point, after Kat's sister, Beth, was sent to live in a girl's home, her new stepmother kicked her brother, Mark, out of the family's house. Kat recalled that once her stepmother began wielding her power over the Bradley children, no one talked much to each other. Over the next few years, as Kat grew into a teenager, she and her second adoptive mother experienced a rocky relationship. She explained that her stepmother packed a bag and handed it to her, and Kat left. Within a short time, Kat said her stepmother called the local police and had her picked up as a runaway, an incident that caused her to be placed in jail at twelve years old. When Kat's parents picked her up at the jail, they drove her to Houston to live with her older sister, who had already married. By 1984, Kat's health had deteriorated, and her diabetes was out of control. Since she could not afford to get medical assistance, she moved back in with her parents. Before Kat's adoptive mother agreed that Kat could move back into the household, she prepared a contract and demanded that Kat sign the document. The agreement stated that Kat could live in the household for one year and that she would enroll in GED classes and get her health under control during the twelve-month period. Kat explained that she was diagnosed as insulin dependent when she was about eleven years old, a diagnosis that required checking her blood sugar and injecting insulin several times each day. In recent years, Kat has wondered if the diabetes could have gone undiagnosed for years, and if the "failure to thrive" syndrome shown on her hospital nursery records might have been an indicator of the condition that developed during her childhood.

As a child, Kat said she was always conscious that she did not look like her brother, sister, parents, or other relatives, and she often wondered if her personality, her likes and dislikes, and the way she walked and talked were like those of her birth parents. But what concerned Kat most of all as she grew older, was the need to know and understand her medical history and that of her biological family. Kat's journey to find her birth mother was a long one, and like so many other Homestead adoptees, it had many twists, turns, and dead-ends. She said, "It took twenty-three years of searching. The adoption agency used fake names, made up information, and burned records. I found my birth mom in April of 2006, and we met face to face the following September. After I met her when I was forty-six years old, I finally understood what a MOM is."

In July of 2010, Kat met her birth father, and she realized he was definitely "my other half." She explained, "After meeting my birth parents and siblings, I finally have an identity. I always had one, but now I know why I never fit in with my [adoptive] family. I know why I do things that I do and why I walk, talk, and think the way I do. It was such a wonderful experience to finally get my answers. I am now an adoption Search Angel who helps others locate their birth families (for free), and I have helped reunite many others in hopes of wonderful outcomes. I've learned the majority of people touched by adoption are willing to meet, greet, talk, and get to know each other. There are reasons things happened as they did in my life, but going full circle and finding my real roots has made my life so complete and whole. I walked through life for forty-two years wondering every time I saw someone I resembled, if we were related."

Kat's reunion with her birth mother was a day that neither of them will ever forget, and she still remembers how surprised she and her mother were when they saw how much they resembled each other. Interestingly, Kat learned she is her birth mother's only child. Although the two live in different states and are many miles away from each other, they continue to communicate often. The reunion with her birth father, Kat recalled, was successful, too, and she quickly learned she had inherited his walk and his quick wit. Sadly, Kat's father passed away a few months after her interview, but she remains happy that she was able to meet and know him for at least a few years before his death.

Tami Dawn Bratcher Brown

Charles Bratcher, a farmer, and his wife, Tommie, a homemaker, from Muleshoe, Texas, were already raising a baby boy they had adopted through the Homestead Child Placement Agency when the couple applied for another child. Their second adoption was approved, and the couple picked up Tami in early 1964, when she was three weeks old. Tami said her adoptive mother was unable to have children, and when the couple decided to adopt their first child, her adoptive father's aunt, a local teacher, directed them to

Homestead. After Tami's parents picked up their baby in Fort Worth, they drove her home to Muleshoe, where she grew up with an adopted brother, who was two years older.

According to Tami, she was born in late 1963 at Harris Hospital in Fort Worth, Texas, and her adoption became final on January 10, 1964. After the hearing was held, Tami's parents received an amended birth certificate. Tami said she also has a hospital birth certificate, but it includes no identifying information other than her footprints. Her adoptive parents are still living, but neither remembers much about the paperwork they completed during either of the two Homestead adoptions, or the names of the people at Homestead who assisted them during the process. Tami's adoptive mother does recall that she and her husband picked up one of the two babies at the Tarrant County Courthouse, but she's unsure if it was Tami or her brother.

Although Tami had always known she was adopted, she did not start searching for her birth mother until 1999. She said, "I had great parents, and they still are." When she began her search, Tami discovered her mother had kept several documents related to her adoption. Among these documents was a statement of charges submitted to Tami's parents for payment before they took their baby home, as well as a copy of the adoption decree they were given after the final hearing in Fort Worth in January 1964. Reimbursable expenses shown on the statement of expenses presented to Tami's parents included these items and charges: Room and Board for Mother at Homestead, $300; OB/GYN, $100; Harris Hospital, Mom & Baby, $300; Harry Womack, Pediatrician, $25; Court Costs, $100; Flowers, $5; Layette, $20; Medicine, $50; Ambulance, $10. Charges on the statement totaled $910, which Tami's parents paid, and they made a separate payment of $50 to the attorney for his legal costs incurred.

Tami is married and the mother of two boys, and she and her family live in Lubbock, Texas. Tami and her husband "run a dirt track," and she is employed as the manager of an agricultural testing lab. Tami's life is a busy one, she said, but she has spent countless hours searching for her birth mother's identity. Some time ago, she talked to Thomas Wilder, Clerk of the 67th District Court in Fort Worth, who told her that Homestead records were burned by Dr. Thomas Durham's family members after his death. The judge explained that Dr. Durham was Homestead Maternity Home's Executive Director before the facility closed. Later, Tami wrote a letter to the Texas Department of Human Resources in Austin and eventually talked to Winiford O'Hara, Administrator of the Division of Special Services. Ms. O'Hara referred Tami to the Texas Bureau of Vital Statistics in Austin, where a staff member informed her that she could request a copy of her original birth certificate, if she knew her birth mother's name. And with that information, Tami said she was back at "square one." A few months after Tami was interviewed for this book, another Homestead adoptee urged her to have her DNA tested, and she submitted a sample to Ancestry DNA. When her test results came in, Tami was amazed to find a second and a third cousin match, as well as another "close match" she soon learned was a sister. Tami contacted the second cousin match, who lives in another state, and after discovering he was Tami's paternal second cousin, he enlisted other relatives to help him identify Tami's birth father. His collaborative effort succeeded, and Tami soon learned she has three half-sisters who were born to her birth father and his first wife before they divorced in the late 1960s. Sadly, Tami's birth father passed away in 2012 before she had learned his identify or knew where he lived.

Although Tami's paternal relatives do not know the entire story about her birth father's relationship with her birth mother, they shared the small amount of information family members have known for years. According to Tami's three half-sisters, their parents separated in 1964, when their mother was pregnant with the youngest of the three girls. Tami said she was amazed to find that she is just eleven days younger than her youngest half-sister. Family members told Tami her birth father allegedly had an affair with a military officer's daughter who became pregnant. When his wife, their mother, learned of the affair and the pregnancy, she took the two older girls and left her husband. Tami's paternal relatives never knew the name of the young woman who is likely Tami's birth mother, so they had no information to share with Tami, not even her age or where she lived. Tami's adoptive parents, her husband, and her children all share her happiness in finally knowing her birth father's identity. She especially feels fortunate that her half-sisters and their families have accepted her.

Tami believes her DNA test results provided some of the missing pieces of who she is, and she feels as if she almost has come full circle in her search. She still wants to locate her birth mother, however, and hopes that she will be willing to talk to her. "There are so many questions I want to ask," Tami said. But for now, Tami is savoring the ongoing relationship she has developed with her three half-sisters and other paternal family members who have accepted her with warmth and love. In the weeks to come, Tami said she plans to petition the Tarrant County court to open her adoption file with the hope that she can be reunited with her birth mother.

Bucky

Born in 1968 and adopted by a North Texas couple, Bucky grew up in the Texoma area. According to Bucky, he was born at All Saints Hospital in Fort Worth, Texas, and his parents picked him up directly from the hospital. He has never known how his adoptive parents learned about Homestead's child placement agency, through which he was adopted. Bucky was raised as an only child, something that he admitted always made him feel "odder than being adopted." As he was growing up, Bucky often wondered about his looks, the color of his hair, and as he grew older, about his medical history.

Bucky recalled that he purchased a computer when he was around "forty or so," and shortly afterwards, he "got curious" and started searching around online for information about his adoption. As he often did, Bucky said he visited his parents for a weekend soon after he began searching. After his parents had gone to bed, Bucky said, "I checked out their file cabinet and dug through some paperwork until I found my Homestead papers. I also found the baby clothes I wore when they took me home. My Mom had kept some hair locks, a baby cap, and some other items, too, and among all those things, I found some correspondence written on Homestead's letterhead, including a letter from Harold Valderas, the attorney who apparently handled my adoption."

According to Bucky, the letter from Homestead to his adoptive parents advised them to "show up at court to finalize my adoption in civil court." Another letter from Homestead was what Bucky deemed a "thank you for shopping with us" letter signed by Rev. Durham. Bucky also found a canceled check in the amount of twelve hundred dollars, the same amount his parents paid Homestead for his adoption. Another document in his parents' file was a "non-id information page" for a "single-birth, male child," listing the baby's weight, length, and head size. The information sheet also stated the baby boy was born after a "normal term pregnancy," and that he was "healthy." Bucky said he has an "adopted birth certificate," but no other information from All Saints Hospital. Later, when Bucky sent a letter to the hospital requesting details of his birth, he received a response telling him the medical records no longer existed.

Bucky's initial search effort to locate his birth mother was to enlist the assistance of a search angel, who soon determined the first letter of his birth mother's surname began with a "K." Sometime later, the search angel talked to another birth mother who lived at Homestead around the time Bucky was born, and she remembered Bucky's birth mother and her name. With his birth mother's name in hand, Bucky requested a copy of his original Texas birth certificate from the state records office in Austin, and soon he discovered his mother was nineteen years old when she gave birth to him in Fort Worth. Since other details on the birth record indicated Bucky's mother lived in Tennessee before she was admitted to Homestead, he searched through Tennessee property records and located her name on ownership documents. As a result of the search, Bucky also discovered the woman who gave birth to him had been married to the same man for forty years. At that point, Bucky had a name and address, and he decided to write his birth mother a letter. Within a reasonable time, Bucky explained, she called him and acknowledged the letter. During this first contact, Bucky said his mother denied she had ever been in Texas, but after a few more conversations, she began to talk to him more freely and admitted she had given up a child for adoption in 1968 in Fort Worth, Texas. However, she did not disclose his father's name or volunteer any details at all about the man's family.

After several additional phone conversations, Bucky and his mother met in person in Grapevine, Texas. During that meeting, Bucky said she shared a few details with him about her experiences at Homestead, including that Dr. Parchman was "good-looking" and that she liked him, and how she had made friends with some of the other girls at the maternity home. In addition, she told Bucky that she was heavily anesthetized and remembered nothing about his birth. According to Bucky, she also said Homestead staff promised her and other girls their babies would never know they were adopted. She also believed giving her baby up for adoption would give her "a chance for a fresh start." Bucky said his birth mother did not explain, and he did not ask, why she chose to live at Homestead in Fort Worth rather than a maternity home near her home in Tennessee.

Bucky did not tell his adoptive parents that he had searched for his birth mother until after he met her in person in Grapevine. His adoptive mother, however, was "not comfortable" to learn that he found "that woman," the name she used to refer to Bucky's birth mother. To further complicate matters, his newly discovered half-brother was unhappy about Bucky's addition to his mother's family. Eventually, the half-brother's attitude toward Bucky caused his birth mother to abandon the relationship with her newly-found son. Bucky admitted that he is sad things did not "work out," with his birth mother and her family. But he added with fondness, "I grew up with loving parents and I loved them, too. Overall, I think my adoption was a pretty good deal."

Jani Leigh Merchant Burnett and her Adoptive Parents

Jimmy Nolan Merchant and Joyce Barrow Merchant married in 1960, and after three years of marriage, Joyce had not conceived. The couple said they began discussing adoption and heard about Homestead from a Denison minister and his wife, a local teacher. According to Jimmy and Joyce, the minister and his wife knew a couple who had adopted a baby from the Fort Worth adoption agency. Joyce said she mailed a letter to Homestead in early 1963 and "expressed an interest in adopting." A short time later, Joyce and Jimmy received a reply from Homestead requesting a personal meeting, and on August 1, 1963, the couple traveled to Fort Worth to meet with Homestead staff. The couple said they were interviewed at 714 Dan Waggoner Building, one of the "tall buildings in Fort Worth at the time." Although neither Joyce nor Jimmy remember the names of Homestead staff members who interviewed them, Jimmy said the people they met with were "all women." The couple later learned their interview had taken place in the law office of Mike Powell, Homestead's attorney. They never met Powell, Jimmy explained, either at his office or at Leigh's final adoption hearing at the Tarrant County courthouse the next year.

Jimmy and Joyce said they will always remember getting the phone call from Homestead saying their baby had been born. The call came in on a Tuesday, and a Homestead staff member said their baby was a little girl who was born the day before. When their adopted daughter was born in late December 1963, several weeks before her February 1964 due date, she weighed five pounds, five and one quarter ounces. The staff member told Jimmy and Joyce they could pick up their baby the following Friday at Mike Powell's office. On Friday, Joyce and Jimmy took off work and drove to the law office in Fort Worth, where they waited for the baby to be "brought over from the hospital." While the couple waited, Joyce said, "I filled out some papers a woman who worked in the law office told us they needed before we could take the baby home." After she gave Joyce the paperwork, the woman walked away, but quickly turned around and said, "Do not turn the paper over." Joyce said she waited until the woman was out of sight and immediately turned over the paper, where she saw the name "Essie Thomas," written in the top corner. Joyce said "I've always believed the name belonged to our baby's mother."

About six months later, someone from Homestead called the Merchants to notify them of the date set for the final adoption hearing. Jimmy remarked that he and Joyce were expecting a letter notifying them of the date, but the phone call was the only notice they received. On the designated date,

Joyce, Jimmy, and baby Leigh traveled to the Tarrant County Courthouse in Fort Worth, and Jimmy's parents accompanied them to help with the baby. While the family was in the elevator that would take them to the court room, another couple with a baby got on the elevator. When the couple saw the Merchants and their baby, they quickly told Joyce and Jimmy that Homestead's adoption lawyer, Mike Powell, had passed away. The couple also said three other Homestead adoption hearings were scheduled that same day, and these couples had been redirected to a Tarrant County courtroom on a different floor. When the Merchant family arrived in the courtroom, they observed a female attorney presiding over another adoption hearing.

When their case was called, the Judge asked Jimmy and Joyce a few questions, and the hearing was over within minutes. According to Jimmy, he and his family left the courthouse without papers of any kind or copies of the documents they had signed before the hearing was held. Jimmy said he and Joyce did not question the proceedings at the time and assumed that Leigh's amended birth certificate and final adoption decree would be mailed to them. But the courthouse visit, Jimmy recalled, was the last contact he and Joyce ever had with Homestead, the law office, or the Fort Worth adoption court. They received no correspondence, no adoption decree, and Leigh's only birth record was a Harris Hospital birth certificate showing only her tiny footprints. When asked about the total cost of the adoption, Jimmy said the couple paid between $1,000 and $2,000. According to Jimmy, the cost included reimbursement of the birth mother's room and board, the birth mother's emergency dental work, hospital charges for labor and delivery, and a small charge for the baby's pediatrician.

In early 2016, Leigh requested her original birth certificate from Texas Vital Records in Austin, using the name her adoptive mother saw on the back of the adoption paperwork. The state office denied Leigh's request, since the name she provided did not match the name on her original birth record filed with the state shortly after she was born. Leigh said she has been fortunate to have the help of her adoptive parents in searching for her birth mother, and she is thankful they have been her best advocates. Recently, Leigh participated in DNA testing, and her adoptive father reviewed the results and sent out emails contacting some of the matches. Leigh's adoptive parents also helped her file a petition in early summer of 2016, requesting that the Tarrant County court open her Homestead adoption file. A follow-up interview with Jimmy revealed that Leigh's petition to open her file was granted, and the file had been transferred to a court-appointed intermediary. Within weeks, the intermediary located Leigh's birth mother in another state, and in July of 2016, Leigh and her birth mother met during a phone conversation. In September of 2016, Leigh, her husband, and her daughter traveled to North Carolina to meet her birth mother, stepfather, and extended family members for the first time. During the visit, Leigh's birth mother acknowledged she gave birth to twins at Homestead in late 1962, about a year before Leigh was born. She also explained that she allowed the babies to be placed for adoption and returned to North Carolina, where she became pregnant with Leigh about three months later. When Leigh returned home, she and her adoptive parents initiated a search, including a posting on *G's Adoption Registry*, for her twin half-siblings that Homestead may have placed with different adoptive parents. At the time this book went to press, Leigh and her parents had been unable to locate the twins.

Carla

Her adoptive father was stationed at Carswell Air Force Base when he and his wife adopted Carla. The couple made a decision to adopt a baby through Homestead's child placement agency after Carla's adoptive mother experienced several miscarriages. According to Carla, she was born at Harris Hospital in the summer of 1970 and was raised as an only child. In 1984, her adoptive mother passed away, Carla added, but her adoptive father, now eighty-four years old, is still living near her and her family. Although Carla's adoptive mother told her very little about her adoption from Homestead, her father recently shared some memories about the day he and his wife drove to Fort Worth to take Carla home. In addition, Carla's father shared copies of three letters, one from a Homestead staff member who informed the couple they had been moved into the "final stage of adoption," and a second letter from Teri Davidson, who Carla later learned had been her Homestead foster mother before she was adopted. A third piece of correspondence was a letter of recommendation to Homestead from her adoptive father's commanding officer at Carswell.

Carla's parents told her at a very young age that she was adopted, and her adoptive father said she was "picked out of a big room of babies." Carla admitted she "wholeheartedly believed that was the way it happened." When her adoptive parents first took her home, and when her adoption was finalized about six months later, Carla said she and her parents lived in Fort Worth. According to Homestead documents in her possession, Carla was adopted when she was four weeks old. Her birth weight was normal, and there are no available details that establish why the baby was not adopted shortly after her birth. Homestead staff members whose names appear in her adoption documents are Mary Jo Maruda, a social worker, and Harold Valderas, the Fort Worth attorney who processed Carla's adoption. When she was still young, Carla's adoptive father was transferred to a U.S. Air Force base in Alabama before he retired about a year later. Carla said she grew to adulthood in that state and married her husband there in 1992. The couple have three children and currently live in northern Alabama. She said, "I feel immensely blessed that I ended up in the family that I did, and I really appreciate my birth mother for having the courage to give me up for adoption."

Around 1995, before her children were born, Carla began searching for her birth mother. Initially, she requested a copy of her own original birth certificate from the state records office in Austin. At the time of her request, she was totally unaware that she needed to provide her birth mother's first and last names. "They turned me down," Carla said. "At first it was a curiosity thing, and I thought I just wanted to see a picture of her. But after I got older, it weighed on me that I couldn't fill out information on medical forms for me or for my kids. I just had to leave that side of the form blank." She added, "Also, I would like to tell my birth mother I had a good life. Over the past couple of years, I've thought about the guilt she must have felt, and it makes me sad to think she may be sad on my birthday each year." Carla admitted she stopped searching for her birth mother until about ten years ago. She explained, "When online search capabilities increased, I was able to read about Homestead and the stories of other adoptees. That's also when I started asking Dad questions about Homestead. My husband became interested in my search, and he has been incredibly helpful, especially with analyzing the DNA test results that I received about two years ago. I was initially reluctant to have my DNA tested, but I went into the process with a 50-50 feeling, thinking nothing is going to happen, and what if it does? At this point in my life, if I don't find her, it may be too late. And I wanted to take advantage of the science and technology out there. I really didn't have anything to lose."

When her DNA test results came in, Carla was very disappointed to find that her close matches included only a second and a third cousin. She did make contacts with each and said, "I was disappointed as well that nothing came from them, because they had no knowledge of any family adoptions." Through one particular cousin match who shared her own family tree, Carla's husband began analyzing and comparing the people in that tree with his wife's other cousin matches. Around the same time, Carla joined the Homestead Yahoo Group online, and communicated with some search angels who "coded" her birth certificate number and filing date in the Texas birth index. The "coding" process gave Carla the first letter of her birth mother's surname. With that very small detail, Carla's husband continued to review his wife's DNA matches, specifically searching for names beginning with that particular letter. Within a short time, he discovered a couple whose daughter was the right age to have been Carla's birth mother. Carla and her husband also discovered the woman's father, like her adoptive father, appeared to have retired from the Air Force. Carla said she located the woman on Facebook and soon learned she lived in Texas and was married, but she had no other children. To her surprise, Carla also learned the woman was a twin, a finding that complicated the DNA identification process Carla's husband had used. Through additional research, Carla and her husband identified the woman's twin and found that she had given birth to four children before she passed away. These findings caused Carla's husband to rebuild his wife's family tree on the Ancestry website, where he included her as the daughter of the Texas woman who had no children. Although she and her husband felt certain they had identified her true birth mother, Carla said she wanted more proof before attempting to make contact and possibly disrupting the woman's life.

To satisfy Carla's need to remove any doubt the Texas woman was her birth mother, she petitioned the Tarrant County court to open her adoption file. The petition was easy to file, Carla recalled, and her hearing date was scheduled shortly thereafter. The day before the hearing, Carla flew to Fort Worth and met the next day with the judge assigned the case. He talked to her a bit and asked a few questions before he granted her petition. He also recommended that she use the services of a court-appointed intermediary to review her file. "My adoption file was very thin," Carla recalled, "and I was quite surprised to see it didn't include a hundred pages or more." Later, when she called the intermediary, Carla said, "My file is sitting here. What do we do now?" At the time Carla was interviewed for this book, she and her husband, as well as their three children, were anxiously waiting to see if Carla's birth mother wants to meet the daughter she had given up for adoption over forty years before.

Michele Eugenia Powell Casey

The adopted daughter of Homestead attorney Mike Eugene Powell and his second wife, Mavis Roberts Powell, Michele was born in Fort Worth in early 1960. Michele's adoption was processed through Homestead's child placement agency, and uniquely, she was named "Michele Eugenia" for her adoptive father. According to Michelle, her father passed away when she was barely four years old, and she was raised by her adoptive mother. She first learned of her adoption when she discovered a piece of paper inside one of her mother's books. The paper, Michele added, included the names of her birth parents. Michele remembers asking her mother if she really had been adopted, and her mother answered "yes." At the time, Michele's mother told her "what little she knew" about her adoption. Later, Michele asked one of her aunts, who said she knew nothing more than what her mother had told her. Michele said she searched for her birth parents, allegedly Dennis Breen and Eileen Manning, according to the notes in her mother's book, and for other adoption-related information, too. Also, she posted on various adoption registries for a long time. Several years ago, Michele said she located her birth mother in Colorado, but sadly she had passed away before Michele found her.

Taud Cheslock

According to his sister, Lanelle Cheslock Dorough, Taud was adopted by her biological parents, Stanley and Naomi Ross Cheslock shortly after her biological sister's death in 1966. Lanelle said each of her parents came from large families and wanted several children themselves, but her mother had Rh-negative blood and experienced difficulties during her pregnancies. In addition, her mother already had lost two babies soon after they were born due to "failure to thrive" syndrome. During the several months her baby sister was hospitalized at All Saints Hospital in Fort Worth because of major birth defects, Lanelle was a nursing student at nearby John Peter Smith Hospital. She and her parents made almost daily visits to All Saints to see her baby sister, and during those visits, they noticed a baby boy, just a few months old, who also was a patient in the neonatal unit. The nurses who cared for Stana Rae, Lanelle's baby sister, also cared for the baby boy they had nicknamed "Eric." One of the nurses present at Eric's birth told Lanelle and her parents Eric had weighed only four pounds when he was born to a twelve year mother who lived at Homestead Maternity Home before giving birth. The nurse said Eric had been in the hospital for much of his young life, beginning with extended nursery care after his premature birth, and most recently, he was recovering from surgery to repair a bi-lateral hernia.

After the loss of their baby daughter, Lanelle's parents expressed an interest in adopting a child, but they knew their chances of adopting at forty-five and fifty years of age were not favorable. In addition to wanting another child, Lanelle said her parents also wanted a sibling for her who would be around when they were gone. The nurses at All Saints who knew Lanelle and her parents said to the best of their knowledge, Homestead's adoption agency had no prospective parents waiting to take Eric home. When Eric's doctors decided he could leave the hospital, Lanelle's parents contacted Homestead staff and made application to adopt six-month old Eric. According to Lanelle, Homestead's child placement agency immediately approved her parents' request to adopt the baby. Even though Lanelle understood her Dad's railroad wages were enough to pass the agency's income test, she never understood why Homestead made an exception for her parents' ages. Although her new baby brother had been known as "Eric" during the time he spent in All Saints Hospital and with his foster parents, Teri and John Davidson, her parents named him "Taud." She said the name was of French origin, and her parents chose that particular name because they believed the baby's mother may have been from Louisiana.

Homestead's adoption agency gave Mr. and Mrs. Cheslock a non-id information sheet indicating Taud's birth mother was a single nineteen year old bank employee who became pregnant during "an affair with a married man." No information about Taud's birth father was listed on the document. At some point, Lanelle and her parents discovered the surname of Taud's birth mother was "Boushley," but without a first name, they were never able to locate his mother. Lanelle believes Taud suffered what she termed "abandonment issues" throughout his entire life. He frequently "got into trouble," and her parents did their best to help him. Lanelle said they offered Taud educational opportunities and allowed him to travel all over the world. She added that Taud passed away on May 12, 2015, and that she still misses her brother very much. Taud is survived by his widow, whom he married in 2010, and by two older sons.

Author's note: Soon after Lanelle's interview, Taud's birth mother was identified as a nineteen year old woman who lived in Chalmette, Louisiana when she became pregnant. Originally, her father's family was from Wisconsin and was of French-Canadian descent. Unfortunately, Taud's birth mother passed away in Louisiana before his own death. Lanelle said she plans to pass the information about Taud's ancestry on to his sons.

Carla Deneal Crabb and Her Adoptive Mother Gwen Crabb

Gwendolyn Sells Crabb and her husband, Jimmie Walter Crabb, worked at Texas Instruments north of Dallas when they adopted "Baby Girl Cole" through Homestead's child placement agency. Jimmie Crabb served in the Air Force and attended college before he began work at the Texas employer. Gwen also was employed by Texas Instruments, but she followed Homestead's adoption guidelines and left her job to care for their baby girl. According to Gwen, Carla was only five days old when she and her husband took their daughter home. When the couple adopted in 1961, they already had a biological son born in 1957. Between 1957 and 1961, Gwen lost a three month old baby and had undergone surgery for uterine cancer. Gwen said she and Jimmie applied to several adoption agencies before they learned about Homestead's child placement agency from her next door neighbor, the minister of First Methodist Church in Richardson.

According to Gwen, Homestead responded to her letter with a questionnaire asking for family background, medical history, and income information. She completed the questionnaire, returned it, and soon received a phone call from someone at Homestead whose name she does not remember. During the phone call, the Homestead employee informed Gwen that she and her husband were tentatively approved to adopt a baby, but final approval was subject to a home inspection, which she scheduled during the phone call. A short time later, a female Homestead staff member visited the couple's home in Richardson, Texas, and examined each room in the house before deeming the residence suitable for a baby. Carla's mother said she will always remember the day she and her husband picked up their baby daughter at the Homestead lawyer's office in a "tall building in downtown Fort Worth." She said, "The lawyer buzzed someone who brought her in." When asked if she remembered anything about the woman who brought the baby to her, Gwen said the woman wore "street clothes," and Carla was wearing "booties and a knit sweater, a white bonnet, and she was wrapped in a yellow knit blanket." It was an "emotional moment," Gwen recalled. Their young son, who was present when she and her husband visited the lawyer's office, wanted to hold his baby sister, and she said someone in the office took a photo of him holding Carla.

When Carla was ten days old, she became very ill, and Gwen took her to a doctor in Richardson who said she had viral pneumonia. The doctor admitted Carla to Children's Hospital in Dallas, where she continued to have labored breathing. According to Gwen, the doctors kept Carla in an incubator until she improved enough to go home. She does not recall the exact number of days Carla remained in the hospital, but she believes it was between one and two weeks. "I was frantic with worry," she said. "I was concerned that Homestead might take our baby away because she had become ill after we took her home." As the Homestead adoption guidelines instructed, Gwen reported her baby's hospitalization to Homestead, and six months later, she and Jimmie were questioned about Carla's illness by the Tarrant County judge who presided at the final adoption hearing on August 18, 1961 at the Tarrant County courthouse.

Carla said she always knew she was adopted. She had not searched for her birth parents because she was afraid of "dishonoring" her adopted parents whom she respected and deeply loved. But when she became pregnant with her first child, Carla said she talked to her adopted mother and asked for details about her adoption. Gwen said she could never understand why Carla did not want to know the identities of her birth parents, and over the years, she had often encouraged her to search. During Carla's talk with her mother, she looked over various Homestead documents and correspondence that Gwen shared with her. Most of the documents were letters from Homestead's attorney, Mike Powell, to Gwen and her husband, notifying them of the final hearing date in Fort Worth and informing them of legal expenses they were required to pay before the final hearing was held. Carla shared the itemized list of reimbursable charges during her interview, and the onion skin copy of the expense statement listed these items and their respective costs: Upkeep for birth mom, $325; Room and Board at Homestead, $250; Upkeep for Mother and Child - Dr. Turner, $122; Dr. Womack, $15; Legal Proceedings and Court Costs, $100; Layette, $20; Flowers, $5; Ambulance, $10; Dental Care, $50; Medicine, $50. Carla's father had added a handwritten note on the expense statement saying the couple paid an additional $250 for "legal."

At the time of her interview, Carla said she had not actively searched for her birth mother. She added that "giving me up for adoption was the best thing my birth mother could have done for me. I thank her every day for being strong enough to give me the life she couldn't provide." According to their own statements, Carla and Gwen are very close and talk on the phone almost every day, and although Carla said she may decide to search for her birth mother at some point in the future, locating her is not an important issue at the present time.

Kimberlie Owen Currier

At the time Kimberlie's parents contacted Homestead, they had attempted to have a baby for almost ten years. At first they tried to adopt a California baby born with spina bifida, but Kimberlie's mother told her "the state of California stopped the adoption." When asked how her adoptive parents learned about Homestead's adoption agency, Kimberlie said her mother's doctor in Odessa, Texas, where her adoptive parents lived when she was adopted, referred her to the Fort Worth agency. Kimberlie laughingly recalled the story her mother told her about the call she received in 1970 from a Homestead staff member telling her that she and her husband could pick up their baby. Her mother was so excited when she hung up the phone, she immediately picked up the receiver again to call her husband at work to tell him the good news. Before she could dial her husband's number, the phone rang again. When she answered, she heard the voice of her doctor's nurse who told her not to bring in another urine sample, because the last one indicated she was pregnant! Kimberlie's adoptive mother told her how she had experienced absolute shock and total joy within a few short minutes, and how excited she was when she shared the news with her overjoyed husband. She added that he was also shocked to learn they would be welcoming not one, but two babies to their household. Shortly after hearing the good news, the couple left Odessa and drove to Fort Worth to pick up their baby. Kimberlie's mother said she was amazed to discover the entire adoption process had taken only nine months and eight days. Kimberlie said she was five weeks old when her parents took her home, but they never knew why she had remained in foster care for those first few weeks. Kimberlie had been named "Anne" by her foster mother, Teri Davidson, and when her adoptive parents took her home, they found a letter from Teri in the baby's diaper bag explaining the infant's feeding and sleeping schedule.

Kimberlie did not search for her birth mother until 1996 when she petitioned the Tarrant County court to open her adoption file. Her justification for the petition was to learn about her medical history, since one of her three children is disabled. The judge denied Kimberlie's petition, and she recalled how disappointed she was with the decision, and she stopped searching for some time. However, in recent years Kimberlie registered on an adoption site and has participated in DNA testing with one of the three well-known companies. Through her DNA test results, she discovered a second cousin match and learned her genetic ancestry is 99.9% European and .1% Japanese. Although she was hopeful that DNA might help identify her birth mother, Kimberlie said her only finding to date is that her mother's surname when she gave birth was "Cunningham." Although she has been unsuccessful in her search attempts, so far, Kimberlie still has hope she will find her birth mother.

"Linda"

When Linda was two days old, she was adopted by a West Texas couple. Both of her parents, Linda added, are now deceased. "I always knew I was adopted," Linda said, but when asked if she knew why her adoptive parents chose Homestead Child Placement Agency, she answered "I do not." Linda explained that her parents were married for ten years when they adopted her in 1963, and in 1965 and again in 1968, they had two biological sons. After Linda's adoption, her mother no longer worked so that she could stay home to care for her daughter. According to her adoptive mother, Linda was born at Harris Hospital in Fort Worth, but she does not know where she was picked up by her parents. A volunteer search angel who assists Homestead adoptees in searching for their birth parents told Linda that her mother's surname likely began with the letter "N." In recent years, and at the urging of two additional search angels who have assisted in her search, Linda participated in DNA testing. Although the test results included a half-sibling match linked to her birth father, who she and volunteer search angels have now identified and located, the results initially did not help identify her birth mother.

In the early summer of 2016, Linda filed a petition in the Tarrant County court requesting that her Homestead adoption file be opened. A judge granted the petition and transferred Linda's file to a court-appointed intermediary. By July 4, 2016, the intermediary had located Linda's birth mother and was preparing to mail her the initial contact letter. Within a few weeks, the intermediary informed Linda that her birth mother refused contact. She did agree, however, to send medical information for the intermediary to share with her daughter. Based on a non-id information sheet contained in Linda's adoption file, she discovered her birth mother was from Texas and that she had completed three and a half years of college when she became pregnant. With additional help from search angels, Linda identified her birth father and learned that she has three paternal half siblings. Interestingly, Linda and each of her birth parents have lived in Texas most of their lives. At the time of her interview, Linda had not spoken with or met her birth father, although she said she plans to initiate contact with him in the near future.

Marlana Robertson Deatherage

Born in the summer of 1967, Marlana was delivered by Dr. Jack Turner at All Saints Hospital in Fort Worth. The math teacher at Cooper High School explained that her parents chose to adopt her after they were married for ten years and her mother, Margaret Robertson, had miscarried at least once. A friend of Marlana's adoptive mother, Mary Eunice, referred Margaret and her husband to Homestead and explained they would need a letter from a doctor stating they were unable to have a child. According to Marlana, her adoptive parents wrote to Homestead and included a letter from their doctor. Within a few weeks, the couple received a reply from Homestead Child Placement Agency, signed by Mary Jo Maruda, Supervisor of Social Work. Marlana still has the letter, and she said the letterhead shows the adoption agency's address as 1028 5th Street, Fort Worth, and Homestead Maternity Home's location as 1250 W. Rosedale. Maruda's letter included an "Application to Adopt," that she asked the couple to complete, sign, and return to the 5th Street address. Soon after the couple returned the application, they received a phone call from someone at Homestead who asked them to meet at Homestead's adoption office on 5th Street for a personal interview with Judith Kelley, another Homestead social worker. Margaret told Marlana that Judith Kelley was pregnant at the time she interviewed them and that she understood the social worker left the job at Homestead to have her baby. Shortly after the interview, a Homestead staff member notified Margaret and her husband they were approved to adopt and would be notified when a baby became available.

Marlana recalled the story her adoptive mother shared about the day she and her husband learned their baby had been born and was ready to be adopted. At the time, Marlana's adoptive parents were living in a rural area of Delta County, Texas, between the towns of

Cooper and Paris. The couple had no phone, but one of their parents living next door did have phone service, and that number was listed on Homestead's records as their contact number. The Homestead social worker called that number on July 21, 1967 and left a message with the phone's owner. Marlana's adoptive mother said she will always remember the message saying, "We have a baby girl that we think is yours." Margaret immediately returned the call and made an appointment for herself and her husband with Ms. Maruda on July 26, 1967. As they were instructed, the prospective parents drove to Homestead's office at 1028 5th Ave. in Fort Worth, where they anxiously arrived about thirty minutes early. According to Margaret, they were met at the door by Ms. Maruda and another Homestead social worker named Sharon Dowden. While the couple talked a few minutes with Ms. Dowden and Dr. Durham, the director, Ms. Maruda left the office and returned "with a bundle in her arms." When Margaret and her husband took Marlana home, she was about three days old.

According to a letter Marlana's adoptive mother kept, Ms. Dowden made the requisite post-adoption visit to the Robertson home in November of 1967. On January 10, 1968, the new adoptive parents received a letter from Harold Valderas, Homestead's attorney, notifying them of the final adoption hearing scheduled on February 9, 1968, at the Tarrant County courthouse. Other Homestead documents kept by Marlana's adoptive mother throughout the years establish the hearing was held in Tarrant County Domestic Relations Court #2, and Judge Harold Valderas signed Marlana's final adoption decree. In 1970, Mr. and Mrs. Robertson adopted another baby girl, Diane, whom they later learned was mentally challenged. Diane is now forty-six years old and lives with Marlana, who explained that her adopted sister is legally blind and deaf, but she is able to work in a sheltered workshop near their home. In 2009, Diane successfully underwent a liver transplant. The next year, Marlana's adoptive father died, and her mother's death followed in October of 2012. When her adoptive father died in 2010, he and Margaret had been married fifty-three years.

Over a decade ago, Marlana and her adoptive mother attended a Homestead reunion in Fort Worth, where they met Teri Davidson, her Homestead foster mother, and other Homestead adoptees, adoptive parents, and birth mothers. During the reunion, Marlana and her adoptive mother heard rumors that Homestead records may have been burned and that Dr. Durham promised Homestead birth mothers he would take their secrets to his grave. Marlana said she does not know if the rumors are true and added that she has not searched for the truth about the records or the fire.

Years ago, Marlana petitioned the Tarrant County court to open her Homestead adoption file, and the judge agreed to send the file to Pat Palmer, a court-appointed intermediary. At that time, Palmer contacted Marlana's birth mother, but she never received a reply from the woman, and the file was closed. A few years ago, a Homestead search angel "coded" Marlana's birth certificate file number and told her that her birth mother's surname began with the letter "G." In 2015, Marlana participated in DNA testing, and through a first cousin match, she learned the name of her birth mother and her birth mother's husband. With that information, she requested and received a copy of her original Texas birth certificate showing that her birth mother was a thirty-four year old married woman named Norma Dean Gardner. Norma's husband, Richard Gardner, was identified as Marlana's father on the document, and other details on the birth certificate indicated Norma already had given birth to three other children. Within a short time, Marlana learned the full story of her birth mother's pregnancy from relatives she met through DNA matches. These relatives told Marlana that Richard Gardner was stationed at Carswell Air Force Base in Fort Worth before he was sent overseas during the Vietnam era. While Gardner was out of the country, Norma worked as a night manager at the Western Hills Hotel on Camp Bowie Boulevard near Carswell Air Force Base, a popular Fort Worth destination at the time. While she was employed at the hotel, Norma met Charles Campbell, a professional pianist who performed in the lounge, and she became pregnant during their relationship. Since Norma was married when she became pregnant, she arranged with Homestead's adoption agency to give up her baby at birth and before her husband returned to Fort Worth. The legal presumption that a child born to a married woman was the child of her husband, absent evidence to the contrary, required the name of Norma's lawful husband, Richard Gardner, to be listed on Marlana's original birth certificate filed in Texas birth records shortly after she was born.

When Norma's husband returned from his overseas tour of duty, it appears he never learned about his wife's pregnancy or about the baby's adoption. Gardner was an air traffic controller at the time, and since his job was in high demand, he received yet another overseas assignment. With Norma's husband away again, she and Charles Campbell resumed their extramarital affair, and Norma became pregnant by him for the second time. Her due date with the second pregnancy, however, was after her husband's scheduled return home, so Norma was forced to explain the pregnancy to her husband when he returned. It seems that Norma's husband must have been a very caring and totally forgiving man, since he made an agreement with his wife that he would not file for divorce if she would give up the baby for adoption. Apparently, he never learned about his wife's previous pregnancy or that she had placed the baby for adoption through Homestead's agency. According to relatives who told Marlana the story of her birth parents, Norma and her husband remained married until she died. Unfortunately, her birth mother had passed away before Marlana learned her name or heard the story of her birth and adoption.

The three children Norma had with Richard Gardner are Marlana's half siblings. She met her half-brother Mark in June of 2015, shortly before he died of lung cancer, and she met a half-sister in July 2015. At the time of her interview, Marlana had not met her oldest half-brother, but she hopes to do so one day. Marlana's birth father, Charles Campbell, also had a daughter, and although the two women have talked on the phone, they had not met before Marlana's interview. Since Marlana's birth father,

Charles, has Alzheimer's, she realizes it may not be in his best interest to meet him. But thanks to Charles's wife who sent her a clip of a Dallas TV Channel 5 news story about the longtime local musician, Marlana was able to see and hear her birth father play the piano during his last professional performance. Marlana ended the interview by saying she had a great upbringing, and her adoptive parents gave her a wonderful life. And she will never forget the moment her adoptive mother told her "Thank you for my three wonderful grandchildren."

Leona Kay Urbanovsky DeBaun

Born at All Saints Hospital in the summer of 1965, and delivered by Dr. Jack Turner, Leona was adopted at birth by Leonard Charles Urbanovsky, a master plumber, and Della Mae Eller Urbanovsky. The couple married when they were in their late twenties, and each was thirty-five years old when they adopted Leona. The marriage was a second one for Leona's adoptive father, who already had a young daughter, and her adoptive mother previously had given birth to a baby girl when she was fifteen years old. According to Leona, the father of her adoptive mother's daughter moved to another state, and she lost custody of the child when she was still very young. Leona added that her adoptive mother's loss of her first child haunted her throughout her entire life. Leona's adoptive parents chose to adopt after her adoptive mother had cancer and underwent surgery that prevented her from having another baby. When asked how the couple heard about Homestead, Leona said her adoptive father's friend told him about Homestead's child placement agency, and he stopped by the agency's office after work one day and picked up an application to adopt. When her adoptive father went home that day, he gave his wife the paperwork and said, "I think you need a baby." About a year after Leona's adoption, her parents also adopted a second child, a baby boy, from Homestead.

According to her adoptive parents and verified by an invoice her mother maintained throughout the years, Leona's adoption cost $3,000. Her mother also saved the little outfits Leona and her brother, Roger Dale

Urbanovsky, wore home from Homestead, and Leona later found names written underneath each of the collars. Written underneath Leona's collar was her birth mother's name, *"Sandra Ann Jones,"* and *"Baby Boy Curtis"* was written under the collar of her adopted brother's outfit. After the 1983 death of her adoptive father, and with the help of her adoptive mother, Leona paid three hundred dollars to Pat Palmer, an intermediary in Irving, Texas, to help search for her birth mother. Palmer soon located Sandra Ann Jones and mailed a letter to her last known address, where Sandra's brother received it and contacted the intermediary. Unfortunately, he told the intermediary that Leona's birth mother had been killed by a drunk driver when she was only nineteen years old. Eventually, Leona learned the names of other maternal relatives, including her grandmother who lived in Benbrook, southwest of Fort Worth. During a contact with her maternal grandmother, Leona discovered her birth mother had returned to Homestead the year after Leona was born and had given birth to a second baby girl. According to her grandmother's account, Leona's birth mother married shortly before her death, but she had no other children. Leona said her birth mother is buried near Granbury, Texas, and at some point, she hopes to learn more about her mother by talking to the man she was married to when she died in the accident. Although her maternal grandmother did not recall the name of Leona's birth father, she did say the young man lived in the Arlington Heights area of west Fort Worth and was nineteen years old when Leona was conceived.

Leona described her birth mother's family as a "very tight, Catholic, Czech family," who gathered at her maternal grandparents' house in west Fort Worth each Sunday after church to have a family meal together. Although Leona has searched through Fort Worth high school yearbooks for a picture of her birth mother, at the time of her interview she had found nothing. The intermediary also sent a letter to Leona's birth father, who never responded, but she did not share his name with Leona. At the time of her interview, Leona said she remains hopeful that she will find her birth father someday. And she looks forward to the possibility of learning more from him about her birth mother.

When Leona was fifteen, she became pregnant. At the time, few schools offered home-bound study or other alternative education resources for teenage mothers, and officials at the Fort Worth suburban high school she attended recommended her adoptive mother enroll her in a nearby church-sponsored school. Leona said her adoptive father wanted her to have an abortion, but her birth mother stood up for her and told him their daughter would be "keeping her baby." Leona said she never revealed the name of her baby's father to her adoptive parents, and added, "Things didn't work out with him anyway, because I found out he was dating another girl at the time I became pregnant." Leona said she is extremely thankful her parents were willing to take on the responsibility of raising her child, and she is even more grateful now that she is raising a fourteen-year old granddaughter of her own.

Scott Dillinger

Born at Harris Hospital in Fort Worth, Texas, during the summer of 1963, Scott was adopted from Homestead's adoption agency by Royal K. Dillinger, an Air Force navigator and his wife, Julie Fream Dillinger. According to Scott, his adoptive mother was unable to have children. Scott said he followed in his adoptive father's footsteps and is currently a flight engineer in the California Air Reserve. When asked how his adoptive parents learned about Homestead's child placement agency, Scott said his father was stationed at Roswell Air Force Base in New Mexico when Mike Powell, Homestead's attorney, visited the base "to solicit adoptive parents." Before his adoptive father learned about Homestead from Powell, he and his wife already had submitted an application to adopt a baby in New Mexico and were on a waiting list. Scott knows nothing about the details of his adoption, who his adoptive parents talked with at Homestead, or where he was picked up when they took him home. Although his adoptive parents did give him some documents at one time, Scott said the paperwork is "long gone" due to numerous military moves he has made over the years He does remember having a sheet of paper at one time that showed his unnamed birth father was twenty-five years old, unmarried, and worked as an "aircraft mechanic." His birth mother was listed on the same sheet of paper, also without a name, as a twenty-five year old single woman, whose occupation was shown as "legal secretary."

Scott said he was raised in a German-American family and had a "great childhood and encouraging parents." Although his adoptive parents are still living, they are divorced. According to Scott, his adoptive parents emphasized academics, supported him in sports activities, and paid for his education at Wichita State University. Scott has been married to his wife for twenty-six years, but they have no children. He jokingly said they are childless "because I'm gone too much." Sometime during the 1980s, Scott began searching for his birth parents, and in recent years, he participated in DNA testing. He explained that his DNA results indicate he is primarily English, with some Irish and Iberian Peninsula ethnicity, too. Although Scott has contacted a few second and third cousin matches, he has not yet identified the surnames of his birth mother or birth father. At the time of his interview, Scott was not actively searching for his birth parents. He is encouraged, however, to learn from the interview that some Homestead adoptees have been successful in petitioning the Tarrant County court to open their adoption files. And he was even more encouraged that some adoptees have been reunited with family members.

William Stanley ("Bill") Dittman, III

Bill's adoptive parents were living in Lubbock, Texas, when Doris Jean Malone, a housewife, and William Dittman, Jr., a food broker, adopted him through Homestead's child placement agency in Fort Worth. Although Bill doesn't remember the name of his adoptive mother's doctor in Lubbock, he did recall his parents said the doctor referred them to Homestead when they decided to adopt a baby. Bill said his family lived in Lubbock until he was two, when they moved to Pleasant Grove, southeast of Dallas, where he grew up. Bill said his adoptive parents' marriage began when Bill, Jr. married Doris, who already had two daughters and was pregnant with her ex-husband's baby. The baby was born after she married Bill, Jr., and was six years older than Bill. Although his parents never told him that he was adopted, Bill said he always thought he might have been. His suspicion was confirmed when he was very young and heard his mother telling someone that he was not her biological son. However, neither of his parents ever discussed his adoption directly with him. Although his adoptive father loved Doris, his adoptive mother, Bill described their marriage as one of much discord that was often fueled by Doris's drinking. When Bill was about eleven or twelve, his parents divorced. After the divorce, he lived with his adoptive father, and they grew very close, but his father never divulged to Bill that he was adopted.

As an adult, Bill became a Dallas, Texas law enforcement officer and married his wife in May of 1997. Because they were older when they married, the couple began talking about having a family right away and even discussed it with their parents and siblings. After Thanksgiving dinner in 1997, Bill's sisters and their spouses stayed behind after everyone else left the family gathering. The youngest of his sisters, six years older than Bill, asked him and his wife if she and the others could talk to the couple about something important, and they agreed. Very early in the conversation, the he and his wife were shocked when Bill's sister told him that he had been adopted. His immediate response was, "Why has no one ever told me?" His sister, speaking on behalf of Bill's siblings, said their Dad "threatened" them and their mother if any family member told Bill he was adopted. His sister explained that she believed he and his wife should know the truth, since they were planning to have a baby as soon as possible.

After Bill got over the initial shock, he decided to search for his birth mother. He explained that when he began searching for his birth parents in 1997, he told his adoptive parents he would always love them and that no one could ever replace them. His adoptive Dad, however, felt threatened and told him that he had kept the adoption information from him because he was afraid of "losing" Bill. His adoptive mother was cooperative, although she did not have any paperwork that might help him initiate his search. Initially, Bill said his adoptive father refused to help, but at some point, he found the adoption papers Homestead had given the couple when they adopted their son. His father, Bill explained, shared only a few of the documents at the time over an extended period.

Since Bill had such a small amount of information on hand, he decided to petition the Tarrant County court to open his adoption file. Although the judge denied his request, he transferred Bill's file to an intermediary in Fort Worth named Joyce Buzbee. Within a short period of time, Ms. Buzbee faxed copies of the adoption paperwork to Bill, but she "blacked out" the names of his birth parents. According to Bill, his work-related expertise in reviewing documents caused him to examine the blacked-out names by holding the document up to the light, and he was able to read the name. Once Bill learned his birth mother's name, he requested and received his original birth certificate from Texas Vital Records in Austin.

After he had searched for several months, Bill discovered his birth father was a published author and psychologist who lived and practiced in San Antonio, Texas. Emotionally driven to meet his birth father in person, rather than on the phone, Bill made an appointment with the psychologist under the pretense of needing marriage counseling for himself and his wife, Tina. Bill said they drove from Dallas to San Antonio and arrived on time for the appointment with the man he believed to be his birth father. Once the couple were seated in the counselor's office, Bill confronted the man and said he believed he was his son. Although the psychologist remained calm the entire time Bill and his wife were in his office, he adamantly denied he was Bill's birth father. According to Bill, the man became defensive and explained to him that he had been married twice and had a son with his first wife who was two years younger than Bill. The psychologist also claimed he was happily married to his second wife, and the couple had a son and a daughter together. Since the meeting was going nowhere, Bill said he and Tina left, and chuckled when he said that he did see a slight resemblance to himself in the man's appearance – "we stared at each other in the same way." Bill added, "The trip back to Dallas that day was a very long one, but I felt more determined than ever to locate my birth mother."

After Bill's very emotional and disappointing meeting with the man identified as his birth father in the adoption file, he admitted he became reluctant to search for some time. However, he said his undying hope to meet his birth mother kept him searching for her for almost sixteen years, the entire time he and Tina had been married. During those years, Bill registered on a state adoption registry site, located and talked to his foster mother, Teri Davidson, and received search advice from a Homestead birth mother, Mary Schwitters Knudsen, who had been reunited with her son. Bill said he learned much about Homestead adoption practices during that time and also heard rumors that Dr. Durham, the maternity home's director or his son had "warehoused the adoption agency's records in another state because of his activities with Black Market babies." Bill explained he also "got cross-wise" with an adoption site's coordinator while he was attempting to communicate with a birth mother who might have known his mother while the two women lived at Homestead.

After so many years of disappointments, false starts, and dead-ends, Bill eventually decided he needed serious help and contacted Kinsolving, a professional search company located in North Carolina. "The company was expensive, and I paid $4,500 to them. Amazingly, they found three generations of my birth mother's family in less than four days. In fact, the company found some information about my birth and my foster care that I later discovered my birth mother didn't even know." Within a short time, the investigator gave Bill his birth mother's phone number, and he said it was "scary as hell," when he called the number. In hindsight, he said, "I think I felt so scared because I was rejected by my birth father, and I had believed for so long that my birth mother was either dead or that she just didn't want to be found."

Initially, Bill called the number, reached his birth mother's voicemail, and left a message that included his name and number. "I tried not to sound like a bill collector," he jokingly added. The next day, after his birth mother had failed to return his call, Bill called the number again and left a second message very similar to the first. On the third day, when he still had not received a response, Bill called again, and his birth mother picked up the phone. When she said "hello," Bill immediately handed the phone to his wife and told her, "Here, take this….I can't breathe." When he calmed down and was able to talk to his birth mother, Bill said he was overcome with joy to hear her excitedly tell other people in the room, "It's my son from Texas!"

In 2014, Bill, Tina, and their children drove to Arkansas to meet his birth mother and her family in person at a local restaurant. According to Bill, the reunion was a very happy one, and he was pleased to meet his birth mother's husband and a half-brother, one of his three half-siblings. At the time he was interviewed, Bill had not met his other half-brother or half-sister, although he had plans to do so. While the family gathering was a joyful one, it was also intensive at times, Bill said, especially when his birth mother shared a few memories of the time she spent at Homestead Maternity Home. Her comments were positive, he said, when she recalled a Christmas party that Dr. Durham and his wife hosted for Homestead girls at their personal residence in Fort Worth. The most humorous bit of information his mother shared during the family reunion, and definitely an "icebreaker," Bill remarked, was that he was conceived during the Alaskan Earthquake of 1964. After searching for almost two decades, Bill said he often finds it difficult to believe he finally found his birth mother.

> *Author's Note:* Bill Dittman, a long-time Deputy in the Dallas County (TX) Sheriff's office, died on September 2, 2016, in a head-on auto accident near Forney, Texas. He was on his way home from work at the Dallas County Courthouse in downtown Dallas, Texas, when the accident occurred just a short distance from his home. Bill is survived by his widow, Tina, and their two children.

Thomas Faltysek

Born in the summer of 1963, Thomas was born at Harris Methodist Hospital in Fort Worth. He has never known the name of the physician who delivered him. When Thomas was three days old, he was adopted by

Manuel Joseph Faltysek, a thirty-eight year old Tenneco employee, and his wife, Geraldine Loehr Faltysek, thirty-six years old. His adoptive parents already had an eleven year old biological daughter, who traveled with the couple to Fort Worth when they picked up Thomas at Homestead's adoption office on 5th Avenue. Before she and her husband decided to adopt a child, Thomas's adoptive mother had given birth to six other children, including their eleven year old daughter, another child, and two sets of twins. According to Thomas, four of the five babies born after his adoptive sister were stillborn, and one of the twins lived for only a few days. Thomas's sister told him years ago that she sat outside the adoption office when her parents met with Homestead staff the day they took him home. She said she overheard one of the Homestead staff members tell her mother and father that Thomas's parents were an "older couple who had too many kids." Thomas's parents drove him home to Victoria, Texas, where he grew up with his older sister. When he was in the third grade, one of the other students told Thomas he was adopted. After he got home from school that day, he asked his parents if the story was true. They explained to Thomas that he was adopted and shared their very small amount of adoption information with him. Thomas said his parents were friends with the student's parents, and the boy who teased him may have overheard his parents mention Thomas's adoption. Both of Thomas's adoptive parents are now deceased.

In 2005, after Thomas learned one of his daughters was diagnosed with a medical problem that could be hereditary, his older sister encouraged him to search for his birth parents. Over a period of several years, he talked to various individuals, including Patricia Molina, who worked at the time for the State of Texas, several adoption search angels, and a court-appointed intermediary. Thomas recalled a telephone conversation with Molina more than a decade ago in which she told him his mother's last name. He recalled hearing Molina say "Holland," but when he asked her to repeat the name, she refused. Currently, Thomas is enrolled in a Master's program through Liberty University, and in recent years, his family life and completing his education have taken precedence over searching for his birth parents. In recent months, he has considered DNA testing to help identify his birth family, to discover his genetic ethnicity, and hopefully, to learn more about his medical history he plans to share with his daughters. Thomas added, "My adoptive parents were my Mom and Dad. I had a good life, which is not a bad thing. But I would like to let my birth parents know what kind of man I turned out to be."

Claudia Hinds Fazio

Born at Harris Hospital in late 1961, and delivered by Dr. Jack Turner, Claudia was adopted by an older Dallas couple who used Homestead's adoption agency. She said her adoptive parents learned about Homestead's adoption services from Carol Frank, a social worker, whose father was a Dallas minister. She believes Ms. Frank may have known her adoptive father's parents when they were Baptist missionaries living in Mexico. When Claudia's adoptive parents drove her from Fort Worth to her new home in Dallas, she joined an adopted brother named Donald who had been adopted from Homestead about two years earlier. Mr. Hinds worked as a structural engineer in the Dallas area, and Claudia's adoptive mother was employed by Braniff Airlines before she and her husband adopted their son. Claudia and her adopted brother grew up together in Oak Cliff and attended Skyline High School. After Claudia graduated, she attended the University of North Texas.

Claudia said she and her brother always knew they were adopted, but the only information she has about her birth parents are details listed on a non-id information sheet her mother shared with her when she growing up. According to the document, Claudia's birth mother was fifteen years old, with red hair, and she was five feet four inches tall. Her birth father was described as a tall, dark-haired sixteen year old. Claudia's mother told her when she was younger that Homestead had "matched up" Claudia with the couple's request for a "baby girl with strawberry blonde hair." Claudia said she had a great life growing up, and she always felt that being adopted was special. She laughingly recalled skipping down the sidewalk when she was a child and proudly proclaiming to others around her, "I'm adopted, and you're not!" Her parents assured Claudia they would support and assist her with any search efforts she made to identify and locate her birth parents, but each time they offered assistance, Claudia said she delayed the search and never really made a serious effort to locate her birth parents. Years ago, she did talk to someone who told her she was the only baby girl born on her birth date in Fort Worth. According to Claudia, Donald also was not interested in searching for his birth parents. She believes, however, a lifelong addiction problem that began when Donald was a young teenager may have contributed to his lack of interest. "We loved our parents so very much," Claudia added, "so there was no real reason to search for our birth parents at the time."

Claudia's parents and her brother are now deceased, and her only child, a son, is an adult. In recent years, especially on her birthday and the anniversaries of the deaths of her parents and brother, Claudia often wonders about her birth parents. Recently, she has considered participating in DNA testing or petitioning the court in Tarrant County to open her adoption file. "I'd really like to know the names of my birth parents and to know more about my medical history." She quickly added, "And I also would like to thank them for giving me the gift of life."

Sally Fielder

Adopted by Audrey Turner and Roger Fielder, Sally was born in early 1962 and delivered by Dr. Jack Turner at Harris Hospital in Fort Worth, Texas. Sally's adoptive mother was unable to have children, and when she and her husband were about forty years old, they decided to adopt a baby through Homestead Maternity Home's child placement agency. According to Sally, her family lived in Fort Worth until she was about four years old, when her adoptive father was transferred by his employer to another state. During her early years in Fort Worth, Sally distinctly remembers her mother taking her when she was sick to Dr. Harry Womack's office near John Peter Smith Hospital in downtown Fort Worth. Sally explained that Dr. Womack was the pediatrician who saw her in the hospital when she was born and that he seemed to be a friend of her parents when they lived in Fort Worth. Sally grew up as an only child, and she knew that she was adopted from the time she was very young. "My parents adored me," Sally said, "and I adored them. I had an idyllic childhood and was just as happy as a clam." When she was old enough to ask questions about her adoption, Sally noticed her mother "became very nervous," and often trembled in response to her daughter's questions. Since her mother seemed so uncomfortable, Sally said she talked primarily about her adoption with her father. When she was about sixteen years old, Sally asked him about her biological parents, and he shared with her the only details she ever knew. According to her adoptive father, Sally's birth mother was a "very young flight attendant who became pregnant by a neurosurgical medical resident," who her father said "could not marry." He further explained to Sally that her birth mother's pregnancy and placing her baby for adoption were "kept secret for a reason." But he never shared the reason with Sally, nor did she ask him additional questions.

Although Sally wanted to believe what her adoptive father told her when she was a teenager, she questioned the circumstances and the validity of the story throughout her adult life and continues to do so. She said she always felt one of her adoptive mother's sisters and her husband treated her like one of their own children. Although she loved them, and they loved her, the care and concern her aunt and uncle showed for her seemed very "parental" in nature. As she grew older, Sally began to notice how much she resembled her cousins, and she often wondered if her uncle might have been her biological father. She recalled the close relationship that existed between her adoptive parents and her aunt and uncle throughout their lifetimes even though they lived in different states, and she explained the closeness prevented her from asking questions about a possible relationship to her uncle. Sally's parents and her aunt and uncle are now deceased, and she said the mystery remains unsolved.

At the time of her interview, Sally indicated she may participate in DNA testing. Her rationale for doing so is twofold – she would like to know the identity of her birth parents, and she wants to learn about her birth family's medical history. The latter is very important to Sally, since she would like to better understand the hereditary diseases of her two children, one of whom is now deceased, and the other is seriously ill. Sally has also considered filing a petition with the Tarrant County court requesting that her Homestead adoption file be opened.

Charlotte House Franson

Charlotte's adoptive parents, Charlene Pierce and Colby House lived in El Paso, Texas, when they adopted her shortly after her birth in late 1967. According to information shared with her by her adoptive parents, Charlotte was born at All Saints Hospital in Fort Worth and was delivered by Dr. Hugh Parchman. Her adoptive parents, Charlotte added, had adopted a baby boy from Homestead two years before they adopted her. Charlotte said her adopted brother has never expressed a desire to search for his birth family. After her adoptive mother passed away after by-pass surgery in 1995, Charlotte enlisted the services of Ms. Pat Palmer, an intermediary who lived in Irving, Texas. According to Charlotte, Ms. Palmer reviewed Charlotte's Homestead adoption file and mailed a letter to a woman in Louisville, Kentucky who was identified in the file as her birth mother. Although the woman never responded, Charlotte knew her birth mother's name and continued to search for her. Later, Charlotte learned that her mother had died of cancer.

During the search process, Charlotte discovered that she shared her birth mother with a half-sister named Kristen, seventeen years younger, who had received the letter intended for their late mother. Charlotte explained that when Kristen read the letter from the intermediary, she did not believe the information that said her mother had given birth to an older daughter who was adopted at birth. Since Kristen's grandmother suffered from dementia and was living in a nursing home at the time, she turned to her father for information about her mother's older daughter. Reluctantly, Kristen's father admitted he knew about his wife's first child, but he quickly added that she had "sworn him to secrecy" about the baby's birth and subsequent adoption. According to Charlotte, her birth mother's name was Judith Marie O'Leary, and she was twenty-one years old when she gave birth to Charlotte in Fort Worth, Texas. Judith grew up in a Louisville, Kentucky household that Charlotte described as "hard-core Irish Catholic." Based on information her birth mother's family shared with Charlotte, Judith worked as a certified public accountant for her entire life. At the time of her interview, Charlotte had participated in DNA testing in an effort to identify and locate her birth father, and when this book went to press, her search was still ongoing.

Celia Spencer Frizzell

In the fall of 1964, long-time Fort Worth residents, Charles Windall Spencer, thirty-one years old, and his wife, Marilyn Pannill, also thirty-one, adopted Celia through Homestead's child placement agency. Celia said she was raised with an older sister who was also adopted from Homestead. According to Celia, each of her adoptive parents graduated from Texas Christian University in Fort Worth. Her adoptive mother stayed home, and her adoptive father, who was first employed by General Dynamics, later worked in the banking industry. She and her sister attended Arlington Heights High School, and Celia said, "I had a beautiful upbringing. I remember our adoptive mother telling us we were adopted one day as we drove home from Galveston, when I was about eight years old. The fact that I was adopted, however, didn't really register with me at the time." She added that her birth mother always told her and her sister they were "chosen" and "loved." However, when Celia and her sister became teenagers and asked questions about their adoptions, their mother provided very little information and seemed to consider the adoption subject "taboo." One detail her mother did share with Celia was that someone from Homestead called her a day or two after Celia was born and said, "Your baby is here!" Although Celia's parents had not officially notified Homestead they were ready to adopt another child, the couple wanted another child, so they readily accepted Homestead's proposal to adopt the baby offered by the Homestead staff member. When Celia and her sister were old enough to understand, their mother explained that she and her husband chose to adopt them because their adoptive father had suffered complications from a childhood illness that prevented him from fathering a child. But in later years, Celia's elderly father told her a different story, when he explained his wife was concerned that pregnancy would affect her looks and that she only wanted to raise daughters. In 2002, Celia's adoptive mother passed away, and she lost her adoptive father, with whom she was very close, in early 2017.

Celia married in the late 1980s, and several years later, she gave birth to two children, a son and a daughter. Her search to find her birth mother began shortly after her children were born, at least in part, from having a need to know her own background and her medical history that she could pass on to her children. Initially, Celia and her husband visited the Fort Worth Public Library and searched through microfiche archives containing Tarrant County birth records. Later, Celia posted her adoption information on several adoption registries. In 1997, after a reasonable period of unsuccessful searching, Celia and her husband hired an attorney who assisted her in petitioning the Tarrant County court. The petition was granted, and a court-appointed intermediary soon located her birth mother, Jylle (*pronounced Jill)* Copeland. Within a short time, Celia and her mother had signed papers stating they wanted to be in contact with each other. After communicating through a series of letters and phone calls, Celia and her birth mother decided to meet in person. For Mother's Day that year, Celia and her husband sent Jylle a round-trip ticket to Fort Worth so they could spend the holiday together. Celia said she and her husband, along with their two young children, were very excited when they met Jylle at the airport, and their reunion was a time she will never forget. Later, Jylle and her family, along with Celia's birth father's family, two groups of people who had not spoken since they learned about Jylle's pregnancy years ago, hosted a homecoming in California for almost two hundred close and extended family members. Although Celia's reunion with her birth mother was the beginning of a close personal relationship that endured until Jylle's death in 2016, the relationship with her adoptive mother effectively ended when she met her birth mother. Celia said her adoptive mother "disowned her" because she searched for her birth mother and developed a relationship with her and birth family members.

During a period of almost two decades, Celia learned about her birth mother's pregnancy at seventeen years old, the time she spent at Homestead Maternity Home, and her life after she gave up her only child for adoption and returned to California. According to conversations with Jylle, Celia heard the story of her birth father, a young California man named Billy, who her mother described as the love of her life. Interestingly, Jylle's parents chose to send her to the Fort Worth maternity home after a referral by "someone connected to Homestead." Jylle said she flew to Fort Worth early in her pregnancy and checked into Homestead Maternity Home, where she was known as "Jylle Cone." After Jylle's baby girl was delivered in the fall by Dr. Jack Turner at Harris Hospital, she returned to Homestead for a brief period before flying back home to California. Celia said Jylle never married, and although Billy did later marry, he has no other biological children. Celia remains thankful that she had the opportunity to meet and to get to know her birth mother, and she continues to enjoy frequent contacts with a paternal aunt. She is also thankful that she and her adoptive father, whom she loved very much, were able to renew their relationship in the years following her adoptive mother's death. She added "I never intended to hurt my adoptive parents by searching for my birth family, and I told each of them from the beginning they would always be my Mom and Dad."

Ramona Kay Wolfe Gaines

Margaret Nash Wolfe and James Wolfe, owner of Bowman & Wolfe Construction Co., were living in Fort Worth, Texas, in 1969 when they adopted Ramona. Earlier in the couple's marriage, Margaret Wolfe had given birth in a western state to her first child, a baby girl, and the baby became sick. The doctor told Mrs. Wolfe that her baby should be transferred to another hospital in a nearby town where she could receive the care she needed to recover. One of the nurses at the hospital allegedly attempted to warn Mrs. Wolfe that something might happen to her baby if she allowed the infant to go to the other hospital. However, the young mother heeded the doctor's advice and allowed her baby to be transferred in order to receive the treatment he said she needed. When Mrs. Wolf was discharged from the hospital where she gave birth, she went to the other hospital to see her newborn baby. But when she arrived there, she learned her baby girl had died. Later, Ramona's adoptive mother discovered her firstborn child allegedly had been sold on the Black Market. Over the next ten years or so, Ramona's adoptive parents had two biological sons and became foster parents to another son whose parents signed over custody to them. Since the couple still wanted daughters, they decided to adopt.

Ramona weighed less than five pounds when she was born at All Saints Hospital in Fort Worth. According to her adoptive mother, she was born with the umbilical cord wrapped around her neck and remained in the hospital for five weeks before she was adopted. Two years after Ramona was born, her parents adopted another Homestead baby girl and took her home when she was two days old. When asked how her adoptive parents learned about Homestead's adoption agency, Ramona said she never asked her parents nor did she hear them say anything about why they chose Homestead.

Ramona's adoptive parents divorced when she was about five years old, but she continued to live with her adoptive mother and her siblings in Fort Worth until she was about twelve. At that time, Ramona's mother moved with her children to Oregon, where her mother was ill and needed help. Her adoptive father passed away about fifteen years ago, she said, but her adoptive mother who is now in her eighties, lives near her. When she and her sister were old enough to understand what adoption meant, their mother told the two girls some "basic stuff" about their birth mothers. According to her adoptive mother, Ramona's birth mother was an actress, and her biological father was a student. She does recall seeing a Homestead non-id information sheet that confirmed those details. Later on, she heard her adoptive mother say Mike Powell was the Homestead attorney who handled her adoption, but she thinks her parents actually picked her up at the office of Jimmy Hinds, the attorney who represented her father's construction business. Although Ramona never knew exactly how much her adoption cost, her adoptive mother said she and her husband sold an airstream trailer to pay for her adoption. At some point, Ramona saw the expense statement, but the only thing she remembers is there was no charge listed for her birth mother's room and board. Her adoptive mother also kept a letter written by Mary Jo Maruda, a Homestead social worker who made a home visit to her adoptive parents' house before she was born. For years now, Ramona has searched sporadically for her birth mother, but after so long with no success, she is no longer searching.

Gala French Harris

Born in 1969 at St. Joseph's Hospital, Gala, a lifelong resident of Texas, was adopted at seven days old by Earl French, now deceased, and his wife, Gladys Hunt French. According to a copy of the receipt for her adoption expenses kept throughout the years by her parents, they paid four thousand dollars when they picked up Gala at the office of Homestead's attorney, Harold Valderas. Gala's adoptive mother said she and her husband made only one visit to Homestead prior to the adoption, and the remainder of the adoption details were handled by Harold Valderas. According to Gala, her adoption was finalized in Tarrant County court in April of 1970. The only details Gala's adoptive parents knew about her birth parents were listed on a single typewritten sheet of paper given to them by the attorney. The document, entitled "Non-ID Information" indicated Gala's birth parents were twenty and twenty-one years old, Caucasian, and each had dark hair and either brown or green eyes. Although she is not certain, the occupation of her birth mother was shown as either secretary or waitress. In years past, Gala said she searched for her birth mother and helped organize a reunion in Fort Worth for more than one hundred Homestead adoptees, birth mothers, and adoptive parents. But she has been unsuccessful in identifying or locating her birth mother.

Michael Roger Harrison

Mike, known as Baby Boy Cash, weighed six pounds when he was born in the fall of 1965 at All Saints Hospital in Fort Worth. He was adopted when he was two weeks old by Eddy Daniel Harrison and Blanche Joanne Teague Harrison, who were already parents to a young daughter they had adopted from Homestead a few years earlier. Although his adoptive father worked at General Dynamics in Fort Worth as a mechanical engineer when his parents adopted him, Mike said his family moved back to Nashville, Tennessee, where they had relatives, when he was still fairly young.

According to Mike, who is a teacher, he always knew he was adopted. When he was old enough to ask questions about his birth mother, Mike's adoptive parents showed him the one page non-id information sheet they received from Homestead when they adopted him. According to details listed on that document, Mike's birth mother was fifteen years old when she was admitted to Homestead. His birth father was a twenty-one year old freshman in college. When Mike began a serious search for his birth parents, his wife, Amy Puckett Harrison, who is also a teacher, enlisted the assistance of a Texas search angel named Connie Gray. Initially, Gray suggested Mike participate in DNA testing, and his test results included a second cousin match. That match, as well as Gray's search expertise and experience in analyzing DNA results, helped locate Mike's birth mother and his birth father, who are still living. Further analysis and additional contacts with Mike's DNA matches surprisingly revealed his birth parents are first cousins. At the time of the interview, Mike's birth mother had declined to meet him, and he had not met his birth father. Several months ago, after learning his father and his wife had two children together, Mike, Amy, and their family met the two half-siblings. As the interview ended, Amy remarked, "Regardless of the outcome, this has been a blessing for my husband to find his half-siblings, meet them in person, and to develop relationships with them."

Tammie Noblett Harvey

A married mother of two girls, twenty-two and twenty-five, Tammie always knew she had been adopted. According to Homestead documents kept by Tammie's adoptive mother throughout the years, she was born at All Saints Hospital in Fort Worth in the early summer of 1966. Dr. Jack Turner, who delivered many other Homestead babies, was present at her birth. Tammie's adoptive father, J. B. Noblett, age 46, and her adoptive mother, Patricia Benton Noblett, 30 years old, already had a three year old son when they adopted Tammie. Noblett was an employee of Greyhound Bus Lines, where he eventually retired after thirty-four years with the company. A few years after her parents adopted Tammie, they had a baby boy.

In May of 1966, Mr. and Mrs. Noblett mailed a letter to Homestead requesting to adopt a baby girl, something Tammie's mother said was her husband's preference. In early June of 1966, an unidentified member of Homestead's staff sent a short form application to the couple, and they returned the completed document to the child placement office in Fort Worth. By mid-June, Homestead recontacted the couple and asked them to meet with staff members for an interview scheduled in the child placement agency's office at 1028 5th Avenue. A copy of a letter from Mary F. Barrett, Supervisor of Social Work at Homestead, to Mr. and Mrs. Noblett, confirmed the interview had been scheduled for June 17, 1966, but the appointment was delayed until the following week. On July 25, 1966, Judith Kelley, another Homestead social worker, wrote a letter to the couple informing them they were approved to adopt a child as soon as a baby girl became available. Since Mr. Noblett was away on an extended bus trip, Tammie's adoptive parents did not pick up their baby girl until about five weeks later. Other Homestead documents in Tammie's possession indicate she was listed on one of the agency's non-id information sheets as "Baby Girl Baker." Her birth mother was identified on this same sheet as a twenty-one year old high school graduate who had attended some business classes. Details on the sheet also indicated Tammie's birth mother enjoyed music and singing and that she worked as a secretary for a government agency on the east coast. Tammie's birth father was identified on the same sheet as a twenty-three year old Air Force radio operator. Additional information showed Tammie's birth father was five feet eight inches tall, weighed 160 pounds, and was "very neat, intelligent, and ambitious." Another document, Tammie mentioned, was a receipt for legal fees totaling one hundred fifty dollars, paid by her adoptive parents to Harold Valderas, a Fort Worth attorney who presented Homestead during the adoption process.

Growing up in a household with two brothers, Tammie recalled how pleased she was to be the only girl. And since her adoptive father had wanted a girl, he always made her feel special. However, Tammie's relationship with her adoptive mother was different, and she never felt as if she could please her. The couple's marriage was a troubled one, Tammie explained, and her adoptive parents divorced when Tammie was seven years old. Eventually her mother remarried, but Tammie's relationship with her did not improve, and she said her teenage years were not happy ones. At sixteen, Tammie became pregnant, but she delayed telling her mother for about three months. When she finally told her, Tammie said her mother "got drunk" in order to deal with the news that her daughter was pregnant. As soon as the initial shock was over, Tammie's mother took her to Planned Parenthood where the staff confirmed her daughter's pregnancy. Immediately after that visit, Tammie's mother scheduled an appointment for her with an obstetrician. During the time Tammie was in an exam room discussing pregnancy options with the doctor and his nurse, her adoptive mother stood in the hallway outside the door and listened to their conversation. At one point, Tammie said her mother "burst through the door and told me she would ship me off somewhere if I refused to have an abortion." Tammie still remembers how upset she was after the abortion and how her mother treated her "like dirt." When she returned to school, Tammie learned she had been "removed from the cheerleading squad," and she admitted she had "no self-esteem." Later, Tammie became pregnant for a second time and gave up the baby for adoption. She explained that her mother was "worried about what people would think" and would not allow her to keep the child. "I was suicidal after I gave up my son," Tammie recalled, "and I thought about driving off every bridge that I crossed for a long time." She added, "I had abortion remorse feelings, too, about ten years ago," but the support of her husband's family and a few close friends has helped her deal with the difficult times.

A few years ago, Tammie was reunited with the son she placed for adoption almost thirty years ago. Tammie candidly explained that her adoptive mother's attitude toward her, as well as the many criticisms she endured as a teenager, greatly impacted how she raised her own daughters. "Although I've been a very straight-forward mother to my girls, I've experienced some of the same things with my youngest daughter."

Susan Hendrix

Born in the fall of 1968 at Harris Hospital in Fort Worth, Texas, Susan was delivered by Dr. Jack Turner and adopted from Homestead Child Placement Agency by Marvin Hendrix and his wife, Brenda Joyce King Hendrix. Five years before Susan's adoption, her parents adopted a son from Homestead. Susan believes her adoptive parents learned about Homestead from the pastor of Saginaw Baptist Church, where they were members. According to Susan's conversations with her parents, Homestead notified them when she was born, and they went to see her in the Harris Hospital nursery. Before they took Susan home at five weeks old, her parents paid adoption fees totaling $1,260, plus $50 in legal fees they paid directly to Homestead's attorney. Susan said her Homestead foster mother included a picture she had taken of her as a baby in the diaper bag given to her adoptive mother. Susan treasures that picture even now, since it was the only one taken of her during the first five weeks of her life. When asked why she was five weeks old when her parents adopted her, Susan said she does not know. Susan's adoptive parents were thirty-five and forty-four years old when they adopted her. Her father was a World War II veteran, who worked forty-two years at General Dynamics in Fort Worth before he retired. "My Dad was a very honest, stand-up man," Susan recalled, "and my Mother was an "opinionated woman who stood up for herself." When she was a child, Susan's parents told her she was special and provided her with a wonderful childhood.

When Susan was about seventeen years old, she began searching for her birth parents. She said, "I was never looking to replace my adoptive parents. I just wanted to know about my birth family and to understand the circumstances surrounding my adoption." She said her Dad always called her "the curious one" and gave her copies of her adoption papers that included a non-id information sheet given to her adoptive parents when they took her home. According to Susan, details on the document indicate Susan's birth parents were married when she was born. Other descriptive information on the document indicates Susan's birth mother was a twenty-six year old stenographer with Irish ancestry, and her birth father was a twenty-seven year old member of the U.S. Air Force. Susan explained her initial attempts at searching for her birth parents began before the availability of the internet and included numerous trips to the library. In addition, she posted information on several adoption registries and communicated with other Homestead adoptees and search angels. The only significant finding, she added, was that someone said her birth mother's surname began with the letter "B." At the time of her interview, Susan said she was contemplating DNA testing and has considered filing a petition with the Tarrant County court to open her adoption file.

Leslie Shives Hinkle

Before Leslie successfully petitioned the Tarrant County Court to open her adoption file in late summer of 2016, the Lufkin, Texas native knew very little about her adoption. According to conversations she had with her adoptive parents and documents her adoptive mother maintained throughout the years, Leslie was adopted at five days old from Homestead Child Placement Agency in Fort Worth, Texas. When asked how her adoptive parents learned about Homestead, Leslie said her adoptive mother's distant cousins in Fort Worth knew Dr. Durham, the maternity home's director, and when they learned her parents planned to adopt a baby, they referred them to Homestead. Leslie explained that her adoptive parents grew up during a "time of secrets" and did not tell her she was adopted until she was about five or six years old. Leslie remembers asking her mother several questions, including "where did I come from?" and "why do I look this way?" In response to Leslie's questions, her adoptive mother explained she and her husband had adopted her when she was a baby.

In the years that followed, Leslie's adoptive mother provided her with more details about her adoption, including that Homestead said her birth mother was a concert pianist. According to Homestead's information, the concert pianist was widowed and already had several children when she became pregnant by an engineer she met at a Fort Worth event. In addition, Homestead staff said Leslie's maternal grandfather had once conducted the Vienna Symphony and that she was about forty percent European. Also, according to Homestead, Leslie's birth mother specifically requested the adoption agency place her baby with a musical family. Since Leslie's adoptive mother performed as one of The Norris Sisters on a well-known radio show in East Texas, the adoption agency staff "matched up" the pianist's child, known as "Baby Peters," with Leslie's adoptive parents. She said her adoptive mother enrolled her in piano lessons about the time she started school, and she continued lessons through high school. But according to Leslie, she could never "play by ear" like her adoptive mother, and she never considered herself a "true musician."

Documents maintained by Leslie's adoptive parents include the name of the doctor who delivered her, Dr. Jack Turner, his delivery nurse, Ruth Hamilton, and Dr. Harry Womack, Homestead's pediatrician. However, Leslie said she first saw the "consent to adopt" document for "Baby Girl Peters" after her adoption file was opened by the court. That particular document indicated Leslie's mother used the pseudonym "Betty Peters" when she gave birth, and her baby was identified as "Baby Peters The signature on the relinquishment document, however, read "Olivia Bertha Peterson," although "Betty Peters" appeared in parentheses beside Olivia's legal name. This document is an example of numerous other consent to adopt forms reviewed during research and interviews for this book that included both the pseudonym used at the maternity home and the hospital and the legal name of the birth mother. The use of pseudonyms on Homestead adoption documents, including an unknown number of original birth certificates, is one example of a variety of obstacles Homestead adoptees encounter when searching for their birth mothers. In fact, Leslie discovered she has no original birth certificate on file with the Texas Bureau of Vital Statistics in Austin.

Leslie said she grew up as an only child in a wonderful home, where she was raised by loving parents, both of whom are now deceased. She attended Lufkin High School, graduated from Texas A&M University, and married a military guy. She and her husband have no children together, but he had a son before they were married. Leslie and her husband traveled all over the world when he was in the military, and they ended up in Killeen, where she has worked for the City of Killeen for twenty-two years. In July of 2016, Leslie filed a petition with the Tarrant County court to open her adoption file. The following month, a Tarrant County judge agreed to open the file and transferred it to a Court-Appointed Intermediary (CAI). Through this process, Leslie learned her birth mother was Olivia Bertha Cmajdaka, a woman who grew up in Rosenberg, Texas, and was widowed twice by the time she was forty years old. Olivia first married an older man, John Donlin, with whom she had a son born in 1941. Several years after Mr. Donlin died of a heart attack, Olivia married her second husband, Gene Peterson, and gave birth to three more children born in 1946, 1950, and in 1956. After Mr. Peterson died in 1958, Olivia Peterson became the sole support of four children between two and seventeen years old. In 1960, she became pregnant by a man who is listed on a Homestead non-id information sheet as a thirty-eight year old single employee of General Motors. Since Leslie's birth mother was a forty-four year old widow who already had four children to support, it appears Olivia chose to place her baby for adoption with Homestead's agency. Sadly, Olivia was already deceased when Leslie petitioned the court and first learned her birth mother's name.

The contents of Leslie's adoption file were revealing in other ways, as well. Not only did Leslie discover her birth mother's name, she was overjoyed to discover she has three half-siblings who currently live in the Dallas-Fort Worth area. Leslie recently talked to one of her two half-sisters, who knew nothing at all about their mother giving birth to a child in 1961, and sadly, she also learned that one of her two half-brothers died in 1965 in an Arlington swimming pool accident. According to Leslie's half-sister, their mother took her and the other young children to live temporarily with two aunts, now in their eighties, who cared for them while she was away. Leslie and her half-sister believe their mother may have been at Homestead during that time, and Leslie hopes to discuss the matter with her aunts when she meets them during the coming weeks. At the time of her interview, Leslie had made plans to meet her half-sisters, half-brother, and their families for the very first time. Although she discovered her birth mother was not a concert pianist, Leslie has learned that Olivia's father, her maternal grandfather, was very musical and played the piano and the violin. Ironically, Leslie's half-sister described family gatherings that included singing around the piano, much like the ones Leslie remembers from her own childhood. Looking forward now to a future with siblings she never had, Leslie is excited about the possibility of many gatherings with her newly discovered family. She remarked that although it has been "a little surreal," she now has a "sense of peace" in her life. She added, "I feel like I can finally breathe."

Gregory Alan Horn

Born at Harris Hospital in Fort Worth, Texas, in the spring of 1963, Greg was known as "Baby Boy Keith. When he was about five days old, Greg was adopted by a career U.S. Air Force pilot, William Dale ("Bill") Horn, and his wife, Betty Lou Knuth Horn, who lived in San Antonio at the time. When asked how his birth parents learned about Homestead's adoption agency, Greg said he has never known. According to a statement of expenses given to his adoptive parents and maintained in their files, Greg's adoption cost about thirteen hundred dollars.

After nine years of marriage and several miscarriages, Betty Lou and her husband applied to Homestead to adopt and were placed on a waiting list. Over the next several years, each time Homestead called the couple to let them know a baby was available, Betty Lou told the adoption agency that she was pregnant again. Within weeks of each phone call, however, Betty Lou suffered another miscarriage. According to the story Greg's parents told him, after his mother experienced her seventh miscarriage, and the couple had turned Homestead down several times because Betty Lou was pregnant, Greg's father said "To hell with all this, I'm ordering a new Corvette." Before the Corvette was delivered, Homestead called again, and Bill answered the phone. As soon as the staff member identified herself, Bill handed the phone to his wife, who he knew would say she wanted the baby. Later, he told Greg that he left the decision making about his son's adoption to his wife, because he could see the new Corvette slipping away before his very eyes.

A year after they adopted Greg, Bill and Betty Lou adopted a baby girl from Homestead who would be their one year old son's only sibling. His adoptive sister was a beautiful child, he said, but she grew into a troubled teenager and adult. As far as Greg knows, his sister has never searched for her birth parents. Greg recalled how wonderful his adoptive parents were and how happy he was as a child. He described his adoptive father as a "man's man," much like John Wayne, he said, who served as a rescue helicopter pilot in Vietnam. Although his adoptive father took on difficult assignments and had a tough exterior, Greg described him as a loving and caring husband and father who had a really big heart.

According to Greg, his father's transfers with the Air Force allowed him to experience a variety of academic and athletic opportunities as he grew up in the U.S. and in Italy. Greg said he was an accelerated student and a stand-out athlete, and his parents always supported him in his school activities. After his father retired from the Air Force and moved their family to Washington State where the couple had relatives, Greg became an All-State football player. Eventually, Greg gave up the sport to attend Stanford, where he graduated. After college, Greg moved to the east coast to attend graduate school and later, he met his current wife with whom he has two children. Presently, Greg is a Presbyterian minister in New Jersey and teaches theology at Columbia University in New York City. According to Greg, his adoptive mother is now deceased, but his adoptive father, who he says is his all-time "hero," is still living.

Although Greg loved his parents, he began to notice as he got older that he looked nothing like anyone around him. Also, he became acutely aware of the special bond that most biological families seemed to share. As a young adult, his adoption awareness became more profound, and he admitted that he often felt as if "something was missing." Greg said he first began searching for his birth mother when he registered on several "adoption boards." After years of posting his adoption information without contacts from anyone, he decided that no one was looking for him, and he gave up searching for a number of years. Earlier this year, Greg resumed searching, and after he received the results of a DNA test, a gift given to him by his wife and thirteen-year old son, Greg became more hopeful that he might find his birth family. In fact, he still remembers the hope he felt when he realized his DNA results included a first cousin match. He said that he immediately contacted the cousin, who lived in North Dakota and admitted that he was filled with doubt that anything positive would result from the contact. But his doubt soon turned into elation when his cousin responded to his email with "Honey, we're from Texas!" After conversations with this first cousin and subsequent communications between the cousin and other family members, Greg discovered his birth father was Stanley Vickers from Floydada, Texas. Sadly, his birth father was already deceased when Greg learned his name. Over the next few weeks and months, Greg learned that Stanley was one of thirteen children and that two of his brothers were All-State football players, just as he had been. In addition, Greg discovered he has two half-brothers, forty and forty-four years old, who were born during Stanley's marriage before the relationship ended in divorce years ago. According to Greg, he has thirty-three paternal first cousins and numerous other Vickers relatives in Texas and in several other states.

In June of 2016, Greg traveled to Ruidoso, New Mexico for a Vickers family reunion. Although he asked his paternal relatives if they knew the identity of his birth mother, no one seemed to know who Stanley might have been dating at the time Greg was conceived. He learned from relatives at the reunion that when he was born, his birth father was a twenty-four year old single guy who had recently graduated college and was working as a salesman for an oilfield supply company. Interestingly, one of Greg's half-brothers visited him in New Jersey, and according to Greg, the visit went very well. Before his half-brother left, he told Greg something that he will always remember. He said, "If my brother and I had known about you, we would have searched for you." Greg feels extremely fortunate to have learned his birth father's identity and to have met so many wonderful members of the Vickers family. He added that he continues to be amazed at how family members have welcomed him and have accepted him into their large, extended family.

Several days before Greg's interview, he learned that a Tarrant County judge had granted the petition he had recently filed with the court to open his adoption file. And he is very positive and extremely hopeful that he will learn the identity of his birth mother, too, in the very near future.

Ronna Sue Quimby Huckaby

Evert Quimby, an oilfield worker, and his wife Frances Quimby, were living in Bowie, Texas when they adopted Ronna, their only child, in early 1963. Ronna explained that her adoptive parents were childless after twelve years of marriage, and they decided to adopt a baby. When asked how her adoptive parents learned about Homestead, Ronna said the pastor of Calvary Baptist Church in Bowie, Texas, where her parents attended services, referred the couple to Homestead. According to her adoptive mother, the minister knew Pearl Slaughter, the executive director of the Fort Worth facility.

Ronna's parents told her they applied to Homestead's adoption agency and were given a brochure about the maternity home and the adoption process. Once they were approved to adopt, Homestead staff informed Mr. and Mrs. Quimby that adoption expenses would range between seven hundred fifty and twelve hundred dollars, and they were advised to bring the money with them when they picked up their baby. Ronna's parents told her they had been saving money for the adoption, but when Homestead called sooner than expected to let them know she was ready to be taken home, the total amount they had saved was not enough to cover the anticipated cost. Her adoptive mother explained that her husband quickly went to their local bank and requested a loan that he received on the spot. The next Monday, after what Ronna described as "the longest weekend ever for Mom," the couple drove to Fort Worth to meet their baby girl for the first time. Mrs. Quimby saved her adopted daughter's Homestead documents and shared them with Ronna when she began searching for her birth mother. Among the documents was the statement of expenses due and payable by Ronna's adoptive parents before they could take their baby home. The total charge for reimbursable expenses related to the mother and baby was $872. This amount included $220 for room and board at Homestead Maternity Home, $327 for "care of mother;" $15 for the pediatrician; $100 for non-attorney court costs; $20 for layette items; $5 for flowers; $10 for ambulance costs; and $5 for transportation. Her parents also paid an additional $750 for legal fees to Mike Powell, Homestead's attorney, at the time Mr. and Mrs. Quimby picked up their baby.

After Ronna's father passed away, she began a serious search for her birth mother. Early in the process, she and her adoptive mother, who supported Ronna's search efforts, attended a "reunion" of Homestead adoptees and birth mothers in 1999 at Luby's Cafeteria in Fort Worth. Interestingly, another birth mother present at the reunion remembered Ronna's mother, who lived at Homestead during the same time she was a resident. Soon after the reunion, Ronna petitioned the court to open her closed adoption file and hired a court-appointed intermediary (CAI) to receive and review the contents of the file. According to Ronna, the intermediary mailed a letter to Elizabeth ("Betsy") Wilson Lockhart, identified in the file as her birth mother. In the letter, the intermediary explained to Lockhart that her daughter had successfully petitioned the Tarrant County court and asked if she would like to be contacted by her daughter. The intermediary received no response, Ronna explained, and followed up with another letter that also asked for family medical information. During this process, Ronna learned her birth mother had used the fictitious name, "Betsy Lamb," during her stay at Homestead Maternity Home and that Ronna's "hospital name" was "Baby Lamb." After Betsy received the second letter from the intermediary, she replied and included medical information, but she declined contact with Ronna, stating she was not ready to meet her daughter. Once Ronna's birth mother stated she wanted no contact, the intermediary closed the adoption file.

Ronna's personal investigation identified her birth mother's sister, and she contacted the woman she discovered was her maternal aunt. And it was her aunt who later convinced Lockhart to communicate with her daughter. Over a period of time, Ronna and Betsy exchanged emails and photos, and Betsy told her daughter how much she resembled her maternal grandmother. Just as Ronna was her adoptive parents' only child, she discovered that she was Betsy's only child. During the communications with her birth mother, Ronna learned the name of her biological father, who Betsy said never knew she was pregnant. Betsy explained to Ronna that she and Donald Auld, a young Hawaiian man known to his family and friends as "Ducky," had a several weeks' long love affair during an extended holiday in Hawaii. Betsy worked as a Braniff flight attendant at the time, and she and a few female friends were headed to Asia for a vacation. During a two to three day layover in Hawaii, Betsy became acquainted with Ducky at the beach, where he worked, and stayed behind to be with him when her friends flew away to their group's final vacation destination. When Betsy returned home a few weeks later, she learned she was pregnant and sought the advice of a close friend, who referred her to Homestead Maternity Home in Fort Worth.

After a period of exchanging photos and family information during phone calls and emails, Ronna flew to New Jersey to meet the woman who gave birth to her. Before Ronna left Texas, her adoptive mother wrote Betsy a personal letter, and her adopted daughter hand-delivered it to her birth mother. During that first visit, Ronna met Betsy, her stepfather, and Betsy's sister and her family. Ronna was overjoyed that each new family member accepted her into the Lockhart family, and while she was in the area, her aunt and uncle drove her to visit the old family estate in Pennsylvania, where their family had deep roots. At the time of her interview, Ronna said she and Betsy were still in touch, and her maternal aunt and uncle, who live in California, have stopped over in Texas several times to visit with her and her family.

Several months later, Ronna made contact with a paternal cousin in Hawaii, who directed her to an aunt who wanted to become acquainted with her newly-discovered niece. After meeting some of Ducky's relatives on the phone, Ronna traveled to Hawaii to meet members of her birth father's family. It was a bittersweet reunion, Ronna recalled, since Ducky had no other children, and his family saw such a strong resemblance in her to the loved one they lost in an auto accident in 1979. Ronna was delighted and very proud to learn that her paternal great-great-great-grandfather once served in Hawaii's government, and she also discovered one of her second cousins taught hula dancing in Hollywood and was somewhat of a celebrity back home in Hawaii. Ronna said she feels very fortunate to have met not only her birth mother, but members of her maternal and paternal families, as well.

A few years ago, Ronna published a book entitled *"Somewhere Out There"* that chronicles her early life as an adoptee and the search for her birth families. The book is a heartfelt story that is beautifully told in text and in photos. For those adoptees who are still searching for their birth families, Ronna's book is definitely a must-read.

Jimmy Shannon Hunt

Born in early 1966 at All-Saints Hospital in Fort Worth, Shannon always knew he was adopted. At the time of his interview, he lived in Midland, Texas, with his wife and two older children. According to Shannon, his adoptive parents, Jimmie and Jackie McNeil Hunt, of Brownfield, Texas, were in their thirties when they decided to adopt a baby. Before he was adopted, Shannon said, his adoptive mother had given birth to a stillborn child, and she was never able to have another baby. When his parents decided to adopt, Shannon's mother told him they talked to an attorney in Brownfield, and he referred the couple to Homestead Maternity Home and Child Placement Agency in Fort Worth. Shannon's adoptive parents also adopted a second child, a daughter, in Lubbock, Texas, but he does not believe an agency was involved in his sister's adoption. Shannon added that he grew up in a "loving home with caring parents," and never considered searching for his birth mother until he was older and his mother gave him copies of some Homestead documents. Included in the paperwork was a Homestead letter outlining parental adoption requirements for the six-month period preceding the final adoption hearing. Additional paperwork included a letter from Harold Valderas, Homestead's attorney, notifying Shannon's parents of the final adoption hearing date in Fort Worth. Another document included in the paperwork was a non-id information sheet and an itemized statement of adoption-related expenses totaling twelve hundred and sixty five dollars, the amount Shannon's parents paid for his adoption. Dr. Harry Womack, pediatrician, and Dr. Durham, the maternity home's director, were identified as Homestead staff members in the paperwork maintained by Shannon's adoptive mother.

Before his adoptive mother passed away, Shannon said he "dabbled" into searching for his birth mother and other family members. He recalled the reason for his search was that his older child, then in seventh grade, was diagnosed with Type 1 diabetes. Initially, he "googled" Homestead and learned the agency's records had been burned. When asked if he had participated in DNA testing or had considered petitioning the Tarrant County court to open his adoption file, Shannon said he has considered doing each of those things, but he had not done so at the time of his interview.

Tammie Lane Cooper Jacobi

A current resident of Houston, Texas, Tammie has lived in that city since her adoptive father, a former government employee, went to work for NASA when she was five years old. Tammie was delivered by Dr. Jack Turner at Harris Hospital in Fort Worth in the summer of 1959, and her adoptive parents took her home when she was six days old. According to family stories, Tammie's adoptive grandmother traveled with her parents to Fort Worth to meet Tammie and to help with the baby during their trip back home to Lubbock. At the time she was adopted, Tammie said her adoptive parents were living in Lubbock, Texas, where her mother worked as an executive secretary for IBM, and her father was employed by the General Services Administration before transferring to NASA in Houston. According to Tammie's adoptive mother, she and her husband made one visit to Homestead's child placement agency in Fort Worth to complete the adoption paperwork. Two weeks later, the couple received a phone call from Homestead saying they should drive back to Fort Worth to pick up their baby. Tammie's adoptive mother explained that Robert Gilchrist, a Homestead social worker, drove to Lubbock to visit their home once before she and her husband adopted the baby, and he returned twice more after Tammie was placed in the Cooper's home.

Tammie, the mother of three adult children, grew up as an only child. Although she admitted that she enjoyed not having to share her parents' attention with older siblings, Tammie said when she was in her mid-twenties, she began to wish she had a brother or a sister. Since Tammie suffers from a rare, hereditary autoimmune disorder, she has searched for her birth family since 1980. She further explained the various avenues she has pursued during numerous attempts to learn her medical history. This effort is extremely important to Tammie, since her son, daughter, and a granddaughter all have been diagnosed with the same disorder. In the mid-nineties, Tammie talked to a judge in Fort Worth and obtained the services of Joyce Buzbee, an intermediary. Although Ms. Buzbee identified Tammie's birth mother as Shirley Lea Wright, a 17-18 year old Colorado woman, the only clue about her birth father was the word "military" that appeared on the non-id information sheet. Tammie said the judge told her at the time that he really doubted she would ever find the information she wanted. Shortly after her experience with the Tarrant County judge and the intermediary, Tammie said she met a Colorado birth mother online who had lived at Homestead Maternity Home in Fort Worth and was searching for the baby she had given up for adoption in Fort Worth. Apparently, the Colorado woman remembered Tammie's birth mother, who she recalled living at Homestead for only two weeks before she gave birth. This same woman also remembered how upset the young mother became when the nurses at Harris Hospital would not allow her to see her baby. According to the woman Tammie met online, the young Homestead mother was unable to speak for two entire days. Although Tammie has searched unsuccessfully for more than three decades now, she still remains hopeful that one day she will find her birth mother.

Kimberly Kaye Jacobs

Polly Ann Stacy Jacobs, a housewife, and her husband, Claude Dean Jacobs, an auto mechanic, adopted Kimberly from Homestead's adoption agency in the summer of 1966, when she was two weeks old. According to Kimberly, her original birth certificate identified her as the "Infant of Patricia Murphy" and showed Dr. Jack Turner delivered her at All Saints Hospital in Fort Worth. At one time, Kimberly possessed a copy of the non-id information sheet that Homestead gave her adoptive parents, but she has misplaced the document in recent years. When Mr. and Mrs. Jacobs adopted Kimberly, they already had a nine-year old biological son, and four months before her adoption, the couple lost a baby girl to Sudden Infant Death Syndrome (SIDS.) After Mr. and Mrs. Jacobs lost the baby, Dr. Blanche Terrill, a female physician in Stephenville, Texas, where the couple lived at the time, suggested they adopt a baby and referred them to Homestead's child placement agency in Fort Worth. Kimberly's adoptive mother said her adoption took only four months from the application until the day they took her home.

When Kimberly was twelve years old, she was the victim in a life-altering accident. She and her eleven-year-old cousin were sitting in her parents' car, and her cousin opened the glove compartment where she found a .22 caliber derringer. Later, Kimberly would learn that her older brother left the weapon in the glove compartment. While the two pre-teens attempted to determine if the item was a car cigarette lighter or a gun, Kimberly was shot in her left eye. The loss of her eye, Kimberly said, has severely limited her employment opportunities, and throughout her adult life, she has been able to work only part-time jobs.

At thirteen, Kimberly's older brother told her she was adopted, and she became so upset that her adoptive mother called her father at work and asked him to come home to help her deal with the situation. Kimberly remembers her Dad saying he and her adoptive mother "chose" her and that she was "special," but Kimberly admitted she was still confused. Over time, however, she said her feelings of concern and confusion improved, and as an older teenager, she had no problems dealing with her adoption either at home or at school. Kimberly's adoptive father died in 1995, and she lost her adoptive mother in 2006. In 2012, she also lost her older brother.

Currently, Kimberly is a divorced mother of an adult son and daughter. She recalled a story her daughter shared about a conversation with "Nana," her grandmother and Kimberly's adoptive mother. According to the conversation, Nana said she and her husband met with Dr. Durham, Homestead's director, during an interview that Homestead required of prospective parents before they were allowed to adopt. Nana also told her granddaughter that she and her husband allegedly met their baby's birth mother during that same interview. Kimberly believes the incident may have occurred just as her adoptive mother recalled, since she was born four months later, about the same length of time many birth mothers lived at Homestead before giving birth. Kimberly added, "I could not have asked for a better family. I feel special, because I have one mother who gave me Life and another mother who gave me Love."

Jennifer

Born in late 1970 in Fort Worth, Jennifer was adopted by a San Angelo, Texas, couple who worked as mental health professionals. Her adoptive mother, Jennifer said, found out about Homestead Maternity Home and Child Placement Agency from her best friend, a nurse, who previously had adopted a baby from the Fort Worth agency. Jennifer, who grew up as an only child, was between eight and ten years old when her parents told her she was adopted. According to Jennifer, her adoptive parents gave her a book entitled *"Where Did I Come From?"* and during a family meeting, they explained she was adopted. Jennifer said she really didn't pay much attention when she was told about her adoption, but when she was in her early to mid-thirties, after her parents had retired and moved to another state, she began to think more about the fact she didn't know anything about her birth family. Her desire to learn her birth mother's identity, Jennifer admitted, may have been triggered by the fact that she is unmarried, childless, and has no close relatives. Jennifer added that she has often wondered what her birth mother is like and why she was given up for adoption.

Jennifer said she knows very little about her adoption, except a few things her adoptive mother told her over the years. She was one week old, Jennifer was told, when her adoptive parents drove to a Fort Worth hospital to take her home. Her adoptive mother's best friend worked as a nurse at the hospital and brought the baby out to her new parents who were waiting in the car. Jennifer said her adoptive parents apparently had become friends with Mary Jo Maruda, the Homestead social worker who processed the couple's application to adopt, and she still remembers a stuffed blue elephant her mother said was a gift from the social worker. Jennifer recalled seeing a copy of a check in the amount of twelve hundred dollars for adoption costs that one of her parents had written to Homestead. She laughingly recalled the check's "memo line" simply said "Baby!!" When Jennifer was younger, her adoptive mother also shared the non-id information she was given by a Homestead staff member. According to the document, Jennifer's birth mother was twenty-one years old, five feet four inches tall, and her ethnicity was English and Irish. The same document showed her alleged birth father was twenty-two years old.

After making no progress during several previous search attempts, Jennifer admitted she has mixed feelings about searching again for her birth mother. A decade or so ago, she sought out the services of Pat Palmer, an Irving, Texas based researcher and President of "SearchLine of Texas," a group that helped adoptees reunite with their natural parents. The search was unsuccessful, Jennifer said, and Ms. Palmer told her there was "a problem with Homestead records." Although Jennifer eventually wants to identify and locate her birth mother, she has accepted that she may never meet the woman who gave birth to her. She quickly added, "After forty-six years, though, I'm not looking for a Mom and Dad. I already have my Mom and Dad."

Author's Note: In early 2016, Jennifer participated in AncestryDNA testing, and her results revealed several close cousin matches, including every adoptee's hope, a first cousin match. With the help of a search assistant, Jennifer analyzed and contacted the cousin matches and soon learned her birth mother's name. Although the initial contact with her birth mother was made by Jennifer's research assistant, a series of phone conversations between Jennifer and her mother soon followed. During their early talks, Jennifer learned the name of her birth father, who is still living, and was surprised to learn she has six half-brothers. Several months after Jennifer and her mother heard each other's voices for the first time, the two women met in person and spent several intensive weeks getting to know each other. Jennifer proudly said, "She welcomed me with open arms, unreservedly, and I feel as if we are best friends." And she also remarked how amazed she was to see how much she and her mother resemble each other in physical appearance and personal mannerisms. Although Jennifer and her birth mother live many miles apart, they continue to maintain a close relationship and are hoping to arrange a family reunion of Jennifer's half-siblings, their families, and numerous other maternal and paternal relatives.

Karen

When Karen's parents adopted her, she was about eight days old. Born in early 1966 at All Saints Hospital, she was delivered by Dr. Jack Turner, Homestead's obstetrician. Before Karen's parents adopted through Homestead when they were thirty-seven and forty years old, they were turned down by several other agencies, most likely due to age requirements. Karen said she had a "happy childhood" and her parents were "great providers" during the years she grew up in the Houston-Galveston area, where her adoptive father worked for a local civil engineering firm.

When Karen graduated high school, her parents offered her higher educational opportunities that included college and law school. At the time she was interviewed, Karen practiced law in the Midwest, where she lives with her husband and children.

When Karen decided to search for her birth parents, she had very little information. When asked if she ever saw a non-id information sheet that Homestead gave her adoptive parents, Karen said she had not. She explained that she located her birth mother with the assistance of a court-appointed intermediary (CAI) in Tarrant County, and she also participated in DNA testing. As a result of the intermediary's review of Karen's adoption file, she learned that her birth father was an Air Force pilot, and her mother was a teacher. Karen also learned her parents were married when she was born, and each of the two was thirty-three years old. According to public records, Karen added, her parents were married in 1965, had a son four years after she was born, and divorced in 1973. Since neither of Karen's parents were born in Texas, it seems likely her father may have been stationed at Carswell Air Force Base during the time her mother was pregnant and when she gave birth. Even more likely, Karen's birth father may have been deployed to Vietnam during the time she was born. Based on Karen's original Texas birth certificate, her birth mother did not live at Homestead Maternity Home in Fort Worth, but instead, lived in a privately-owned apartment building on Handley Drive in east Fort Worth. Interestingly, research for this book revealed that Sharon Dowden, a former Homestead social worker, now deceased, also lived in the same apartment complex.

Based on Karen's search, her birth mother later remarried and moved to another state, and her birth father remarried and had other children. Unfortunately, he passed away before Karen's began her search. She explained that she wrote her birth mother a letter but "she rejected me in the beginning." Later, her birth mother admitted to Karen she had "never told anyone" she gave a baby up for adoption, and she told her daughter she did not "want to be found." Although Karen was very disappointed, she reluctantly accepted her birth mother's position. But over a period of months, Karen's brother, who is four years younger and lives with his mother in another state, began emailing her. Through these email contacts and Karen's subsequent responses, her brother conveyed how his mother felt about her own situation and attempted to explain her reluctance in meeting Karen. "I can't step into her shoes," Karen said, "but I'm trying to understand why she has delayed meeting me." At the time Karen was interviewed, she seemed hopeful about a future meeting, since she believes her brother has convinced their mother to meet Karen and her family in the months ahead.

Terri Hopkins Langan

Robert Lee Hopkins and Alice Elizabeth McKinnon Hopkins adopted Terri when she was several days old and took her to live in Sweetwater, Texas. Both of her adoptive parents, Terri said, were truck drivers when they adopted her, and she is currently a truck driver herself. According to Terri, she found a copy of a check in the amount of twelve hundred and fifty dollars, made payable to Homestead for her adoption costs, among her adoptive parents' belongings. When Terri was about three years old, her parents moved to Baytown, Texas, where her mother worked as the director of a daycare center. When Terri was about five years old, her adoptive parents "sat her down at the table" and told her she was adopted. Since she was so young and did not understand what the word adopted meant, Terri said the information meant very little to her. Several years later, her parents attempted to adopt another child, but the baby had physical disabilities and emotional issues, and the adoption was unsuccessful. When she was a teenager, Terri said her parents asked her if she wanted to know the names of her birth parents, but she told them she was not interested at the time. She explained during the interview that she delayed searching for her birth mother because she believed it would have been disrespectful to her adoptive parents. However, in recent years, Terri started searching again for her birth parents and consulted search angels and others who assist adoptees in finding their birth families. To date, her efforts have been unsuccessful, and at the time of her interview, Terri said she is no longer searching.

Wiley Lastor

Born in 1971, Wiley is married, has five children, and currently lives near Sherman, Texas, the town where his adoptive parents lived and where his adoptive father owned an air-conditioning company. According to Wiley, his adoptive parents, Wiley William Lastor and Hazel Frances Frank Lastor, arranged his adoption from Homestead's child placement agency in Fort Worth before he was born. The couple received special help with his adoption from Carol Lee Frank, a social worker at Homestead and one of his adoptive mother's older sisters. When Wiley was about ten years old, his parents told him he was adopted. "They caught me off guard," he said, and quickly added "I was disappointed to learn that I hadn't been made by my parents like the other kids." Wiley's adoptive father died when he was twenty-one years old, but his adoptive mother is still living.

When Wiley was an adult, he began searching for his birth mother. After learning her name from some volunteer search angels, he requested a copy of his original birth certificate from the Texas state birth registry in Austin. He recalled a lady named Rosa Hyde, who helped him obtain a copy of the document. Later, Wiley located his birth mother, a Texas resident, and she shared details of her pregnancy and his birth with him. According to his mother, she was 15 or 16 years old and living with her father in Fort Worth when she became pregnant for the first time. Her father, she explained, "made her go to Homestead." She also told Wiley the name of his birth father and explained the man died in 1972, during what she referred to as the "drug raids in Fort Worth." Sadly, his birth mother did not remember Wiley's date of birth.

Meeting his birth mother was not what he expected, Wiley explained, since he soon learned she had dealt with addiction issues most of her life and had served time in jail more than once. Although a relationship with his mother did not work out, Wiley is happy that he now knows his birth family's medical history, including the fact that his mother's father and her grandfather each died of bone cancer. He also discovered his maternal great-grandmother was diagnosed with Alzheimer's disease shortly before he met his birth mother. Wiley acknowledged that his birth mother continues to call him from time to time, and he talks to her when she calls. But his concern for his wife and children prevent him from becoming involved in his birth mother's life.

"Liz"

A native of Florida, Liz was one of six siblings. She became pregnant by her high school sweetheart soon after she graduated. Liz said she had planned to delay sex until she was married, but injuries received during a serious automobile accident in the fall of her senior year caused her to feel differently about herself and possibly weakened her mind and self-control. In late summer of 1969, Liz left Florida to attend college in Virginia, and early into the semester she developed morning sickness and learned she was pregnant. When she told her boyfriend about her pregnancy, he asked her to marry him, but she turned down his offer. Later, Liz wrote letters to her parents and to the parents of her boyfriend and explained she was pregnant. As her morning sickness worsened, Liz said her grades fell, and just before the Christmas break, she realized that she would not be returning to college the next year. Liz said her appearance surprised her parents when she arrived back home in Florida, since she had "put on some weight," and her siblings were upset, too, because she needed her room back. Soon after her arrival, Liz said she and her parents had a discussion about her pregnancy and what she should do. They also told her there was no room at home to raise another child. At the recommendation of an uncle, a local attorney, Liz's parents made arrangements for her to stay at Homestead Maternity Home in Fort Worth until she gave birth and her baby could be placed for adoption.

Liz said she flew alone to Fort Worth, where she arrived after dark in the middle of a rainstorm. Since there was no one from Homestead waiting at the airport to meet her, she took a taxi to the maternity home on West Rosedale. Although she doesn't remember who met her at the maternity home when she arrived that night, she said someone, maybe Mrs. Durham, directed her to her first floor room. Although Liz described her twin bed as very uncomfortable, she had no other complaints about the facility, and was not bored, since she tried to stay busy. Each girl, Liz recalled, was assigned simple chores that included washing dishes and doing her own laundry, but there was still plenty of free time to read, play cards, and to go on occasional shopping trips with other girls, such as her suite mate, who had a car. Once each day, Liz read Norman Vincent Peale's writings in an effort to retain a positive attitude and thought process, and she also talked to her baby and expressed her love. Some of the girls, she added, attended Bible study groups held at private homes. Each Homestead resident required permission from Mrs. Durham to leave the premises, but Liz does not recall being subjected to an evening curfew. Liz said she and other Homestead residents enjoyed healthy meals and took daily prenatal vitamins that were kept in the dining room. During the months Liz lived at Homestead, she completed two college credit correspondence courses, learned to sew, and made a dress while she was there. Dr. Parchman was the Homestead obstetrician who saw Liz for routine prenatal exams, and he also delivered her baby at All Saints Hospital in the late spring of 1970.

Liz recalled an exam Mrs. Durham administered at Homestead in between her doctor's visits that indicated her baby was already in place to be born. When Mrs. Durham notified Dr. Parchman, he decided to induce Liz's labor two weeks before her due date, since he was scheduled to be out of town the next week. Details of Liz's labor and delivery are unclear, since she apparently was heavily medicated and remembers very little. She does remember that another Homestead mother occupied the same hospital room she was assigned after delivery, and she vaguely recalls someone visiting her room on the second day after she gave birth to have her sign paperwork. Liz also recalls falling and hurting herself as she walked from the hallway bathroom back to her bed. To help with pain she experienced after the accident, Liz was given Demerol for almost two days and remembers very little during that period, as well. When asked if Dr. Durham visited her in the hospital, she said he did not. Overall, Liz believes she remained in the hospital for three or four days before she returned to Homestead, where she remained for another two weeks before the return airline ticket arrived that her parents had mailed from Florida.

When Liz returned to Florida, her parents picked her up at the airport and exchanged greetings, but when she began talking about her stay at Homestead, her confinement in the hospital, and giving up her baby for adoption, her father quickly told her she could talk about those things on the drive home, but once they arrived, "that was it" for talking about the events of the past few months. Soon after she returned home, Liz enrolled in summer classes at a local junior college, and in the fall, she enrolled in a state university and moved on campus. She explained that she did not do well in her classes at the university, since she was dealing with questions about her self-worth after giving up her baby for adoption, and it was not long before she decided to return to the junior college she had attended earlier. It was not until 1986, Liz added, that she received her college degree. Although Liz dated several young men in the years that followed her baby's adoption, she did not marry and have another child until the mid-eighties. Looking back on her life, Liz believes her post-adoption feelings of guilt and unworthiness, coupled with the fact that she felt undeserving of another child, contributed to her delay in becoming a mother for a second time. Including her oldest daughter born in 1970, Liz is the mother of three children and is still married to her husband and the father of her younger children.

As the years passed, Liz never forgot the baby girl she gave birth to in Fort Worth. She remembered thinking about searching for her child when she walked out of Homestead, and she knew in her heart she would search when her daughter reached legal age. Years later, when Liz began her initial search, she engaged the services of a Dallas-Fort Worth area intermediary and learned her adoptive daughter's parents had divorced when the child was four years old. Liz also discovered her daughter's adoptive mother remarried, and her daughter was adopted for a second time by her mother's new husband. Since her daughter's second adopted name created a serious search problem, Liz hired a Miami friend, another birth mother who helped reunite adoptees and birth mothers, to assist with her search. Liz said her daughter was twenty-three years old when they met for the first time, and she still recalls the excitement, joy, and happiness she felt when they first saw each other. As the two women became acquainted, Liz told her daughter the name of her birth father, and the two later met each other. Eventually Liz's daughter married and had children, and the families have spent treasured moments together.

"Lola" (In her own words)

"Many years ago, in the late 1950's, my adoptive mom found out that she was unable to have children. At that time, my adoptive dad's brother and his wife were facing the same situation and had already adopted two children through the Edna Gladney Home. After a while, my adoptive parents decided that was the path they also would choose, so they went to Edna Gladney and filled out the necessary paperwork. Unfortunately, they were turned down due to my adoptive dad's health. He had internal issues that finally caused his death in 1979. They were heartbroken, to say the least. At the time, my adoptive parents were members of Castleberry Baptist Church in the River Oaks section of Fort Worth, Texas. They also were very close to the pastor at the time, Dr. Victor E. Sears. He was the one who introduced them to Dr. Durham, the pastor at Arlington Heights Baptist Church and a board member at Homestead. In November of 1960, they completed the necessary paperwork that Homestead required of prospective adoptive parents and paid a processing fee of one thousand dollars. Then they went home and waited to see if they would be accepted as adoptive parents. Much to my adoptive mother's surprise, she soon received a call from a woman who said she was calling from the office of an attorney by the name of Powell. She informed my adoptive mother they had a two-day old baby girl in the office, and if she and her husband were interested, they had three hours to get there and pick her (me) up. They were told to bring an additional three hundred dollars in cash for the birth mother's expenses. In shock, my adoptive mother hung up the phone and immediately called my adoptive dad at his work, and they raced to the bank and then to the attorney's office. Once there, a Homestead staff member rushed them inside a small room, where they were asked for the cash. After my adoptive parents paid the money, someone handed the baby (me) to them. Very quickly, they were ushered out of the office and sent on their way. There were never any home visits before or after my arrival, and my adoptive parents and relatives told me they were never even required to go before a judge to finalize my adoption. I have always known that I was adopted, and my adoptive mom supported me when I started my search. But she would get angry at the 'system' every time I told her that I had hit another brick wall. I've been searching since mid-1980, but I've been unsuccessful, so far, in identifying my birth mother."

Marie Lizette LeMarquand

Marie's parents were living in Midland when they adopted her in late spring of 1961 from Homestead's adoption agency in Fort Worth. When they adopted Marie, the couple already had a daughter who was twelve years old. Two years later, the couple adopted another daughter. According to Marie, she and her younger sister always knew they were adopted, and their mother referred to them as "chosen children." Marie's father worked for The Shield Co., an oilfield chemical supply company, and about the time she was born, he started his own business. Marie said she grew up in Midland, married a "Midland boy" and moved to Fort Worth, where her husband worked for years. In 1984, Marie's adoptive father passed away, and in 1998, she lost her adoptive mother. Although Marie was always aware she did not look like the rest of her family, she never had what she referred to as a "burning desire" to search for her birth mother. After her father's death, however, Marie and her adoptive mother talked at length about her adoption, and she learned her birth mother was about sixteen years old when she gave birth in Fort Worth. Even though Marie's adoptive mother told her she would be supportive if she decided to search, Marie decided against it, since she had seen how disappointed her adoptive sister was when her search for her birth mother had been unsuccessful.

According to Marie, her life changed about twenty years ago when she received a letter from her birth mother. She recalled feeling shocked and overjoyed when she read the letter from her mother, who had hired a private investigator to locate her daughter. When the two women met each other for the first time, Marie said the resemblance was so strong. Their husbands were totally amazed, because they looked alike and they even dressed alike. During the first few months after they met, the two women and their husbands forged close relationships, and Marie's birth mother freely shared the events surrounding her pregnancy and subsequent stay at Homestead. She told Marie that shortly after she learned she was pregnant and broke the news to her family in New Mexico where she lived, her grandmother drove her to an abortion clinic in Juarez, Mexico. When they went inside the clinic, her grandmother decided she did not like what she saw and drove her granddaughter back home. Soon after Marie's birth mother returned home, her mother told her she would be going to Homestead and would stay there until her baby was born. She never understood how her mother learned about the maternity home or why she chose to send her to Fort Worth. During the time Marie's birth mother lived at Homestead, her mother told anyone who asked about her whereabouts that she was staying temporarily with a relative in Fort Worth who "needed some help."

Marie's birth mother recalled that someone at the hospital told her she had given birth to a baby girl, but she was not allowed to see her child. After a few days, she was discharged from the hospital and returned to Homestead for a short time before leaving Fort Worth to return to her family's home in New Mexico. Once she was back home, Marie's birth mother attempted to talk to her parents about the baby, but she said it was obvious they did not want to discuss anything about her pregnancy or the baby she gave up for adoption. Her parents' primary concern, Marie's birth mother said, was that neither of her parents wanted anyone in their hometown to know about her pregnancy or that she had given up a baby for adoption.

Marie's birth mother said she did complete high school, but it was very difficult, since she felt as if "everyone knew" what had happened to her.

After graduation, she did not attend college, but instead, married her first husband, with whom she had two children, a boy and a girl. She also told Marie that her birth father was killed in an automobile accident a few years after she was born.

According to Marie, her adoptive mother and her birth mother met and got along very well with each other. During the years that followed, Marie and her birth mother enjoyed a wonderful relationship that lasted for almost a decade. She and her husband and her birth mother and her husband also maintained a relationship that included mutual care, concern, and respect. Their families enjoyed each other's company and spent lots of time together, and her birth mother and stepfather were wonderful grandparents to her children. Marie recalled how her stepfather mentored her husband in a new profession he began during that time, and how happy her children seemed to have a new set of involved grandparents. As the years passed, Marie said she discovered her birth mother, as well as some of her maternal family members, had issues with alcohol abuse and depression, and the relationship she had with her mother ended after some irreconcilable problems arose. Marie feels sad the relationship did not endure, but she also understands that when her birth mother gave up her baby for adoption, her outlook on life, as well as her self-esteem, was never the same.

Deanne Martin Loftis

Delivered by Dr. Jack Turner at All Saints Hospital in the summer of 1966, Deanne was adopted by Doyle Martin and Yvonne Waller Martin. Deanne is a married mother of two young adult children and works in radiation therapy at an East Texas oncology center. She said her adoptive mother told her that she and her husband chose adoption because she had been diagnosed with hyperthyroidism and was unable to conceive. She also told Deanne they learned about Homestead Maternity Home and Child Placement Agency from a book containing the names of Texas adoption agencies. When Deanne was adopted, her parents were thirty-two and twenty-nine years old, and when she was interviewed, she said both adoptive parents were deceased.

Deanne always knew she was adopted and recalled hearing her adoptive mother tell her many times that she was "special" and that she had been "chosen." When Deanne turned eighteen, her adoptive mother gave her a "non-id information sheet" containing details about her birth mother, her alleged birth father, and her maternal grandparents. From that sheet, Deanne learned her birth mother was an eighteen-year-old high school graduate, of Presbyterian faith, whose ancestry was Irish. She was five feet two inches tall, with red hair, green eyes, and fair skin. Deanne's alleged birth father was identified on the document as a twenty-two year old college sophomore. According to the document, he had one sibling, was Baptist, and was of Irish ancestry. Deanne's alleged birth father's physical description said he was five feet ten inches tall, weighed one hundred fifty pounds, and had black hair, brown eyes, and a dark "complexion."

According to Homestead letters Deanne's adoptive parents received and her mother retained throughout the years, the couple received a letter dated March 16, 1966, acknowledging their inquiry about adopting an infant. An application form outlining Homestead's requirements to adopt was included with the letter. On April 7, 1966, Deanne's adoptive parents received a letter stating they were approved to adopt. Homestead's letterhead appeared on the second letter signed by Mary F. Barrett as supervisor of Homestead's social workers. The couple received a third letter, also signed by Mary F. Barrett, notifying them of a home visit scheduled for July 6, 1966. According to that letter, the home visit was the final step needed to formally approve the adoption.

Deanne weighed four pounds and four ounces when she was born, and according to her adoptive parents, they took her home when she was about three weeks old. When she was growing up, Deanne said her adoptive mother told her she and her husband had wanted to adopt a second child, but Mr. Martin had a heart attack, and the agency removed their names from its list of potential adoptees. Other Homestead documents in Deanne's possession include a letter from Dr. Womack to Homestead's child placement agency regarding her initial weight loss, a receipt for legal expenses of $150 paid to Harold Valderas, and an itemized statement of reimbursable adoption costs paid by her adoptive parents. Included in the total amount of twelve hundred sixty five dollars were room and board charges of $600 for Deanne's birth mother, $300 due to the hospital, $135 to Dr. Turner, Homestead's obstetrician, and $35 to Dr. Harry Womack, the baby's pediatrician. Other charges listed were for medicine ($50); layette ($15); staff services rendered ($65); flowers ($5); ambulance ($10); transportation ($30); and miscellaneous charges totaling $20.

In an effort to locate her birth family, Deanne participated in DNA testing offered by Ancestry and 23&me. Also, she broadened the search by transferring her DNA results to gedmatch.com. Deanne explained how she began the search for her birth parents "primarily out of curiosity," and "because I had no siblings," and she went on to say, "I thought it would be so cool to walk into a room and see people who looked like me." At the time of her interview, Deanne said a search angel was assisting her in reviewing the DNA matches in an attempt to identify her birth parents.

Patricia Mayo

Her adoptive parents were thirty-two and thirty-eight years old when they adopted Patricia through Homestead Maternity Home's child placement agency in Fort Worth. Patricia was born in the summer of 1965 at All Saints Hospital, but she remained with foster parents until her parents adopted her at six months old. Patricia's adoptive father was stationed at Carswell Air Force Base when he and his wife, a British war bride, who was unable to have children, adopted her. According to a story Patricia's adoptive mother told her when she was young, Homestead notified her and her husband they were approved to adopt. One week later, she said, Homestead notified her parents that she was available to adopt. Patricia grew up as an only child and always knew she was adopted, but when she was asked if she knew how her parents learned about Homestead's adoption agency, Patricia said that she did not know.

When Patricia's father retired from the U.S. Air Force, he went to work for Coca-Cola Bottling Company in Fort Worth. During those years, she and her family continued to live in Tarrant County, and later she attended Everman High School. When Patricia was in seventh grade, her parents separated after her adoptive mother began a relationship with another man. Although Patricia continued to maintain a loving relationship with her adoptive father, she experienced a strained and difficult relationship, one that continues even today, with her adoptive mother. As she grew up, Patricia said that she never felt "connected to anyone," and when she was in her mid-twenties, she decided to search for her birth mother. Initially, she learned how to search by talking to various people, including staff at the Texas Vital Records in Austin. After she discovered the existence of online adoption registries, Patricia posted her information on the Texas Central Adoption Registry and on the Homestead portion of *G's Adoption Registry.* Her searching was sporadic, she said, especially after she and her son's father divorced and she remarried.

In the summer of 2009, just a few days after her birthday, Patricia received an email from the state-administered Central Adoption Registry in Austin, Texas. The email informed Patricia that her birth mother had contacted the registry, and the state contact asked Patricia if she would like to talk to her. Patricia quickly replied "yes" to the email, and the state contact informed Patricia that her birth mother wanted to call her. Within a few minutes, the two women heard the other's voice for the very first time. Their phone conversation lasted for almost two hours, Patricia said, and she knew when the phone call ended, the relationship would continue. Amazingly, her birth mother, Wanda, had posted on the Texas Central Adoption Registry just eight days before she and Patricia first spoke to each other. Patricia and Wanda continued to exchange information during frequent telephone and email contacts with each other. During their conversations, Wanda explained to Patricia that she became pregnant by a young man she met in the Fort Walton Beach, Florida area. Since she was a teenager, her parents made the decision to send her to Homestead Maternity Home in Fort Worth, Texas, where she would stay until she gave birth and her baby was placed for adoption. According to Wanda, she was seventeen when she gave birth to Patricia. When Wanda returned to Florida, she "got back" with her boyfriend and became pregnant for a second time. Since Wanda was eighteen when her second baby, a daughter named Denise, was born, she chose to keep her baby. According to Wanda, her boyfriend and the father of her two daughters, left the state before Denise was born. Wanda later remarried, but the relationship ended in divorce. Soon after the divorce, Denise began what would become a successful search for her birth father, a man named William (Bill) Sheeren. During a series of conversations with her birth father, who was also divorced, Denise initiated a successful attempt at matchmaking between her parents, and on Valentine's Day, about eighteen years ago, Wanda married the father of her first two children.

Several months after that first phone conversation with her birth mother, Patricia met her birth parents. During the visit, she also met Denise, her younger sister, who explained how their parents had reconciled long ago the issue of Bill leaving Wanda before she was born. Patricia also met other extended family members including aunts, cousins, a niece and nephew, and her maternal grandmother, who passed away about two months after their reunion. Since Patricia and her birth family live in different states, they have not seen each other since that first meeting. But Patricia said they continue to keep in touch through phone calls, emails, and social media.

Jamie Hawkins Messenger and Peggy Hawkins, His Adoptive Mother

According to Jamie and his adoptive mother, Peggy Amos Hawkins, he was born in the summer of 1970 at All Saints Hospital. Peggy and her husband, James Wallace Hawkins, now deceased, adopted Jamie from Homestead Maternity Home's child placement agency in Fort Worth. After the couple adopted Jamie, they took him home to Fort Stockton, Texas, where James Hawkins owned a radio station and where Jamie grew up. He was their fourth and youngest child, Peggy added. She explained that when she and

James were younger, she had given birth to two children before they adopted a third child, who was three years older than Jamie. She added that surgery prevented her from having additional children, and adoption was the couple's only option for enlarging their family. In 1967, when Peggy and James decided to adopt Jamie's older sister, they submitted applications to four different agencies, including the Homestead Child Placement Agency in Fort Worth. Homestead responded first, Peggy said, when a social worker named Judith Kelley called to tell the couple they were approved to adopt pending a visit to their home in Fort Stockton. According to Peggy, the home visit went well, and after Mrs. Kelley returned to Fort Worth, she called to say Homestead had a child for them, and the baby should be picked up the next day at Homestead's adoption office on 5th Avenue in Fort Worth. Peggy added that neither she nor James had specified the sex of the child they wanted to adopt, but as it turned out, Homestead chose a beautiful baby girl for them, an infant who had been in foster care for about two and one-half months. When Peggy and her husband arrived at Homestead, Mary Jo Maruda, another social worker, greeted them in the adoption office and sent them to talk to Dr. Durham, the minister, while she went to the back to get the baby from Mrs. McGruder, a Homestead foster mother. Peggy said she will always remember the minute she saw her dark-haired baby girl, "Joanie" dressed in a "pink onesie." About three years later, Peggy and her husband adopted a five-day old baby boy they named Jamie. The couple received several documents from Homestead, and they picked up Jamie directly from the hospital. The documents given to the couple by Homestead included a statement of adoption expenses amounting to twelve hundred dollars, an identical amount paid for their daughter's adoption three years earlier. In addition, Peggy said they received a non-id information sheet indicating Jamie's father had once served in the U.S. Navy. She said Jamie cried more than usual when he was a baby, and the only way she could calm him was to hold him tightly until he stopped crying. During Peggy's interview, she wondered aloud if her son's birth mother may have suffered from an addiction before or during her pregnancy. Her concern was based in part on a 25-year long heroin addiction from which Jamie has recovered after two incarcerations and eleven stays in rehab. At the time of his interview, Jamie proudly said he has been clean and sober for four years and is an active member of a sober motorcycle club.

M.J.

According to information M.J. discovered during ongoing search for her birth mother, she was known by Homestead staff as "Baby Holland." M.J. was born in Fort Worth, Texas, in late 1965 and currently works as a graphic designer in North Carolina. M.J.'s parents, who lived in Aransas Pass, Texas, adopted her through Homestead's child placement agency when she was about a week old. About two years later, her parents adopted another baby girl through the Children's Cradle Society in San Antonio. When M.J. was about four years old, her adoptive father, who had recently completed his doctorate degree in marine zoology, accepted a position at North Carolina State University and moved his family to that state. Although M.J.'s mother had a biology degree from Louisiana State University, she stayed home with her two daughters until after they started elementary school. M.J. said, "Overall, I had a great childhood. I was very lucky to have great parents, and they provided me with every advantage. They taught me about animals and plants and that nature was very important." The things her parents taught her as a child are still important, M.J. added, since she and her husband live on a small farm where they raise animals and grow some of their own food. Her adoptive parents are still living, she said, and live on a farm of their own not far away.

In 2000, M.J. recalled, she began searching online for her birth mother, but the only information she knew was what her adoptive mother had been told by Homestead staff -- that her birth mother was a college student. Along the way, M.J. said she worked with a volunteer search angel who believed her birth mother's name was Kathy W. Holland, but she does not remember how the search angel discovered the name. According to M.J., the search angel also said the name could have been a fake one, since

Homestead frequently assigned pseudonyms to pregnant women who lived at the maternity home. Off and on, for more than a decade now, M.J. has attempted to locate the woman she was told could be her birth mother. At the time of M.J.'s interview, she had requested her original birth certificate from the Texas vital records office in Austin. However, during an update to this interview, she said the request was returned from Austin with a notation that she had provided an incorrect name for her birth mother. Since her search efforts have been unsuccessful to date, M.J. said she is considering DNA testing, and she may decide to file a petition with the Tarrant County court to open her adoption file.

"Monique"

First known as "Baby Girl Vernon," Monique was born at All Saints Hospital in the spring of 1966 and weighed four pounds and twelve ounces. Once Monique weighed five pounds and could be released from the hospital, she was adopted through Homestead's child placement agency by a couple who lived in East Texas. By the time she was four and could read, Monique explained she discovered a poem about adoption in her mother's purse and asked what adoption meant. Her mother responded to her question and explained that she and her brother, seventeen months younger, had been adopted. When Monique turned eighteen, her adoptive mother gave her the Homestead adoption paperwork she had kept since 1966. A statement of adoption expenses included in the paperwork showed Monique's adoptive parents paid a total of twelve hundred and forty-five dollars for her adoption. Reimbursable charges included on the statement were due Dr. Harry Womack, Homestead's pediatrician ($35) and $135 to Dr. Jack Turner, who delivered Monique. Additional documents contained in the Homestead paperwork was a letter from Homestead approving her parents' application to adopt, correspondence from Harold Valderas, the attorney who handled Monique's adoption case, a letter from Homestead approving her parents' application to adopt, correspondence from Harold Valderas about the date and time of the final adoption hearing, and a copy of the adoption agreement. Monique recalled the only birth certificate she had as a child was an All Saints Hospital certificate containing her baby footprints, but spaces on the document for birth details were blank. According to Monique, the certificate was signed by the hospital's administrator whose surname she believes was "Johnson." When Monique was older, she filled in the blanks on the hospital certificate with her personal birth details.

In the months following her eighteenth birthday, Monique began searching for her birth mother. Although she grew up in an "intact home with both parents" who cared for her and "never deprived me of anything," Monique said she felt as if "something was missing." Between 1984 and 1992, she talked to Tarrant County court officials, lawyers, and to state vital records staff in Austin, but all contacts ended in "dead ends," she recalled. Shortly after Monique married in 1992, she contacted Patricia Molina, a state employee in Austin, who told her she needed her birth mother's name to search for her original birth certificate. Since all of Monique's previous search efforts were unsuccessful, she asked a personal friend who was a private investigator if he would help her identify and locate her birth mother. The investigator often traveled to the state vital records office in Austin, Monique explained, and during one of his paid searches, he searched for a copy of Monique's original Texas birth certificate. When he returned from Austin, Monique's friend gave her the name of her birth mother. Although she searched for her birth mother for years, Monique said she was unable to locate her.

In 1996, Monique, as well as other Homestead adoptees, birth mothers, and adoptive parents, attended a Homestead Reunion held at a Luby's cafeteria in Fort Worth. Dr. Jack Turner, Judge Harold Valderas, and Mrs. Teri Davidson, a former Homestead foster mother, also were present at the gathering. After lunch, the doctor and the lawyer participated in a question and answer session with attendees. Although Monique does not recall the question one of the attendees directed to Dr. Turner, she does recall how angry the doctor became before "he got up and left." She added that Judge Valderas "got up and walked out behind Dr. Turner."

After years of unsuccessful searching for her birth mother, Monique decided to participate in DNA testing. Although she received many matches, none of them helped identify her birth mother's family. Shortly after Monique was interviewed for this book, a friend assisted her in locating her birth mother and other maternal family members. Sadly, Monique discovered her birth mother had passed away a number of years ago and is buried in the Houston, Texas area. On a happier note, however, Monique learned she has two half-brothers and plans to meet them in the near future.

Bart Neyman

Born in Fort Worth in the spring of 1969, Bart was adopted from Homestead at six days old by a career military man and his wife. He was the middle child of three, with an adopted older brother and a younger adopted sister. His siblings, Bart added, were not adopted from Homestead. Bart discovered he was adopted by asking his parents, who confirmed his concern, but he remembers very little discussion about specific circumstances surrounding the adoption itself. When he was about eleven, Bart began running away from home, explaining that his adoptive father "drank a lot," and his "mom wasn't mentally stable." After he ran away several times, Bart's adoptive parents contacted child welfare services, a local agency that sent him to a court-appointed foster home. While Bart lived in the foster home, his adoptive parents told neighbors who asked about their son's whereabouts that he was attending a private boarding school. Later that same year, when Bart was about twelve years old, child welfare officials attempted to reintroduce him to his adoptive parents' household. According to Bart, he experienced "a lot of friction with his parents," and things did not go well.

Soon after he returned home, Bart said he and his older brother were playing football in the yard, and his adoptive mother ran out and "yanked a hunk of hair out of my head." Later, he discovered his mother was taking a type of medication that precipitated the outburst. Bart said he called his caseworker who came out to the house and talked to his parents, but she did not remove him from the home. However, the caseworker did tell Bart that he could call her if his mother ever became violent again. Soon after the hair-pulling incident, Bart overhead his adoptive mother tell his grandmother during a phone conversation that "things would be good [around here] if that damn boy wasn't here." After Bart heard his mother's remark, he ran away and called his caseworker, who quickly made a home visit and once again talked to him and to his adoptive parents. For the second time, the caseworker refused to remove Bart from what he considered to be an abusive home. His adoptive parents were extremely upset that Bart had called the caseworker, and after she left, his father angrily warned him that if he ran away again, he no longer would be "part of the household." Bart's family situation continued to deteriorate, however, as his parents continued to drink excessively and get into disagreements with each other, with him, and with his adopted brother. Bart added that his adopted brother's hyperactivity also contributed to problems occurring in the household.

When he was about thirteen, Bart went to live in a foster home for the second time in his life. After several months, he discovered his adoptive parents were moving, and they were taking his adopted siblings with them. In a desperate attempt to say goodbye to his brother and sister, Bart skipped school and trekked fifteen miles across town to visit them at school before they left town. "One of the teachers I knew apparently felt sorry for me and allowed me to sit in my brother's class until school was dismissed. When school was out, I also attempted to talk to my little sister, but she told me Mom said I was a troublemaker and that she should stay away from me." After sadly telling his siblings goodbye, Bart saw his mother parked in front of the school, ready to drive his brother and sister home. After he watched his siblings get into the car, he also saw his mother drive away without ever turning her head to look at him or to wave goodbye. And that was the last time Bart saw his brother and sister for twenty years.

During the next year or so, Bart said he was kicked out of multiple foster homes, and at some point, he learned that his adoptive parents had given him up for adoption. As soon as he heard the disturbing news, Bart talked to his caseworker and asked where he could go or what he should do to keep from being adopted for a second time. He said the caseworker responded by giving him the choice of going to a juvenile home/detention facility or to a children's home, and he remembers asking her to send him to "the best children's home" she could find. That home, Bart added, was the Wesleyan Children's Home in Macon, Georgia. When Bart checked into the Macon home, he was thirteen going on fourteen and very wise beyond his years. He said he liked the children's home and wanted to stay there until he graduated high school. Bart discovered the objective of the children's home, however, was to place him with a "forever family," and he recalled appearing on Wednesday's Child, a television news segment featuring older children who were available for adoption. One of the teachers at his school told him she would like to adopt him, and Bart told her he would like to be part of her family. But during weekend "trial visits" with her family, the teacher discovered her sons were jealous of Bart's athletic ability, so the situation did not work out for him.

Bart remembers "always praying for God's guidance" in everything he did, and based on an event that happened later, he is certain God did answer his many prayers. Before spring vacation the next year, Bart's caseworker asked him if he wanted to go to Daytona Beach, Florida, with the long-time director of the children's home, Joe Neyman, his wife, Shirley, and their children. Bart knew and liked the director and his family, and they often showed their support of him by attending many of his athletic events, including football games. He recalled how excited he was about the invitation and said he readily accepted it. During the Daytona Beach vacation, Joe and Shirley Neyman took Bart aside and asked if he would like for them to adopt him, and he excitedly answered "yes." Bart was almost fifteen when he was adopted the second time, and according to his own statement, Shirley and Joe Neyman were "one of a kind" parents – "top shelf," he added. At the time Bart was interviewed, Mr. and Mrs. Neyman were still living, and their current relationship with Bart includes his wife and children.

Almost a decade ago, Bart recalled a rather strange event. His first adoptive father, by then a retired colonel, called him, and they had what Bart referred to as a "bizarre conversation." The man began the phone call with "Where have you been, and why haven't you called us?" Bart recalled his former adoptive father began talking to him about "letting bygones be bygones" and said he wanted to "make amends." Throughout the years, Bart said he had "attempted to not hold any animosity against his parents," and over the next six months he and his mom and sister "got things reconciled." Not long after, his sister called him and told him that his former adoptive mother had died of cancer. The news was very troubling, Bart recalled, since none of his former family members had told him when they last talked that his mother even had cancer. With sadness in his heart for what might have been, Bart and his wife traveled to Texas to attend his adoptive mother's funeral, and he also saw his father at that time.

Roughly ten to twelve years ago, Bart decided to search for his birth mother and hired a court-appointed intermediary (CAI) in Fort Worth, Texas, who helped him petition the court to open his adoption file. Once the petition was granted, the intermediary reviewed the file's contents and contacted his birth grandfather in an effort to reach out to Bart's birth mother. After several months, his birth mother did contact the intermediary, but she chose to provide very little information other than her family's medical history. Although Bart had no direct contact with his birth mother, he did learn that she never married and had no other children.

Today, Bart is a successful businessman and a happily married father of two teenage sons. Although his childhood was often difficult and certainly lacked the stability that loving and caring parents can provide, his steadfast faith in God and in the future remains strong.

Kimberly Kinkade Prax

Born in the spring of 1963, Kim was adopted through Homestead's child placement agency in Fort Worth, Texas, when she was about a week old. Her adoptive parents, Roy Kinkade, Jr., and his wife, Anita Fern Waites Kinkade, already had a three and half year old biological son at home when they adopted Kim. Interestingly, Kim grew up in northeast Tarrant County about an hour away from where she currently lives with her husband and two college-age children. According to Kim, her adoptive parents were caring and loving, and she experienced a happy childhood growing up in the same house and neighborhood where she lived all of her young life. Although Kim always knew she was adopted, she did not know the name of the Fort Worth agency her parents used for her adoption. Kim's adoptive father, who is still living, once told Kim she was adopted from the Edna Gladney Home in Fort Worth, but when her adoptive mother passed away about a year ago, Kim found an envelope with a return address for "Homestead Child Placement Agency, 1028 Fifth Ave., Fort Worth, Texas" among her mother's personal items and paperwork. Inside the envelope, Kim recalled, was a single sheet of paper that listed non-id information for a baby girl with the same date of birth as her own. Although the information sheet is not identified as Homestead's, the document resembles others provided by the child placement agency to adoptees interviewed for this book. Details included on the sheet show Kim's birth mother was a nineteen year old student, of English, Irish, and Swedish ancestry, who had completed one and a half years of college. Kim's birth father was listed as a thirty-six year old "US Gov't Clerk," with Irish ancestry, brown hair, brown eyes, and olive skin. Maternal grandparents also were listed on the document, and Kim's maternal grandfather was identified as a fifty-two year old "high school principal," whose ethnicity was "Swedish." In addition, all four individuals listed on the information sheet were identified as members of the Catholic faith.

Although Kim often wondered about her birth family, she did not actively search until she decided to participate in DNA testing a few months before her interview. With the help of an adoption search angel, she learned that her birth mother's surname likely began with an "A" or a "B," a bit of information that was useful in analyzing her DNA matches. Later, with the assistance of a friend, Kim discovered the DNA results established her genetic ancestry was much more diverse than the English, Irish, and Swedish ethnicities mentioned on the non-id information sheet found among her mother's belongings.

Even though Kim had several close cousin matches, contacts with the individuals failed to identify relatives who had knowledge of an adoption that occurred in Fort Worth in the early 1960s. Several weeks after Kim's interview for this book, she petitioned the Tarrant County court to open her adoption file. And in early fall of 2016, a judge granted Kim's petition and transferred her file to an intermediary appointed by the court. After reviewing the adoption file, the intermediary successfully located Kim's birth mother, who she learned had never had other children. At the time this book went to press, Kim and her birth mother were planning to meet in person after communicating with each other through a series of letters.

Fred E. Roberson, Jr.

Fred, as he is known to his family and friends, was born in late 1969 at Harris Hospital in Fort Worth and adopted through Homestead's child placement agency. When his adoptive father, Fred E. Roberson, Jr., and his wife, Wilma Maurice Boaz, adopted him at less than a week old, they took him home to Whitesboro, Texas, where they had grown up and where they raised their son. Fred's adoptive father worked for a specialty tool company that was a supplier to the oil and gas industry, and his mother was a housewife. Although Fred's father has been deceased for a number of years, Fred's adoptive mother is still living and has remarried. One of Fred's earliest memories is that his adoptive mother told him he cried a lot after she and her husband brought him home. She also told him their biological daughter, three years older than Fred, was upset by his crying and asked her parents to take the baby back to the hospital. The sibling relationship apparently did not improve, according to Fred's recollection of a later event. According to Fred, when he and his sister were old enough to argue and were involved in some sort of disagreement, his sister suddenly told Fred their Daddy was hers, but not his. The revelation upset Fred, and when he asked his mother what his sister meant by the statement, she told him that he had been adopted. Fred's mother added that his sister remembered when he came home from the hospital because he cried so much. "I always looked different," Fred said, and he admitted his looks created a "big disconnect" with his family. "My mother and sister each had blonde hair and green eyes, and my father's eyes were hazel in color," Fred explained. "My overall look," he continued, "was starkly different. I had dark hair, dark brown eyes, and red skin." In addition, he said his temperament and likes and dislikes were totally opposite, and still are, from his mother and his sister.

Fred does have a copy of the non-id information sheet given to his adoptive parents by Homestead. According to the document, his birth mother was a twenty-one year old "telephone operator," who was five feet seven inches tall and weighed one hundred thirty-five pounds. His birth mother's father allegedly was a "carpenter," and her mother was a "homemaker." Fred's alleged birth father was described on the Homestead document as a twenty-five year old Marine captain, who had dark hair and dark eyes. When Fred was a teenager and considered searching for his birth mother, he sat down with his adoptive mother to share his thoughts. He still remembers what she told him: "Be careful….you may not like what you find." Occasionally, as an adult, Fred often has thought about searching for his birth family, but he thinks about what his mother said years ago and believes her words still ring true. "But maybe I'll change my mind one day," he added.

Reggie Rowe

Born at Harris Hospital in Fort Worth, Reggie was delivered by Dr. Jack Turner. When Reggie was about ten days old, he was adopted by Jessie Wade Rowe and Carolyn Juanita McLarty Rowe, longtime residents of Decatur, Texas, where he grew up. According to his adoptive parents, they picked up Reggie from the Homestead Child Placement Agency's office, but they never told him where the office was located. Eighteen months later, Mr. and Mrs. Rowe adopted a baby girl from the Edna Gladney Home in Fort Worth. His parents owned and operated a dairy farm, Reggie said, and he described them as "hard-working, church going, and caring parents, who instilled in me a good work ethic. I always felt loved and cared for," he said. His adoptive parents' example of a strong work ethic carried over into his own life, Reggie added, since he has worked almost twenty years for the same company. Reggie's adoptive mother passed away in 1997, and his father died in early 2016, a few months before his interview for the book.

According to documents provided by Homestead to Reggie's adoptive parents and shared with the author, his adoption cost twelve hundred and fifty dollars, and the fee was paid directly to Harold Valderas, the Homestead adoption agency's attorney. Other documents in Reggie's possession include a non-id information sheet prepared by Homestead and given to his adoptive parents when they took him home, along with their agreement to adopt a baby from Homestead's child placement agency. According to Reggie, the agreement was signed by his adoptive parents and by Dr. T. E. Durham, Homestead's executive director at the time he was adopted. The non-id information sheet listed Reggie's birth mother as a seventeen year old high school senior, and the document identified his alleged birth father as a twenty-one year old high school graduate who was employed in an oilfield-related job in the Midland-Odessa area. Reggie's older sister petitioned the Tarrant County court to open her Edna Gladney adoption file, and the process, a relatively simple one, cost about five hundred dollars. A few years ago, Reggie also initiated a search for his birth mother and talked to a search angel who reviewed the Texas "birth books" for him. According to Reggie, he never followed through with the search, nor has he participated in DNA testing or petitioned the Tarrant County court to open his adoption file.

Jeffery Earl Smith

Born in early 1961 at Harris Hospital, Jeff was delivered by Dr. Jack Turner. His adoptive parents, Donald Eugene Smith and Mollie Adele Hendricks, who grew up in Fort Smith, Arkansas, adopted him when he was eight days old. At the time he was adopted, Jeff's father worked at the Red River Army Depot near Texarkana. Jeff is married and has children, and at the time of his interview, he was employed by the U.S. Bureau of Prisons. According to Jeff, his parents told him when he was a young child that he was adopted. Later in life, he learned his parents could not have a biological child, since Jeff's Dad had sustained a football injury earlier in life, one that prevented him from fathering a child. Jeff said his parents were in their mid-thirties when they adopted him, and since the couple believed they were too old to adopt again, they raised him as an only child. "My Mom and Dad were wonderful and loving people, and I couldn't have asked for a more wonderful upbringing," Jeff added.

According to Homestead correspondence and paperwork kept by Jeff's adoptive parents and currently in his possession, Carol Frank, a Homestead social worker in 1961, signed an "approval to adopt" letter dated February 21, 1961, and they received the letter just a few weeks before he was born. Included in the adoption paperwork was a copy of the itemized statement of expenses presented to his adoptive parents at the Homestead lawyer's office, an amount that was due and payable before they were allowed to take their baby home. Individual items listed on the invoice are Homestead Maternity Home's room and board charges for Jeff's birth mother ($390); Harris Hospital ($250); Dr. Harry Womack ($15); Dr. Turner ($120); Legal documents ($100); Layette ($20); Medicine ($50); Flowers ($5); Ambulance ($10); Optometrist ($27.75); and Transportation ($7.81). Another piece of Homestead correspondence kept by Jeff's adoptive parents was a letter signed by Mike E. Powell, Homestead's attorney, advising the couple of the final adoption hearing date scheduled on October 5, 1961, approximately six months after Jeff was adopted.

Although Jeff admitted he has thought many times about searching for his mother, he did not know the name of the agency his parents used to adopt him until he recently searched through his parents' old files and paperwork. With the encouragement and support of his wife, Jeff mailed in a DNA test kit about two weeks before his interview, and he said he is very excited about receiving the results and reviewing his DNA matches.

Debbie Rene Solomon

Debbie, a divorced mother of two who currently lives in North Carolina, was adopted from Homestead's child placement agency by James Robert Solomon and Linda Fay Beauman Solomon. Born in the fall of 1970, Debbie remained in foster care for about three weeks before her adoptive parents were allowed to take her home. When asked how her parents knew about the adoption agency operated by Homestead, Debbie explained that her adoptive mother, Linda Solomon, lived in Fort Worth with her mother-in-law, Mary Solomon, while she attended nursing school at Texas Christian University. During the time Linda lived in Fort Worth, she worked as a student nurse at Harris Hospital, and she learned that Homestead babies delivered at the Fort Worth healthcare facility were available for adoption. Homestead documents in Debbie's possession indicate Mary Jo Maruda was the Homestead social worker who approved her parents' application to adopt. According to Debbie, her adoption was finalized in Tarrant County court in April 1971. Debbie always knew that she was adopted, and although she has no documentation of the exact amount paid to the Homestead agency by her parents, she believes the total was between twelve hundred dollars and eighteen hundred dollars.

Although Debbie said her adoptive parents were "great parents," she became interested in searching for her birth parents when she was about sixteen years old. She said her adoptive parents "encouraged" her and were "supportive." As the internet "ramped up," Debbie said she started "digging around online." When she initially began her search, her adoptive parents provided her with the limited information they had, including the non-id information sheet given to them by a Homestead staff member when they took Debbie home. Details on the sheet indicate Debbie's birth mother was a twenty-year old secretary with English/Irish ancestry, who had fair skin, auburn hair, and brown eyes. Her alleged birth father was described as a twenty-six year old "purchasing agent," of English ancestry, who had light olive skin, brown eyes, and black hair. Her maternal grandmother's age was shown as forty-one, and Debbie's paternal grandparents were described as healthy, reputable, with a good education.

After years of unsuccessful searching for her birth mother, Debbie decided to participate in DNA testing. When her test results arrived, Debbie was totally amazed, since she had a valid match on her birth father. In addition, her birth father's user id for accessing his DNA test results included his surname. At the time Debbie was interviewed, she had learned her birth father graduated college in Texas where he still lives, and she had messaged him through the DNA website. In the letter Debbie wrote to her father, she explained to him that she did not want to "freak him out," but her DNA test results proved she was his daughter. During her interview, Debbie shared bits of information about the man she hopes to meet, including that he is married and has a younger child. She intends to give her father thirty days to respond to her email, and if he does not reply, she plans to follow up with him in a yet to be decided manner. In the meantime, she and her two children are very excited about the possibility of meeting her birth father, their grandfather. Debbie added that throughout the search process, her adoptive mother has remained supportive and is excited for her, too.

Dr. Joel Dow Starnes II

Trey, as the West Texas doctor is known to his family and friends, was born in Fort Worth in the early fall of 1970. Shortly after he was born, Trey was adopted through Homestead's child placement agency by Dr. Joel Dow Starnes, Jr., a Midland physician who is now deceased, and his wife, Bobette Rebecca Brooks Starnes. Trey's adoptive mother had no adoption paperwork to share with Trey, but she did recall that a Homestead staff member told her and his adoptive father that his birth mother was a "musician" who was of "German descent." When asked how his parents knew about Homestead Child Placement Agency, Trey said his parents' minister may have referred the couple to the adoption agency.

Although Trey has known his entire life that he was adopted, he had never searched for his birth family. But his sixteen year old son's interest in his ethnic ancestry and that of his father was the impetus for Trey to order an AncestryDNA test kit. When Trey was first interviewed, he was still waiting on his DNA test results. A few weeks later when he received his results, Trey discovered he had a close match he believed might be an aunt. After further analysis and the added assistance of his wife and son, Trey discovered the individual he thought was his aunt might actually be his paternal grandmother. Trey's wife phoned the woman and explained she was a match on her husband's DNA results. Trey also talked to the woman, and after hearing his adoption story, she readily volunteered to help unravel their family connection. After several phone conversations with her sons, the woman learned one of the men was likely Trey's birth father, information that also confirmed Trey was her paternal grandson. With his grandmother as the liason, Trey phoned his birth father. According to Trey's wife, the phone call went well, and the two men discussed ordering a paternity test to remove any doubt they were father and son. Several weeks later, Trey's wife said that she and her husband planned to travel to Oklahoma to personally meet his birth father.

Lisa Stinson

Known as "Baby Girl West," Lisa was delivered by Dr. Jack Turner at All Saints Hospital in Fort Worth, Texas, in early 1966. According to Lisa, her adoptive mother lost her first husband in the Korean conflict, and she already had two young sons when she married for a second time to another "military guy." Lisa said her adoptive parents were unable to have a child together and decided to adopt a baby from the Homestead Child Placement Agency in Fort Worth. Lisa's adoptive father, she recalled, was a "stern man" who served several tours with the Army in Vietnam. When she was nine years old, her adoptive parents divorced, but she and her two older brothers, who were already out of high school, continued to maintain good relationships with each other. Lisa added that she was unaware of her adoptive parents' troubled relationship before they separated and later divorced. She recalled her relationship with her adoptive mother was "fair," and when she initially began searching for her birth mother she had to "search behind my mother's back." Her adoptive mother felt "threatened," Lisa explained. Although her adoptive mother did not help with Lisa's search, she did provide her with Homestead documents she had retained over the years. One of the documents was a letter of recommendation for her parents, addressed to Mrs. Mary F. Barrett, a Homestead social worker, and written by a doctor or pastor whose name she did not recall. A statement of adoption expenses totaling twelve hundred and sixty-five dollars was also included in the paperwork. Although legal fees were not listed on the itemized statement, a copy of a letter from Harold Valderas, Homestead's attorney, to Lisa's adoptive parents, stated $150 was due and payable for legal services and recording fees incurred in connection with their baby's adoption. According to Lisa, her adoptive parents paid an additional $150 to their own Travis County attorney who represented them throughout the adoption process. Lisa's adoptive mother also kept an All Saints Hospital birth certificate containing her baby's newborn footprints. Although the certificate was signed by a hospital administrator whose surname was "Johnson," it contained no vital information. During the spring of 2000, Lisa accompanied her adoptive mother to her family reunion in Mississippi. As Lisa, her mother, and her brother were sitting at the table listening to stories about her adoptive mother's ancestry, Lisa said she "felt out of place," especially as she observed how "gleeful" her mother reacted to family stories her cousins told. She added, "I had a very weird feeling, since my mother had shut down so many times when I asked her questions about my adoption and my birth parents." Later that year, Lisa attended a Homestead reunion held at a Luby's cafeteria in Fort Worth where she met Teri Davidson, a former Homestead foster mother who cared for her and several dozen other Homestead babies before they were adopted. Interestingly, Mrs. Davidson brought an album of baby photos to the reunion and shared them with attendees. Lisa said Mrs. Davidson's album contained a photo of her as a baby, and it was the earliest photo of herself that she had ever seen. As a result of her own searching and with the help of adoption search angels, Lisa connected with her birth mother on Halloween weekend in 2000. Almost immediately, Lisa said, "I began looking on the internet for more information about the man my birth mother identified as my father." In 2004, when Lisa still had not located her birth father, she received a lengthy letter from her birth mother. In the letter, her mother told her the man she had previously identified as her daughter's birth father "may not be your father." She further explained to Lisa that she had a brief encounter with another man she knew at a party held at the end of the college year. At the time Lisa's birth mother was with the other man, she believed she was already pregnant by her college boyfriend, who had recently gone home for the summer. According to Lisa, her birth mother realized soon after she met her that she resembled the man at the party, not her college boyfriend. But she said it took her birth mother almost four years to finally tell her the truth. After Lisa learned the name of the man her mother believed to be her birth father, she attempted to contact him, but at the time of the interview, Lisa said she had received no response.

Jeff Taylor

An electronics tech who works offshore, Jeff was born in the fall of 1962 and adopted through Homestead's agency when he was six days old. His adopted father was in the U.S. Air Force, and his mother was a housewife. When his adoptive father retired from the military, Jeff said his family moved to Robstown, Texas, near Corpus Christi, where his father became a welding instructor in a community college. Before the couple left Fort Worth, they adopted a second baby boy who was born in the spring of 1963. When Jeff and his younger brother were very young, their parents told them they were adopted. But Jeff said he avoided talking to his adoptive mother in "any detail," because he did not "want to hurt her" by discussing his adoption. The only adoption paperwork Jeff has ever seen was a letter from a Homestead social worker about a "pre-adoption social work visit," and some "after-adoption paper work" related to legal fees. In later years, after his adoptive mother was diagnosed with advanced Parkinson's disease, Jeff said he began searching for his birth mother and enlisted the services of a court-appointed intermediary who was able to locate and contact his birth mother in Colorado, where she lived at the time. According to Jeff, his mother told the intermediary that she did not want to have any contact with him. Jeff also learned that his birth father, a Navy man who worked in air traffic control, likely had a "short fling or maybe a one-night stand" with his birth mother, who was a twenty-one year old college student when she became pregnant. Jeff also discovered his birth mother used the surname "Hill" on Homestead records and was of German and Dutch ancestry. Interestingly, Jeff said, he was his birth mother's only child. At the time he was interviewed for this book, Jeff believed his birth mother was still living.

Loren Taylor

Adopted from Homestead Maternity Home's child placement agency in late 1962, Loren grew up in Midland, Texas, with her adoptive parents and their biological daughter, sixteen years her senior, and a sister who was also adopted from Homestead. Loren's parents told her and her adopted sister at a very early age they were adopted and were "chosen" children. After Loren's adoptive father died, her adoptive mother helped Loren search for her birth mother for more than a decade before she passed away. The only information Homestead gave to Loren's adoptive parents about their baby's birth mother was that she was a twenty-two year old woman from Lubbock, who had red hair and blue eyes. Other verbal information provided by Homestead to Loren's adoptive parents indicated their baby's alleged birth father was an attorney from Lubbock. Loren's parents received only verbal information from a Homestead staff member, rather than the usual non-id information sheet. At some point in the 1990's, after Loren's adopted sister's birth mother found her, Loren hired an intermediary to help locate her own birth mother. Although she received a name the researcher believed to be Loren's birth mother, her efforts to locate the woman were unsuccessful, and eventually, the intermediary closed the case.

Throughout the next two decades, Loren worked and stayed busy raising two daughters, and efforts to locate her birth mother were overridden with the demands of daily life. But in mid-February 2016, Loren read about this book project, and several months later, she decided to order a DNA test. After weeks of waiting for the test results, Loren received her DNA matches just a few months before she was interviewed for this book. Much more fortunate than many other adoptees who participate in DNA testing, Loren had a coveted first cousin match. After a few emails, Loren and her first cousin, ironically another adoptee, discovered they shared a common relative – the first cousin's grandmother was Loren's birth mother. A few hours of internet research provided Loren with the names of other relatives, a probable location, and a plethora of other pertinent details before she attempted to contact her birth mother. The most ironic bit of information discovered during the research was that Loren had always lived just a few hours away from her birth mother, half-siblings, and other maternal and possible paternal relatives. A few weeks after she learned her birth mother's name, Loren mailed a personal letter to the woman who gave birth to her years ago in Fort Worth. After three weeks passed, and she had received no response, she mailed a follow-up letter. However, at the time this book went to press, Loren had received no response from her birth mother.

Teresa Lynn Landis Taylor

Born at Harris Hospital in Fort Worth, Texas, in early 1961, Teresa was delivered by Dr. Jack Turner, a local obstetrician associated with Homestead Maternity Home. Teresa's original Texas birth certificate, recorded shortly after she was born, identifies her as "Vallerie Barnes." When she was six days old, Teresa was adopted by Fred Landis, a tool-pusher for an oil company contractor, and his wife Oshia Landis, a housewife. After picking up their baby in Fort Worth, Fred and Oshia Landis took Teresa home to Midland, where they lived at the time. According to Teresa, her adoptive parents each were thirty-two years old when they adopted her, and her mother had already experienced five miscarriages before she and her husband decided to adopt. When Teresa was a baby, her adoptive mother recorded her growth and all of her "baby's firsts" in a baby book especially designed for adopted babies. Teresa's adoptive mother also told her about the day she and her husband drove from Midland to Fort Worth to pick her up from Homestead and how they drove back the same day on treacherous icy roads. About five years later, Teresa said her parents adopted a baby boy from Homestead, and she and her younger brother were raised together as their adoptive parents' only children.

When Teresa was about twenty-five years old, she recalled "digging through Dad's cedar chest" and finding what she believed at the time to be an "amazing document that was like gold to me." What Teresa discovered was the non-id information sheet Homestead Child Placement Agency frequently gave adoptive parents when they took their babies home. Teresa's information sheet described each of her birth parents, including physical descriptions, ethnicity, and religious and educational backgrounds. Her birth mother was identified as a thirty-two year old high school graduate who was five feet six inches tall and weighed one hundred thirty-five pounds. Her hair color was auburn and her eyes were green. According to additional details on the sheet, Teresa's birth mother was Baptist and of English/Irish ethnicity. Teresa's alleged birth father was described as five feet nine inches tall, with brown hair and brown eyes. Occupations were not shown for either of her birth parents. According to Teresa, however, the most interesting detail on the information sheet was that her mother already had five children at home. The folder of documents Teresa discovered in the cedar chest also contained an invoice for her adoption costs of fifteen hundred dollars.

Through her own search efforts and with the assistance of adoption searchers, Teresa discovered her birth mother's name was Virginia Brown. Sadly, her birth mother already had passed away in 2007 in Utah, where she lived. In addition, Teresa learned at least one detail on the non-id information sheet provided by Homestead was correct – her mother had given birth to five other children in Utah and had experienced a "tumultuous relationship" with her husband, a man named Norman Brown, before she became pregnant with her. At the time Virginia became pregnant, she was living near Salt Lake City, where it appears she met Teresa's birth father. Later, the couple came to Texas, and the man stayed for a time before he returned to Utah. At that point, Teresa's birth mother must have known she was pregnant and chose to remain in Texas, where her sister lived. As a result of the search, Teresa met her birth mother's sister, her biological aunt, who welcomed her with the words, "We've been thinking about you all these years. We tried to tell her to just say the baby was Norman's." Teresa also learned from her aunt that within a year after Virginia gave birth to Teresa in Texas, she divorced Norman in Utah, and she later remarried. Ironically, Teresa said, her aunt lived in Midland, Texas, at the very same time she was growing up in the same city. Recently, Teresa hired a genetic genealogist to help locate her birth father, and she remains hopeful the search for him will be a successful one.

Terri

"Jane Smith," a pseudonym used by Terri's birth mother when she lived at Homestead Maternity Home, gave birth to Terri at Harris Hospital in Fort Worth, Texas, in early fall of 1960. Dr. Jack Turner delivered Terri, and Mike Powell, Homestead's attorney at the time, handled her adoption. Although Homestead's adoption agency did not give Terri's adoptive parents a non-id information sheet, they were provided an itemized statement of her adoption expenses that totaled twelve hundred dollars. According to Terri, her adoptive parents were required to pay the entire amount before they took Terri home to south Texas, where her father was a farmer. She said, "I always knew I was adopted," and added that her adoptive mother explained to her the difficulty she and her husband experienced in adopting a child. According to Terri, her adoptive parents were "turned down by every adoption agency in Texas" before Homestead approved them. Interestingly, Terri's adoptive parents were in their mid-thirties at the time they adopted her, much younger than many other Homestead parents who were in their late thirties or early forties when they were approved to adopt. Terri believes the problem existed primarily because her adoptive father farmed and did not make much money. She added that she grew up in a wonderful family with "many cousins."

Eighteen years ago, her adoptive mother passed away, and about three years later, Terri said she hired a court-appointed intermediary (CAI) to assist her in the search for her birth mother. During the search process, Terri learned her birth mother was born in Oklahoma and was sixteen years old when she gave birth to her in Fort Worth. Jane Smith, the pseudonym Homestead assigned to Terri's birth mother when she entered the maternity home, and the same name Homestead required her to use at the hospital was a variation of the young woman's legal name. The pseudonym "Smith" also appears as Terri's birth mother's maiden name on her original birth certificate filed in Austin, Texas. When Terri's parents finalized her adoption in a Tarrant County court in Fort Worth, they received an amended birth certificate that included only her adopted name and the names of her adoptive parents. This amended birth certificate is similar to other amended birth certificates issued to Homestead adoptees, with specific birth details, such as place and time of birth, weight, and length, missing from the document. During the search for her birth mother, Terri learned she has a half-sister. In 2013, her birth mother died without disclosing the name of her daughter's birth father, and in late 2014, Terri participated in DNA testing. In March of 2015, Terri said she received test results that included numerous cousin matches. Although she has a long way to go, Terri said she will continue to use these DNA cousin matches to search for the rest of her birth family.

With her permission, Terri's personal statement summarizing her feelings and concerns in reference to her own adoption search story appears below.

"There was a time when I was angry…angry at the system and with anyone who was keeping secrets. DNA testing and finding more information about my birth mother made me more tolerant, have more empathy, and to be more contented with the family I had growing up. The black hole I had inside me feels as if it is being filled up. And I appreciate my life so much more."

Jeffery Lynn Thomas

Born in the fall of 1959 at Harris Hospital in Fort Worth, Jeffery was delivered by Dr. Jack Turner, one of Homestead's obstetricians. Shortly after his birth, Jeffery was adopted by Eugene Arthur Thomas and Lois Mae Gorman, who took him home to Arlington, Texas, where he grew up. Jeffrey said he was raised with a sister who was adopted through a private adoption, and when the two children still were young, his mother told the two they were adopted. Jeffery said his parents went through a very bad divorce when he was about seven years old and explained that he grew up "not really knowing my Dad. I did experience a good up-bringing as a child who never lacked anything before my parents divorced, and I was the most spoiled child that ever walked the earth." However, after his parents divorced, Jeffery remembers his mother was often verbally and physically abusive to him and his sister. He believes his mother must have suffered from the pressure of being a single parent who lacked the education to obtain a job that paid enough to support her family, and eventually she became addicted to prescription medicine. According to Jeffery, both of his adoptive parents are now deceased.

Jeffery began searching for his birth mother when he was about twenty years old. Each time he asked his adoptive mother for details about his adoption, she rarely answered questions directly, and instead, gave Jeffery "bits and pieces of information." One of his concerns was the absence of baby photos taken of him during his first month, although there were many pictures taken of him during the rest of his babyhood. Another concern of Jeffery's was that he wore a cap in most of these early pictures. When he asked his adoptive mother about the cap, she said she used it to cover "a lot of bruising and scraping on his head," something she believed may have happened when forceps were used during his birth. She also told Jeffery the injuries took several weeks to heal, and because she was so afraid someone might think she had "done something" to her baby, she decided to cover his head with a cap.

During other discussions with his mother, Jeffery said she described three unusual and rather strange incidents, one before he was adopted, an incident involving another baby, and a third incident that occurred after he was taken home from Homestead. The first incident involved an allegedly accidental encounter with Pearl Slaughter, whom the couple first met when they applied to adopt from Homestead, and a young couple who were with Pearl at a racetrack in Grand Prairie, Texas. According to Jeffery's adoptive mother, she and his father ran into Pearl Slaughter and the couple when they attended the races in Grand Prairie, Texas. According to his adoptive mother, when Pearl Slaughter introduced the young couple to her and to her husband, she noticed the young woman was obviously pregnant. Jeffery's mother always thought the incident was "very odd," and in later years, she often wondered if the pregnant woman at the racetrack could have been her son's birth mother. Another incident, totally unrelated to the one in Grand Prairie, also troubled Jeffery's adoptive mother. She told Jeffery that another baby, a little girl, was picked up from Homestead by her adoptive parents at the same time she and her husband took Jeffery home. Although Jeffery said his mother had no proof, she always wondered if he and the baby girl might have been fraternal twins. The third unusual incident, Jeffery recalled, involved a man who told his adoptive mother that he was a friend of a couple she and his adoptive father knew. The man, who appeared to be in his mid-fifties, unexpectedly dropped by his parents' house, mentioned their friends' names, and asked to see the baby the common friends told him Jeffery's parents had adopted recently. Jeffery's father was at work at the time, and his mother was skeptical about allowing a man she had never met into her home, but she allowed him to come inside and to see the baby anyway. According to Jeffery, his mother always suspected the stranger was connected in some way to his birth father.

A conversation between Jeffery and one of his co-workers who was an adoptive mother, caused Jeffery to initiate a search for his birth mother. The co-worker told Jeffery how Pat Palmer, an adoption searcher she had hired, successfully located her adopted daughter's birth mother. After the conversation, Jeffery decided to hire Palmer to help with his own search. In 2014, with Palmer's assistance, Jeffery obtained a copy of his original birth certificate filed with the State of Texas shortly after he was born. The document identified Jeffery's birth mother and indicated she was nineteen years old when she gave birth to him. The name of his birth father, however, did not appear on the document. Although Jeffery has considered DNA testing to help identify his biological parents and their families, at the time of his interview, he had not ordered his test.

Michael Frank Tusa

A lifelong resident of the Waco, Texas area, Mike was born in the fall of 1959 at Harris Hospital in Fort Worth and delivered by Dr. Jack Turner. Soon after birth, he was adopted through Homestead's Child Placement Agency by Frank Charles Tusa, and his wife, Minnie Clarice Brown Tusa, who raised him as their only child. According to Mike, his adoptive parents married "late in life" and were forty-two and thirty-seven years old when they adopted him. Mike said his adoptive father operated a small chain of local grocery stores in and near Waco, known as "Tusa's." During World War II, Mike's adoptive mother worked as a fuse assembler at an area bomb-making plant, and Mike recalled reading an interesting article about his mother and her co-workers that appeared in a local newspaper. According to the article, his adoptive mother and other female plant workers wrote "little love notes" to servicemen, signed them with often unique names, and placed them inside the packages of bombs the plant shipped overseas. Mike said an unidentified U.S. pilot who received one of his adoptive mother's notes must have thought Minnie was really special, since the article reported that he named one of the bombers *"Mischievous Minnie."* Both of Mike's adoptive parents are now deceased.

An itemized statement of expenses given to Mike's parents by Homestead's adoption agency and currently in his possession, indicate he was three days old when Minnie and Frank Tusa adopted him. Mike said his parents told him at a very young age that he was adopted, and his mother also shared with him that he was a "blue baby" who was born with a heart murmur and a "hole in his heart." The expenses listed on the statement and paid by Mike's adoptive parents included $375 to Homestead Maternity Home for reimbursement of his birth mother's room and board; $191.85 to Harris Hospital; $135 to Dr. Turner, obstetrician; $15 to the pediatrician; and $716.85 to Mike E. Powell, attorney. The pediatrician's name did not appear on the statement.

Mike said he began searching for his birth mother in 2009, primarily out of curiosity, but also for health reasons for himself and for his six children. With the help of a search angel named Betsi Westling, he learned his birth mother's name was "Ann Caskey." Once he knew his birth mother's name, Mike ordered a copy of his original Texas birth certificate. When the birth certificate arrived, Mike discovered his birth mother had been born in Louisiana and was twenty-eight years old when she gave birth to him. His birth father's name was not shown on the birth certificate, and a box was checked that indicated his mother was unmarried. In addition, the birth certificate indicated his mother had given birth to two older children. Interestingly, 3600 Crescent in Fort Worth, Homestead Maternity Home's first official address, was listed as Ann Caskey's residence when information for the original birth certificate was provided. Although Mike has not yet located his birth mother, he continues to search, and he indicated he intends to participate in DNA testing in the very near future.

Dock Harrison Vickers

Born "Baby Boy Rakes" in late 1964, he was delivered by Dr. Jack Turner at All Saints Hospital in Fort Worth, Texas. When Dock was eight days old, he was adopted by a forty-year old couple who lived in Shallowater, Texas. He and his family continued to live in the West Texas community until he was twelve years old, Dock said, when they relocated to northeast Texas. According to Dock, his mother had Rh negative blood and already had lost two baby boys before she and her husband adopted Dock and his sister, two years older, through Homestead's child placement agency. When asked why his adoptive parents chose Homestead to adopt, Dock admitted he did not know, but he said his parents may have been referred by the

Baptist church they attended in Lubbock, Texas. When Dock was adopted, his parents named him Bobby Scott Pittiet, in memory of Michael Scott Pittiet, one of the two baby boys his parents lost. In 1984, Dock asked his parents questions about his adoption, and his father became very upset and said, "You've got a nice house, a new car – why aren't you happy?" The conversation soon turned into an altercation, and Dock said he ended up with a black eye and some bruises. When asked if this type of behavior was unusual, Dock admitted he suffered verbal and physical abuse in varying degrees from each of his adoptive parents throughout his early life.

Soon after the violent and disturbing incident in 1984, Dock successfully petitioned the Tarrant County court to open his adoption file. Subsequently, the judge transferred Dock's file to a court-appointed intermediary (CAI) who reviewed the file's contents. Although Dock learned the identity of his birth mother, the intermediary delivered sad news that his mother had died several years before in an automobile accident. The intermediary also told Dock his birth mother was married when she died, and she and her husband had three children together. Additionally, Dock discovered that his birth mother was a nineteen year old nurse who gave birth in Fort Worth and returned to work at the same out-of-state hospital where she had been employed before her baby was born and placed for adoption. Another document in the file, a copy of an investigative report written in advance of Dock's final adoption, identified his birth father as a twenty-seven year old respiratory therapist who worked at the same hospital as his birth mother. During the pre-adoption investigation, the man acknowledged he knew about his co-worker's pregnancy and admitted to the investigator that he was the baby's father. The intermediary also located Dock's aunt, his birth mother's sister, through a contact with one of his cousins. He recalled how special it was to meet his "Aunt Bev," who said she had been "praying for forty-eight years that he would find [his] way home." As a result of the adoption file review, Dock received copies of documents in the file, including the "consent for adoption" signed by his birth mother on November 11, 1964, and a copy of the adoption petition recorded in Tarrant County court records on March 25, 1965. He also received a copy of the final adoption report dated June 2, 1965, and prepared by Mary F. Barrett, a Homestead social worker. Dock recalled how troubling it was for him to find his birth father's name had been physically "cut out" of the page on which it appeared in the adoption report.

Although Dock's search for his birth mother allowed him to meet members of his maternal birth family, the relationships he developed with biological family members also caused his adoptive parents to "disown" him. In response to his adoptive parents' actions, Dock chose to legally change his name. He said his adoptive father died from brain cancer a few months before he was interviewed for this book, and although his adoptive mother and sister still live in Texas, he has no contact with either individual.

Kim Korleski Walsh

A lifelong resident of Arlington, Texas, Kim was born in Fort Worth in the summer of 1969 and adopted shortly after her birth by John Korleski and his wife, Murdale Seger Korleski. Although Kim's adoptive father had served in the U.S. Air Force, by the time she was adopted, he was working as an engineer in the mobile home industry. Kim's parents had three older children before they adopted her and another child, a baby boy, from Homestead's child placement agency. According to Kim, her adoptive parents' biological son, Kevin, died of a heart condition in 1965, when he was fifteen years old, and their two biological daughters, Carmen and Karen, were ten and a half and twenty years old when she was adopted in 1969. When Kim was about fifteen or sixteen, she and her adoptive mother began searching for her birth family. Although the two of them joined an adoption support group at a local library, the internet and other search tools were not yet available, and their search efforts were unsuccessful. After Kim married and had children, she was busy with the requirements of daily living and didn't search for an extended period of time. But in the 1990's, she met other Homestead adoptees who were searching for their birth mothers, and in recent years, she has participated in DNA testing. At some point, Kim also enlisted the assistance of search angels who "coded" her Texas birth certificate number and date of birth and said her birth mother's surname likely began with the letter "C." That particular piece of vital information, combined with an in-depth analysis of her DNA results, finally helped Kim and those assisting her to correctly identify her birth mother's name and ultimately, to determine where she lived.

After several phone conversations, Kim said she met her birth mother for the first time in April of 2016. The visit was not exactly a smooth one, Kim said, since her mother was rather anxious and even became sick early into the visit. However, her mother did discuss her own medical history and the medical histories of family members with her, something that Kim and her children had been missing for many years. In the months following the meeting with her birth mother, Kim also met her mother's younger sister, her aunt, who also became pregnant when she was very young. As a result of her own experience with unwed pregnancy and adoption, Kim's birth mother convinced her younger sister to give up her baby for adoption, too. Kim learned that her aunt and the son she had given up for adoption were recently united through DNA test results. According to Kim, her nephew was one of three adopted children whose parents gave each child a DNA test kit for Christmas the previous year. The adoptive parents told their children the purpose of the gifts was to help them determine their ethnic ancestry. However, one of the children, Kim's nephew, matched as the son of Kim's aunt, who was also in the database.

Kim summed up her adoption, the search for her birth mother, and their subsequent reunion with these words: "My adoptive parents are where I needed to be. I learned that my situation was much better than my birth mother could have provided me."

Todd White

Born in the fall of 1969, Todd was adopted from Homestead's adoption agency by Dr. James Wheeler White, a cardiovascular surgeon, and his wife Phyllis Merritt White, a teacher. His adoptive parents told Todd that an umbilical cord infection prevented them from taking their baby home until he was twenty-nine days old. At the time Dr. and Mrs. White adopted Todd, they were living in Big Spring, Texas, where they continued to live until 1979, when the family relocated to California. When asked how his adoptive parents learned about Homestead, Todd said they were referred by friends who had adopted two children through the Fort Worth adoption agency. Todd said he had not engaged in much discussion with his adoptive parents about his adoption until about a week before his interview, and explained he initiated the conversation because he and his wife were interested in knowing their children's medical history. During the talk with his adoptive parents, Todd learned the couple had misplaced his Homestead documents, but they did share with him a few details about his adoption. According to Homestead information, each of Todd's birth parents had earned a degree in architecture. The couple also explained to Todd they were "good friends" with Dr. Durham, Homestead's director, who told them in confidence their baby's birth mother was allowed to live at Homestead longer than other young women who boarded at the maternity home. When Todd was interviewed he was still deciding if he wanted to participate in DNA testing or if he should petition the Tarrant County court to open his adoption file.

Melissa Kay Young Wofford

Adopted by Thomas Young and Shirley Funk when they were in their mid-late thirties, Melissa was a premature baby and was delivered by Dr. Jack Turner at Harris Hospital in Fort Worth in the late fall of 1960. According to Melissa's adoptive parents, she remained in the hospital for seven to eight weeks until she could go home. When Melissa was large enough to leave the hospital, Thomas and Shirley Young picked her up at Homestead's adoption office and drove her home. The only identifying information Melissa's mother said she knew about her daughter's birth mother was that she had dark hair and was fifteen years old when she gave birth. At home in Dallas, Melissa was welcomed by an adopted five year old brother. Melissa explained her adoptive parents were unable to have children together when they adopted the baby boy in 1955 in Iowa, their home state. Melissa's mother told her growing up that a doctor in Iowa flew out to California and returned with a baby boy that he personally placed in her arms. An Iowa attorney, her mother said, handled the adoption proceeding. Melissa added that when her brother was a teenager, he sometimes threatened to find his birth mother, but as an adult, he has never searched for her.

Melissa said she was always concerned that she did not resemble anyone in her adoptive family, and she felt as if her grandmother may have felt differently about her because she was adopted. As Melissa and her brother grew up, their mother frequently told the two children she did not want them to search for their birth mothers until after she was gone. But when her mother became seriously ill in 2007, Melissa joined an online site for Homestead adoptees, and in 2008, she petitioned the Tarrant County court to open her adoption file. Melissa soon learned the judge assigned to hear her case refused to open the file, and she later discovered his decision might have been influenced by having adopted children of his own. Soon after Melissa's petition was denied, she signed up with the Central Adoption Registry maintained by Texas state employees in Austin. In July of 2008, Melissa received a phone call from Patricia Molina, who worked with the registry and with adoptees who often contacted the state for information about their adoptions. After Molina confirmed the registration was complete, Melissa asked her if she could obtain a copy of her original Texas birth certificate. Molina asked her what she knew about her birth mother, and Melissa gave her the only details she knew – her birth mother was fifteen years old when she gave birth seven to eight weeks before her due date and that she had dark hair. Although Melissa did not understand why Molina volunteered information contained on the original birth certificate and later, the document itself, she was shocked to learn she was a second-born twin. Later, when Rosa Hyde, another state employee contacted Melissa to confirm she was mailing out the original birth certificate, she mentioned the document contained a handwritten notation in the margin stating "Dead born – DC 60-4322." After Melissa received the document, she discovered the referenced death certificate belonged to a man who died eleven months before she and her twin were born. Dr. Turner's signature on the birth certificate verified he was the attending physician when the twins were born, and other details listed showed her birth mother was fifteen years old and lived at 3600 Crescent when she was admitted to the hospital where she later gave birth.

Before Melissa's mother died, she acknowledged that she knew her adopted daughter was a twin. She explained to Melissa the couple had requested twins when they placed an application with Homestead. But when a staff member called them, she explained the twin girls were born prematurely, and one of them had died. Melissa's mother told her she and her husband readily agreed to adopt the surviving baby girl. Melissa later asked her mother's two sisters if they knew she was a twin. One of her elderly aunts confirmed she had known all along, admitting that Melissa's mother warned her that she should tell no one. The other aunt who was eighty-nine years old at the time, said she never knew Melissa was a twin.

Throughout the next several years, Melissa was assisted by search angels who attempted to locate her birth mother. Although there were several women identified with the "Camp" surname, their ages conflicted with information on the original birth certificate. In addition, Melissa learned from state staff and from search angels that "Camp" may have been a fictitious name assigned to her mother when she lived at Homestead. Recently, Melissa's son gave her a DNA test as a gift, and she has already received the results. Although she still has many more matches to review and analyze, Melissa already has discerned two distinct groups of people that possibly relate to each of her birth parents.

Patti Bear Youngblood

William Ray Bear and his wife, Margaret Elizabeth Humbert, adopted Patti through Homestead's child placement agency shortly after she was born at Harris Hospital in the winter of 1959. Her adoptive parents had been unable to have a child and waited for several years, Patti said, before they adopted. When asked how her adoptive parents learned about Homestead, Patti explained that her adoptive father's stepfather worked at General Dynamics in Fort Worth, Texas, and he may have known Mike E. Powell, Homestead's attorney, and told his stepson about the adoption agency. According to Patti's parents, they picked up their baby from Harris Hospital after they paid twenty-three hundred dollars for her adoption. According to details her parents told her years ago, that amount included reimbursable expenses to Homestead, such as charges for her birth mother's room and board, the baby's layette and diapers, and legal fees. Homestead's attorney told Patti's adoptive parents the total also included an amount to cover the birth mother's enrollment in "beauty school" after she left the maternity home. Patti's adoptive parents lived in Texas until she was about two years old, when her father accepted a job with Boeing in the state of Washington, where he worked for twenty-seven years. After the Bear family moved to Washington, Patti's parents adopted a son through an open adoption agency in Seattle. She remembers her adoptive parents telling her when she was about five years old that she was adopted. Later, when she asked her parents questions about her adoption, they said the only information they ever had was that Patti's birth mother was sixteen, unmarried, and that she already had given up another child for adoption.

When Patti was twenty-one, her adoptive father passed away at the age of fifty-three. After he died, Patti said her adoptive mother did not want to talk much about her adoption. She added that her relationship with her adoptive mother had been difficult for many years, and the two women had not spoken for more than a decade when she passed away in December of 2015. About ten years ago, Patti worked with adoption search angels who helped her obtain a copy of her original birth certificate filed with the State of Texas shortly after she was born. She was amazed to see her birth certificate contained information she had never known, such as the time of her birth, the name of the doctor who delivered her (Dr. Jack Turner), and that her birth mother was a twenty-year old woman whose surname was "Joyce." Patti also noted her birth mother's address on the birth certificate was 3600 Crescent Drive, Fort Worth, Texas, the same as Homestead Maternity Home's location before the facility moved to 1250 West Rosedale. According to Patti, the space for her birth father's name on the document was left blank. As Patti's adoptive parents had been told by Homestead, the original birth certificate indicated "Jan Joyce" was unmarried and had given birth to one other child who was deceased.

During the years that Patti searched for her birth mother, she worked with two intermediaries and at least one search angel. Through the efforts of these individuals, Patti said she obtained copies of three letters written on Homestead letterhead, addressed to her adoptive parents and signed by Mike E. Powell, Homestead's attorney. In addition, Patti received copies of other adoption paperwork that included the adoption petition filed with the Tarrant County court. A review of these documents, along with the efforts of those who helped Patti search, revealed her birth mother's name was "Jan Joyce." Individuals assisting Patti agreed the name may have been a pseudonym used at Homestead and at Harris Hospital. For several decades, Pattie continued to search for her birth mother, and at one point, she admitted that she called Dr. Turner at his home one night. She recalled saying, "I'm Patti Bear, and I would like to get copies of my adoption record," and the doctor immediately hung up the phone. Patti said she also visited Harris Hospital, where she was told her medical records might be available. But when she completed the request for the records, she was denied access. In addition, Patti contacted Patricia Molina, who worked with Texas vital records in Austin, and asked if she could confirm her birth mother's actual name was "Jan Joyce." According to Patti, Molina told her "Jan Joyce" probably was not her mother's correct name. At the time of her interview, Patti had participated in DNA testing, but some recent health problems had prevented her from reviewing and analyzing the results. She ended the interview by saying, "I haven't given up searching."

Chapter 10

Adoptive Parents, Siblings, and Other Adoptees

During the course of conducting interviews for this book, I communicated with several adoptive parents, including Peggy Hawkins, Jimmie Merchant, and Joyce Merchant. Although interviews with Peggy and her son and Mr. and Mrs. Merchant and their daughter are included in a previous chapter, the stories of Betsy Ross Dunavant and Mary Willis Rhoden, Homestead adoptive mothers, and Kelly Michelle Money, who is searching for her half-siblings, were not. Their stories, as well as the stories of Karl Schubert and Sharon Weiss, two adoptees who believed they were adopted from Homestead, but were in fact adopted through Volunteers of America (VOA), another Fort Worth adoption agency, are included in this chapter, as well.

Barbara, Homestead Adoptive Mother

At the time Barbara and her husband adopted their son, they were living in Oklahoma, where he worked as a boilermaker and she stayed home. Barbara explained she and her husband were in their mid-twenties and had been unable to have a child. When she and her husband were in their mid-twenties, the couple decided to adopt, and when Barbara asked her doctor to recommend an adoption agency, he gave her Homestead's phone number in Fort Worth. Barbara contacted Homestead and she and her husband completed the application to adopt, but two years went by before they adopted their son. Barbara said the process took so long because the adoption agency told her the couple's application to adopt had been "lost."

According to Barbara, she and her husband learned Homestead had a baby boy for them when an unidentified staff member unexpectedly called her one day. She said the individual told her the adoption office had experienced some difficulty in reaching her and her husband, and the baby boy's birth mother refused to leave the hospital until he was picked up by his adoptive parents. The staff member who phoned the couple told them to go to the office of Homestead's lawyer, Mike Powell, who was located in the Dan Waggoner Building in downtown Fort Worth. Barbara said they immediately drove to Fort Worth, where they met Powell and paid him twelve hundred dollars. According to Barbara, Powell explained the adoption fee covered expenses for the baby's clothes and diapers, dental costs and bus fare home for the birth mother, and legal fees and court costs. Barbara recalled two women and another man also were present at the law office that day, and one of the women handed her the baby, who was dressed in a blue sailor suit and had a blue cap "pulled down over his head." Barbara believes the woman who handed her the baby was a nurse named Ruth Hamilton, and one of the two men may have been Dr. Durham, Homestead's director. Barbara said the couple received no paperwork or information about their baby, except that he had been born at Harris Hospital in Fort Worth eleven days earlier, and his birth mother's name was "Carmen South," a woman who she was told had "French Indian" ancestry. Later, Barbara discovered a bluish spot on her baby's lower back, something she learned was a "Mongolian Spot" and allegedly, an indicator of Native American ancestry.

Approximately six months later, Barbara and her husband returned to Fort Worth for the final adoption hearing. She does not recall if she and her husband were given their son's birth certificate immediately after the hearing, or if they received the document later in the mail. The birth certificate they received, however, only contained her son's name, his date of birth, and the names of his adoptive parents. Although Barbara and her husband were told their son was born at Harris Hospital, she has never known the name of the doctor who delivered him. When asked if her adopted son ever petitioned the court to open his adoption file, Barbara said he had not. She explained that her son has participated in DNA testing, and his results revealed he is twenty-nine percent Native American. But she admitted neither she nor her son understand his DNA matches, since "we don't know what we're looking at."

Betsy Dunavant

She and her husband, from whom she is now divorced, adopted their son, Steven Ross Dunavant, from Homestead Maternity Home in the summer of 1967. When Betsy and her husband discovered they were unable to have a baby of their own, they applied to five different local adoption agencies, including Homestead's child placement agency in Fort Worth. She said they applied to Homestead because they knew a couple at First Baptist in Longview, Texas, who had adopted two children through that agency. Homestead responded first, Betsy said, and they immediately sent the couple a letter that included a questionnaire. She and her husband completed the questionnaire and mailed it back to Homestead. A short time later, Mary Jo Maruda, a social worker at Homestead, contacted the couple and scheduled an in-person visit at the child placement agency's office in Fort Worth. During the phone call, Maruda requested the couple bring letters of recommendation to adopt with them to the appointment. When they later met with Maruda at Homestead's office in Fort Worth, the social worker informed the couple they were approved to adopt and asked if they had a gender preference for their baby. The couple replied, "No," and Maruda quickly looked at Betsy's husband and said, "You need a boy!"

Five weeks later, Betsy recalled, Maruda called the couple's home and told her she had good news – a ten pound, eight ounce, blonde haired, blue-eyed "perfectly healthy" boy would be waiting for them at Homestead's office at 5th Avenue and W. Rosedale as soon as they could get to Fort Worth. She and her husband were overjoyed and immediately drove to Fort Worth to pick up their new baby. When Betsy and her husband arrived at Homestead, they met first with Dr. Durham, who informed the new adoptive parents their baby boy had been delivered by Caesarian section and had a "perfectly-shaped head." Betsy recalled Maruda also was present at the meeting, but she left the room to get the baby while Betsy's husband gave Dr. Durham a check for fifteen hundred dollars. Betsy laughingly explained the adoption happened so fast that she and her husband had quickly "borrowed money for the baby from a bank friend." Betsy said Maruda handed the baby to her, and Dr. Durham gave Betsy's husband an itemized statement of expenses totaling the identical amount of the check he had received. The statement, Betsy recalled, included charges for Dr. Jack Turner, who delivered her son, and for Harold Valderas, the attorney who handled the adoption paperwork.

Kelly Michelle Money

When Kelly was about sixteen years old, her biological mother, Susan Francis Kelly Strickland, told her daughter that she had given birth to two children in Pampa, Texas, that she gave up for adoption. According to Kelly, her mother was fifteen and seventeen years old when the babies, a boy and a girl, were born somewhere between August of 1960 and April of 1963. Kelly said her mother often gave vague and unemotional answers when she questioned her about the circumstances of her pregnancies and giving up the babies for adoption. She does believe, however, that one of the babies was adopted in Pampa, and the other infant may have been sent to Fort Worth and adopted in Tarrant County. In 2013, Kelly's mother passed away from complications of Alzheimer's disease. Kelly explained that her mother was an adopted child herself and had been searching for her own birth mother since she was twenty years old. The story Strickland told her daughter was that she was abandoned by her birth mother at a Pampa motel. When she was about fourteen months old, Strickland was adopted by Charles Lee Kelly and his wife, a local Pampa couple, after her birth mother relinquished her parental rights. Kelly said her mother's adoptive parents passed away before she was born in 1978.

In 1991, when Kelly was about twelve years old, Strickland met her birth mother, Kelly's biological grandmother, who was living in Pahrump, Nevada, at the time. Although Kelly attempted to maintain contact with her maternal grandmother, she said a letter she mailed her was returned and marked "refused." Before and after her mother's death in 2013, Kelly has searched for her two half-siblings, the boy and girl Strickland gave up for adoption in Pampa, Texas. In 2015, Kelly registered a birth sibling search with the Central Adoption Registry sponsored by the state of Texas and coordinated by Tricia Ziegler, a state employee in Austin. Although Kelly has no documentation relating to the two children her mother said she gave up for adoption in Pampa so many years ago, she believes one of the children could have been adopted through Homestead's agency. Recently, Kelly participated in DNA testing, and her test results show a first cousin match and a few second cousin matches. At the time Kelly was interviewed, she had attempted to contact her first cousin match, but she had received no response. In the meantime, Kelly continues to hope DNA analysis, combined with her own search efforts, will be successful and that she will meet her two half-siblings sometime in the very near future.

Mary Willis Rhoden

In 1959, Mary and her first husband, Robert Lee ("Toby") Goforth, decided to adopt a child. Mary, one of nine siblings who grew up in Delta County, Texas, was an employee of Universal Studios on St. Paul Street in Dallas, Texas, and Toby worked for McMath Industries, a furniture manufacturer. Mary said she and Toby had saved about $900, a lot of money in 1959, to pay for the adoption and applied in March of that year to adopt a child through Homestead's adoption agency in Fort Worth.

Initially, the couple made an appointment to meet with Clora Pearl Slaughter, the director, in her office at the Colonial Hotel located at 3600

Camp Bowie Boulevard. When they met, Mrs. Slaughter introduced herself as either Margaret or Elizabeth, Mary recalled, not "Pearl" as she had identified herself on the phone. Mary described Mrs. Slaughter as a *"short, fat, little old lady, about 60 years old, with light brown hair pulled into a bun in the back."* She said Mrs. Slaughter *"came across as business-like, but she was scary to a young woman like me."* Slaughter explained to Mary and Toby that Homestead required a home evaluation be made before the baby was born, and that adoptive parents were required to send a photo of the adoptee, taken at six months of age, to Homestead's office before the final adoption hearing was held. Mary added that Robert Gilchrist, a Homestead social worker, drove over to Grand Prairie, Texas, where she and her husband lived at the time, and evaluated their home to determine its suitability for a baby.

Mary said their adopted son was born at Harris Hospital in late December of 1959, and at birth, he weighed four pounds. Within nine days, he weighed four pounds, eleven ounces, and Homestead called Mary and Toby to tell them they could take their baby boy home. A Homestead staff member instructed the couple to meet at Mike Powell's law office in the Dan Waggoner Building in downtown Fort Worth and to bring with them one thousand dollars in cash to pay for the adoption. Since the couple had saved only nine hundred dollars, Mary called her mother, who agreed to lend her the remaining one hundred dollars needed for the adoption. Mary said she later learned her mother had mortgaged her car in order to lend her the extra money. Soon after the couple arrived at Powell's office on the seventh floor of the downtown building, a nurse wearing a white uniform and a nurse's cap, brought their son into the room. Mary recalled their son was "sick a lot, and the doctor gave him gamma-globulin." When she asked the doctor why her baby was sick, he blamed the child's chronic illnesses on an "immune system weakness" caused by his premature birth.

In early 1960, Mary and Toby received a letter on Homestead letterhead that establishes the maternity home and child placement agency had been in business for less than a year when their son was born in late December of 1959. The letter stated, in part, *"During 1959, we were able to bring happiness to 48 couples during our first year of operation, nearly doubling our fondest hopes."* The letter proudly announced Homestead had placed twenty infants during the last three months of that year (1959.) In addition, the Homestead letter acknowledged the adoption agency's problem in reaching *"Indian"* and *"black"* parents and with *"placing children outside of Texas."* On June 2, 1960, Mike Powell, Homestead's attorney, finalized the adoption of Mr. and Mrs. Rhoden's son, whose "hospital name" had been *"Baby Boy Paul."* District Judge Fisher Flannery, who signed the final adoption decree, rescheduled the hearing several times, since Mike Powell was fighting a cancer diagnosis he had recently received. Soon after the hearing, Mary and her husband were issued a birth certificate for their son, but Mary said she found it strange to see the document did not identify the doctor who delivered him.

Mary said she called Homestead again in 1966 to tell the adoption agency she and her husband were ready for another baby. During the phone call, Mary was advised the cost of an adoption had been increased to fourteen hundred and thirty-five dollars, and the couple would be placed on a waiting list. About eight months later, in early 1967, Mary received a phone call from Homestead saying they had a baby girl ready to be taken home. When she and her husband arrived at the adoption office on 5th Avenue, just around the corner from Homestead Maternity Home at 1250 West Rosedale, they met briefly with a Homestead social worker. After the meeting, an unidentified woman brought the baby out and handed her to Mary. Initially known as *"Baby Girl Wise"* Mary's adopted daughter allegedly was the daughter of a Church of God minister and his wife.

In 1969, Mary and her husband adopted another baby girl who was two weeks old. She recalled receiving a phone call from a Homestead staff member who told her the baby was ready to go home and that she should bring diapers and money to pay the adoption costs. When the couple picked up their baby, they were given a statement of reimbursable adoption expenses due at the time which included charges for the birth mother's room and board at Homestead ($660); hospital care ($300); Dr. Turner ($135); Dr. Womack ($35); Medicine ($50); Layette ($20); Ambulance ($10); Transportation ($30); and flowers ($5).

In later years, Mary said she helped her adopted children locate their birth parents, and one of her daughters successfully petitioned the Tarrant County court to open her adoption file. According to Mary, personal details listed on all three non-id information sheets provided by Homestead were proven to be incorrect.

Karl Paul Schubert

Born at All Saints Hospital in 1966, Karl always believed he was adopted through Homestead's child placement agency in Fort Worth, Texas. A review of Karl's adoption paperwork, however, revealed that his adoption was handled by Cuvier ("Cue") Lipscomb, a partner in the Fort Worth law firm of Jacobs and Lipscomb. Although Lipscomb was not a Homestead attorney, he was known to handle adoption cases for birth mothers who used the services of Volunteers of America (VOA) in Fort Worth.

In Karl's case, one of the documents his adoptive parents maintained over the years was a statement of living expenses for his "natural mother." Letters from Lipscomb to Karl's adoptive parents, Billy Paul Schubert and his wife, Flora Beatrice Schubert, indicate his office prepared the statement of expenses and also was responsible for paying them. Itemized expenses included monthly "living expenses" beginning December 31, 1965, and ending March 25, 1966, and included payments for monthly phone service provided by Southwestern Bell. Other expenses paid by Karl's adoptive parents included those charged by All Saints Hospital, where Karl was born, Dr. A. B. Pumphrey, Jr., who cared for his birth mother and delivered her baby, Dr. R. D. Nyman, a Fort Worth pediatrician who examined the newborn infant, and local pharmacy charges for medicine and supplies for Karl's birth mother. In addition, Karl's parents were charged for the services of Alice Fenimore, a dependency investigator, the subsequent adoption investigation, court costs, legal fees, and the cost of a Texas birth certificate. In total, Karl's adoptive parents paid $1,641.30 to adopt their son, with $1,000.00 paid up front and $641.30 paid out in installment payments over a twelve-month period. At first glance, Karl's adoption documents did not resemble Homestead documents at all. In addition, the itemized "living expenses –natural mother" appeared to be expenses incurred by pregnant women who chose to use VOA services and often lived in private homes until they delivered. Also, medical and legal staff identified in Karl's adoption papers were not associated with Homestead Maternity Home and Child Placement Agency, and charges for a "dependency investigation" were not included on any of the many Homestead itemized statements of expenses reviewed during the completion of this book project.

Karl always knew he was adopted, but his parents did not discuss in detail during his youth and teenage years. He said he grew up in a loving family that included his parents' four biological children and two other adopted siblings. His adoptive father served in the military, and when Karl became an adult, he enlisted in the military, too. Although he had searched for his birth mother for years, often assisted by search angels or other adoption searchers who believed he might have been a Homestead adoptee, it appears no one ever examined his adoption papers. A few years ago, a Homestead search angel "coded" Karl's birth mother's surname using the birth index and found her surname began with a "W." And until the summer of 2016, when Karl provided copies of his adoption documents to the author, he still believed he might be a Homestead adoptee.

Karl's parents are now deceased, and he explained that he wanted more than ever to locate his birth family. Several months before Karl was interviewed for this book, he participated in DNA testing and already had received his results. But since Karl worked full-time, and DNA analysis can be a tedious and time-consuming process, he had contacted only a few of his close cousin matches. Although Karl had made no solid family connection with any of the matches, some information provided by a second cousin who lived in Texas sounded promising. In fact, during this particular cousin's attempt to determine her family link to Karl, she concluded his birth father likely was one of seven brothers in her lineage.

While Karl waited to learn more about his cousin's search for his birth father, he decided to petition the Tarrant County court to open his adoption file. He also enlisted the services of a court-appointed intermediary (CAI) who would review the file's contents if a judge granted his petition. Within a few weeks of filing his petition, a Tarrant County judge granted Karl's request, and his adoption file was transferred to the court-appointed intermediary so she could initiate her review. A short time later, the intermediary contacted Karl with the news that his birth mother was still living and she had located an address for her. Karl said the intermediary suggested he write a personal note that she would include with an initial letter to his birth mother asking if she wanted to be contacted by her son. Karl was overcome with joy, since he had feared his mother might have been deceased, and he spent some time finding exactly the right card and composing a heartfelt note to the woman who gave birth to him. The intermediary mailed the letter and included Karl's personal note, but after three weeks of waiting for a response, his birth mother had not responded. With Karl's permission, the intermediary proceeded with a second, and final, letter. In the meantime, Karl's investigative nature took over, and he began searching in-depth for his birth parents, albeit this time with the help of his paternal second cousin he met through DNA testing. Within weeks, his cousin had identified Karl's father, and with that information, Karl learned his birth mother's name while researching public records. Although Karl's birth parents were not married when he was conceived and born, in the decade that followed his birth, his parents were twice married to each other. Unfortunately for Karl, his birth father died several years ago. Interestingly, Karl and his birth father, as well as several other paternal relatives, have served in the military and have worked as law enforcement officers.

As Karl hoped, prayed, and emotionally prepared for a meeting with his birth mother, he received a phone call from the intermediary. However, it was not the message he had played over in his mind many times – the intermediary advised Karl that his birth mother did not want to make contact with him. Although he was extremely disappointed, Karl said he understands his birth mother must have her own reasons for not wanting to meet him. He said he respects that, and he added that with time, maybe she will have a change of heart. But for now, Karl said he plans to make contact with his half-siblings and cousins on his birth father's side and hopefully, with some of his birth mother's relatives, as well.

Update: During the week following Thanksgiving 2016, the intermediary contacted Karl with the news that his birth mother wanted to write a letter to him.

Heidi Bellows Webb

Born in early 1969 and adopted by Danny and Sally Bellows when she was two months old, Heidi currently believes she may have been adopted from Volunteers of America (VOA) in Fort Worth, rather than through Homestead's child placement agency. Throughout the years, however, Heidi has been assisted by search angels and others who thought it possible she was adopted through Homestead. According to information obtained from Heidi during the interview for this book and personal details posted on *G's Adoption Registry*, she has learned in recent years that her birth mother is now deceased. According to some of her birth mother's relatives, Heidi may have been born while her mother was on the way to Arlington Memorial Hospital. Heidi also learned her mother was transferred to John Peter Smith Hospital in Fort Worth before she placed her baby for adoption with Volunteers of America (VOA.) These same relatives provided a limited amount of background information about Heidi's birth mother, including that she had married in the early 1940's and at age forty-four, she had given birth to seven children, including a baby that was stillborn. Surprisingly, Heidi also learned from relatives that her birth mother's husband, who was fifty years old when Heidi was born, did not believe he was the father of his wife's eighth child. In recent years, as a result of other conversations with one of her half-sisters, Heidi discovered her birth mother's husband was still living. However, the elderly man was very ill, and Heidi was unable to talk to him before he passed away last year. Since Heidi still has many unanswered questions about her birth mother's pregnancy, her birth father's true identity, and factual circumstances surrounding her adoption, she is considering if she should petition the Tarrant County court to open her adoption file.

Sharon Lynn Weiss

Named "Baby Girl Johnson" at birth, Sharon was born in the fall of 1954 at Harris Hospital. According to Sharon, Carlo Weiss and his wife, Emily Witten Weiss, adopted her shortly after she was born. At that time, her adoptive father was a captain in the U. S. Air Force and was stationed at Carswell Air Force Base in Fort Worth, Texas. When Captain Weiss and his wife decided to adopt, he talked to his colonel at Carswell, who told him about "a minister who knew pregnant women who need to give up a baby." Sharon later learned the minister mentioned by the colonel was Dr. Durham, who served for years as the pastor of Arlington Heights Baptist Church in Fort Worth. Sharon's adoptive mother said a friend of hers, Mrs. Gray, who ran an antique shop in Fort Worth and lived in a neighboring apartment at 5300 Bryce Avenue where Sharon's parents lived at the time, also told her Dr. Durham was well-known for "brokering baby adoptions." Although her adoptive parents did not share much information about her adoption with her when she was young, Sharon does recall one occasion when her father jokingly said "we bought you new." Based on information and documents Sharon later discovered, she doubts that she was a Homestead baby and believes she may have been adopted through the services of Volunteers of America (VOA).

When her adoptive mother passed away in 1980, Sharon discovered court papers establishing her birth mother attempted to regain custody of her baby before the six-month temporary adoption period ended. The basis for Sharon's birth mother's lawsuit was her discovery that a woman named Louise Clinton had obtained her signature on relinquishment papers, and the woman was not legally authorized to do so. Court documents in Sharon's possession indicate Clinton lived at 3728 Avenue J, the same address that appears on Sharon's original Texas birth certificate as her birth mother's residence address. The court documents indicate Taylor, Ruff, & Stafford, a law firm located in Fort Worth's Oil & Gas Building, represented Sharon's adoptive parents in the Tarrant County lawsuit filed by their child's birth mother. A review of Fort Worth City Directory listings published in the late 1950's confirm that Louise Clinton and her husband,

Alton Clinton, did, in fact, live at 3728 J Avenue during the general time period Sharon's mother gave birth in 1954.

As part of the lawsuit filed by Baby Girl Johnson's birth mother to halt her daughter's adoption and to have the court return the child to her, Louise Clinton received a subpoena to appear at a court hearing scheduled on November 19, 1954. The hearing was held on the appointed date, but Mrs. Clinton failed to appear. Later that same day, a Tarrant County judge issued and signed an order requiring Sharon's adoptive parents, Mr. and Mrs. Weiss, to return Baby Girl Johnson to her birth mother. However, in order to regain possession of her baby, the judge ordered Mrs. Johnson to pay her legal costs in connection with the lawsuit, as well as all legal fees incurred by the defendants in the lawsuit, Mr. and Mrs. Weiss. Paying hundreds of dollars in legal fees, of course, was impossible for Sharon's birth mother, so she did not reclaim her daughter, an act that allowed Sharon's adoption by Mr. and Mrs. Weiss to proceed and to be finalized later in a Tarrant County court in Fort Worth.

After reading through the court documents, Sharon began a long and intensive search to locate her birth mother, whose married name and the name of her husband, as well as her out-of-state location, appeared in the documents. As a result of that information, Sharon discovered her birth mother already had two sons, about four and six years old, and was separated from her husband when she gave birth in Fort Worth. Through conversations with her birth mother's relatives and other individuals, Sharon also learned her biological father likely was her birth mother's married employer at the time she became pregnant. Later, when Sharon located her birth mother and attempted to make contact, she learned through half-siblings from the woman's second marriage that she did not want to talk to her daughter. And at the time of Sharon's interview, she and her mother had not yet talked or met each other.

Afterword

On January 22, 1973, a decision in *Roe v Wade* was handed down by the U.S. Supreme Court, and maternity homes all over the country felt the impact of the decision. An article published on Sunday, February 18, 1973, in the Corsicana (TX) *Daily Sun* stated:

> *"Rapid decline in occupancy is closing maternity homes from Calif to New York at a rate that leads some experts to predict that maternity homes will be extinct within 10 years. According to our department of health, the state of Texas now has only 12 such homes. Two years ago there were 19. A health department official explains there seems to be less need for maternity homes these days due to the public acceptance of abortion and single parents."*

In the years that followed the landmark *Roe v. Wade* decision, abortion became a legal alternative to giving birth or placing a baby for adoption. Even before the decision became law, hundreds of maternity homes throughout the United States began closing their doors, and Homestead Maternity Home in Fort Worth was one of them. Although many of the facilities still existed, more and more unmarried women chose to keep their babies and raise them, often with help from their parents or extended family members.

As more and more young, unwed mothers made conscious choices to keep their babies, grandparents began accepting the roles of surrogate parents, and in urban areas throughout the country, support groups were formed by grandparents raising grandchildren. Over time, society has become less harsh on single women who make the choice to raise a child, with or without family support, but the life of a single mother often continued to be a difficult one. In years past, employers were less likely to hire a young woman with a child, and even if the young woman did obtain a job, adequate and affordable child care was difficult to find. Most Homestead birth mothers still living today are over sixty years old, and their experiences with pregnancy, adoption, marriage, and motherhood span decades of changes in laws and society's unwritten rules. Each Homestead birth mother's story is unique and belongs only to her, but one single thread ran through so many of the stories Homestead birth mothers shared for this book. For various reasons, each woman felt as if she had no choice at all when she gave up her baby for adoption.

Appendix

Complaints Lodged Against Homestead Agency to Child Welfare Supervisor

Date written – 09/12/1960

(Transcription)

1. Maternity Home not licensed – verified. Report from Social Worker, Carolyn Bradford, that boarding homes are being used that have not been studied or approved by Health Department city ordinance on such.
2. Negro girls not accepted as outlined in original Plan of Operation.
3. No casework services for girls as agreed in Plan of Operation.
4. Psychiatric services as outlined in Plan of Operation not available.
5. Program for older children not developed as originally outlined in Plan of Operation
6. Intake of girls does not come through Social Services Department
7. The original written description of the manner in which records are kept, including location and the custodian of such, is now invalid as reported by Carolyn Bradford and Mary Barrett, Social Workers. Records are in Attorney Powell's office. (Board members should not have access to records.)

8. Infants placed without benefit of proper records. Case records not dictated and only application forms completed, as reported by Carolyn Bradford and Mary Barrett. Home visit and verification are not made prior to placements.
9. A report of change in Board Membership not reported to the agency. Current list not available. According to Carolyn Bradford, there have been resignations.
10. Placement of children are arranged by Attorney Powell and Mrs. Slaughter, Executive, according to Miss Bradford. These placements seem to have to do with financial ability of adoptive parents. In one instance, Mr. Powell offered a child to a couple at one price, and a few hours later, while heavily intoxicated, demanded larger payment.
11. Donations are made to the agency, and according to Carolyn Bradford, are not reported by the Executive and Mr. Powell.
12. Carolyn Bradford reported at a recent Board meeting that the Auditor said the books could not be balanced because of poor bookkeeping practice. Dr. Durham asked that an annual audit be sent to Mr. Winters. Mr. Powell stated this had been done, and since Mr. Winters had not written, he had assumed it was acceptable. The Annual Audit has not been received in the licensing office.
13. According to Mary Barrett, birth records of infants were falsified. Mr. Powell said he would continue to see that this practice was followed.
14. According to Miss Bradford there have been instances of incest and the early placement of the child was questionable; however, information was withheld from the doctor and the social worker.
15. The intoxication of the Executive and Attorney Powell while on duty is frequent, according to Miss Bradford.
16. Attorney Powell uses references to approve items of standards under question. He is very hostile toward Mrs. Piester and Miss Giles. He does not want Mrs. Piester to know of problems because he feels that license was withheld and she is too thorough in her evaluation.

He is very hostile toward the Health Department, which recently removed 26 girls when inspection was planned. They continue to have girls in foster homes after agreement with Miss Jane Williams, Regional Supervisor that they would not.

17. Mr. Powell made decision to remove a child in Lubbock without a casework decision.
18. They do not have a current solicitation license. (How can this be done in light of all complaints - - numerous ones are listed in record.) A recent telephone call had to do with placement of a child through I.S.S. The Agency agreed to do the study. The couple submitted material and were told study mailed to I.S.S. I.S.S. reported to couple. No correspondence received from Agency.
19. (Omitted from report; possible item numbering error.)
20. Director of City Health Department and the Child Welfare Regional Supervisor in conference with City Attorney expressed our concern about complaints and our inability to validate complaints when Board does not involve themselves in responsibility of clarifying complaints. Often, complaints referred by Attorney Powell and Board takes no further action. The Child Welfare Supervisor requested from complainants Barrett and Bradford that information be given in writing. As yet, this has not been done. The City Attorney stated because of city ordinance the situation would be clarified.

/Signature
(Mrs.) Ruby Lee Piester
Regional Child Welfare Supervisor
9/12/60

Discrepancies in the Operation of Homestead Agency
October 21, 1960
(Transcription)

As reported by Mrs. Mary Barrett, Social Worker, who has worked part-time for the Agency doing adoptive studies for them, Mrs. Barrett is willing to discuss any of this with Board Members upon their request.

All of the adoptive files are kept in the Attorney's office. The original plan was to have files in the Social Work Department which originally was in another location.

Mrs. Barrett reported having seen correspondence in Mr. Powell's office from Louis Bond Closser, Box 156, Ysleta Station, Texas. She stated attached to this correspondence was recommendation from Mexico College and El Paso High School as to the character of Mr. Closser. In a letter to Mr. Powell, the correspondent had stated that he had married a Mexican girl and he knew of high-class Mexican people who would marry white girls who had made mistakes.

From the letter, it was implied the Agency would send the girls to Mexico and pay $25.00 per month room and board until such time as permanent plans could be made for them.

In a copy of letter replying to Mr. Closser, Mike Powell Attorney had listed all the Agency employees, including Mrs. Barrett, Miss Carolyn Bradford, and Mrs. Swann, Secretary, as well as Mrs. Slaughter, stating he was sending pictures and when plans were completed, a designated person would accompany the girls to Acapulco. It was Mrs. Barrett's opinion of this was to take the girls into Mexico to place their babies with Anglo Americans. When Mrs. Barrett became angry with Mr. Powell, stating he had no right to list her name and that she did not want to be involved in such activity, he denied any such plans.

Reimbursement

Mrs. Barrett stated that the cost of reimbursement is padded, by putting a date the girl came to the Agency earlier than actual date of arrival and charging room and board to the adoptive parent. She stated reimbursements jumped from almost an average of $900.00 to $1450 in most instances.

No social work is being done with the girls. The girls are in apartments which have not been approved. Mrs. Slaughter is not a social worker but does all of the work with the girls and in addition to this, she does adoptive studies and placements.

Mrs. Barrett gave the name of **[Redacted]** as prospective adoptive couple. She made a home visit. At the time she called on this couple, she called at **[Redacted]** place of business, a service station, which is between **[Redacted]** and found him most hesitant to discuss their application. After some discussion, he referred her to his wife, who is a schoolteacher. Upon inquiry as to what the difficulty was, the couple told her they felt adoption was a serious business. They met Mrs. Slaughter in Fort Worth for an interview, after having completed a detailed application form. They were interviewed in Mrs. Slaughter's guest house, which they reported was filthy and dirty. The focus of interview was how much money they were interested in paying. During this interview, a telephone call was received by Mrs. Slaughter in which she was bickering with a man about the cost of placing a baby with him. They felt the agency was only interested in money and not in selecting good parents. They are now going to a social agency in Austin, and do not want to continue with Homestead. A friend of theirs had insisted that they report this to Miss Leatherman, since the friend was acquainted with Miss Leatherman. She feels that they would be quite willing to discuss the irregularity with Mrs. Slaughter in the selection of adoptive parents. Mrs. Barrett reported that a **[Redacted]**, who is a grandfather, had an infant placed with him, and it was reported he gave $1,000 in addition to regular reimbursement fee.

Mrs. Barrett reported at the time she began adoption studies no medical forms were obtained on adoptive parents and no monthly health reports required on the baby. She discussed this with Carolyn Bradford, social worker, who said she has since had some forms made. Mrs. Barrett stated Miss Bradford had never seen the Plan of Operation of the Agency until Mrs. Barrett insisted that she see same.

Mrs. Barrett stated adoptive couples are paying the attorney fee for handling the adoption at the time of placement when it has not been determined that the final adoption will not be consummated. Mr. Powell told Mrs. Barrett they are meeting the cost of administration from maternity home fees.

Mrs. Barrett gave the name of **[Redacted]**, as a couple who had been told they would have a baby placed with them and had put on their application they could only pay $200.00. Mr. Gilchrist visited the couple and told them he would place a baby. They purchased baby bed and other equipment for an infant. They were contacted again and told they would have to pay more for a baby, after they thought they were approved. The couple finally raked up $500.00 and the agency is still telling them they would have to pay more. Mrs. Barrett stated $5.00 fee for flowers is charged to the expense of each girl since Mrs. Slaughter takes flowers to the hospital. Mrs. Barrett believes they are charging adoptive parents twice for the dependency (investigation) - - once in reimbursement fee for mothers and baby's care and in the attorney fee. He receives $150.00 for placement and $100.00 for dependency, making a total of $250.00. Mrs. Barrett reported she made a home visit **[Redacted]** without the record since she was in that vicinity, and as yet the record has not been located. The baby has been placed with no record of study of the home.

Revalidation of Child Placing License

Homestead Child Placement Agency
1028 Fifth Avenue, Fort Worth, Texas
Date: June 24, 1966
(Transcription)

I. This study represents the joint efforts of Mrs. Mary Elizabeth Power, Consultant Foster Family Care, Child Welfare Division, Texas Department of Public Welfare, Austin, Texas, and Miss Margaret Ann Scott, Regional Director, Child Welfare Division, Texas Department of Public Welfare, Fort Worth, Texas. Only the major changes which have taken place in building, program, services and staff, since the original child placing license was issued in 1955, are presented. Data was collected through observation during four periods of work in the Agency; reading of the records of unwed mothers, their babies and foster parents; working with Mr. Frank Del Rio of our State Office Fiscal Division and Herbert E. Dickey, C.P.A., Ridgelea State Bank Bldg., Fort Worth; Statements from the Executive, staff and Board members; meetings with the Board of Directors; validation of complaints from New Mexico, Louisiana, and Arkansas around placing children in these States without previously agreed terms and a written configuration; reading of the minutes of the meetings of the Board of Directors.

II. Organization and Administration
The Agency is a non-profit corporation governed by a Board of Directors which consists of fifteen members. A permanent record of policies and administrative decisions made by this Board is kept. Ten meetings of the Board are held annually.

The building was formally occupied by Harris Hospital, later by Harris Nursing Home. Prior to Homestead occupying it in February 1963, it was completely remodeled in compliance with all local ordinances relating to safety, fire, health, sanitation, etc. The four-story, fireproof, brick structure consists of an ample number of rooms to comfortably house fifty unwed mothers in single rooms in one wing of the building at the street address, 1250 W. Rosedale. The front wing of the building with the street address of Fifth Avenue accommodates the offices of the total staff of the Child Placement Agency and the Chapel. Accurate accounts of capital resources, receipts, expenditures, and per capita costs of child care are kept. Accounts are audited annually by Dickey and Harrell, Certified Public Accountants. Our office is furnished monthly and annual reports, (see Exhibit No. 2).

The reimbursement fee of $1,265.00 paid by adoptive parents is that approved by Mr. Jerome D. Chapman, then assistant Director of the Child Welfare Division. (Exhibit No. 4 for breakdown.) The total amount is paid at time the placement of a child is made with an adoptive family. In some instances, one-half is paid at the time of placement and the remaining half by the time the adoption is consummated. In a few cases of handicapped infants, the reimbursement fee is waived entirely.

The Agency has had a very crucial experience the past two years of having two rapid a turnover in its casework staff, with too short tenure in most instances:

Carol Frank - - three months after she received her Master's degree in social work, Mrs. Mary F. Barrett began her employment January 1, 1965 and is still currently on the staff; Joyce Skaggs two and one-half months, Catherine Green four months; Madge Tucker one and a half months; Judith Kelley is now in her third period of employment at Homestead (9 months, 1 week,) and hopefully now for a long time); Glenda Signs seven and one-half months; Reyes Petra two months; Stella May Taylor three and one-half months, and Mary Ann Walsh two weeks. With the number of unwed mothers, infants, boarding and adoptive parents, the Agency it serves must have a minimum of three full-time qualified caseworkers on the staff at all times.

The Board must assume responsibility for securing funds for carrying on the work. This past year approximately $10,000 was raised outside of reimbursement fees. This was done primarily by Dr. T. E. Durham, the Executive Director, from the Board, membership, and some of his Baptist friends. I outlined possibilities of getting known, contiguous basic budget support from United Fund, Church sponsorship, and/or foundations. The responsibility of continuous solicitation shall be borne by the Board of Directors or by the appointment of a special officer for this purpose, other than the Executive or the Child placing staff. A predictable, dependable income must be developed so that a working budget can be made at least three months in advance, and the staff does not have to be "hurried" into making placements so that reimbursement monies can be obtained.

III. The placement practices do meet our mandatory expectations for the continuance of the child-placing license, however, the recorded assessment of the motivation for adoption and the capacity for adoptive parenthood must be fully developed. Although the case files include all needed factual information, relationships, feelings and attitudes related to several areas of the study ought to be recorded in greater depth. The written agreements with adoptive parents are designed adequately and cover all necessary points. The assessment of the suitability of foster boarding families need to be more carefully made. The clarification by this Agency to our Regional Child Welfare Director that a family is ready to be licensed as a Boarding Home should not be made until the minimum standards for an Agency Boarding Home have met compliance.

IV. All requested reports are on opposite side of this file as Exhibits:

No. 1 - Homestead Maternity Home Brochure
No. 2 - Financial Reports, October 1965 – April 1966
No. 3 - List of Caseworkers 2-1-61 - 6-24-66
No. 4 – Reimbursement Schedule
No. 5 – Inspection Report Dept. of Public Health and Welfare, City of Fort Worth
No. 6 - Fire Inspection Report
No. 7 - Census – UMM 11-1-65 – 4-30-66
No. 8 - Census – Babies 11-1-65 – 4-30-66
No. 9 - Information sheets of staff members
No. 10 -Tenure, change of staff, and termination of

V. Recommendations

1. Discontinue outside of Texas adoptive home studies and placements, unless they are the result of pre-arranged and written pre-agreed upon plans with the Child Welfare Division of a given state.
2. Move immediately toward developing and stabilizing a known and dependable income above and beyond reimbursement monies.
3. Employ only qualified caseworkers of integrity, with emotional and physical health at prevailing professional salaries so that longer tenure can be expected.

/Signature
Mary Elizabeth Power
July 12, 1966

Homestead Maternity Home and Child Placement Brochure, circa 1964

(Transcribed Text)

Admittance

We prefer that the unwed mother enter our home at four or five months of pregnancy; however, we accept the mother at any stage of pregnancy as we realize that quite frequently she may desire to enter earlier to conceal her condition while on other occasions an unwed mother must wait until a later date to enter the home due to circumstances beyond her control. As we believe an unwed mother is entitled to seclusion and privacy upon entering the Home, the unwed mother takes an assumed name and her legal name and home address is unknown to other residents. All records, including the hospital records bear the assumed name. The unwed mother's legal name is known only to the office that is located at another address and the records are kept locked at another address. We require all girls to share equally and without compensation in the usual duties such as keeping their rooms, cooking, etc. We do not permit girls to work outside the Home. Two housemothers, under the supervision of our Executive Director, are in direct charge of the Home. The housemothers are in charge of meal planning and follow menus suggested by our obstetrician. They direct the care and cleaning of the home and are in direct supervision of the girls.

We have a simple set of rules and regulations and each girl is required to abide by these rules. The girls are not permitted to leave the premises without permission of a housemother and not in groups in excess of two girls without a chaperone. All visitation by parents must be made by special appointment with the Executive Director and we do not permit any visitors except parents. No men, except fathers, are permitted on the premises. No mail is received at the Home, but we have a post office box for the girls' convenience, and the mail is delivered directly from the post office box to the Home. Distribution is made by the housemother. No phone calls are permitted except with permission of the housemother.

A Social Worker is at the home daily to discuss problems with the girls but if a girl does not wish to discuss her problem, she is not required to do so. Our Executive Director, a retired minister, has an office at the home and is present in his office several hours daily for counseling with girls who desire spiritual and moral guidance. He conducts service at the home every Sunday but we do not require girls to attend services. We have a member of our Board of Directors who is a Catholic, and she will take any Catholic girls to mass. The expenses of the unwed mother is an admittance fee of $50 and $30 per month, but if the mother is unable to pay all or part of the expense, we will accept her without payment. Part of the expenses of the unwed mother, such as medical expenses, hospital bills, etc. is paid as reimbursement by the adoptive parents, as part of our agreement with the Texas Department of Public Welfare. A girl desiring to enter our home should request an application blank, complete the application, and mail to our offices at 1028 5th Ave., Fort Worth, Texas. On receipt of the application, we shall advise the girl as to whether or not we can accept her. In emergency cases, a mother should call our office, ED 5-5942, Fort Worth, Texas. The girl should bring with her such personal effects as cosmetics, toothbrush, maternity clothes, Bermuda shorts and pedal pushers, but short shorts are not permitted. We furnish all linens.

General Information

The Homestead Maternity Home is a non-profit charitable corporation governed by a Board of Directors. The Board consists of 15 members holding 10 meetings annually. The Board consists of several doctors, a registered nurse, a minister, an attorney, and other prominent citizens of the State of Texas and is in complete charge of operations of the Home. The Homestead Child Placement Agency, which has the same Board of Directors as the Home, is a non-profit charitable corporation licensed by the Texas State Department of Public Welfare and is in complete charge of placement of the child in an adoptive home. Both organizations are vitally interested in the unwed mother, the child, and the adoptive home. Our source of support is from donations, voluntary contributions, and adoptive reimbursement. We are the only licensed child placement agency in this area with an Executive Director who has a Ph.D. degree. In addition, our Executive Director, Dr. T. E. Durham, B.A., Th.M., PhD, was pastor of Arlington Heights Baptist Church for a period of 30 ½ years, retiring in June 1962 and became our Director in July 1962. In view of Dr. Durham's extensive educational background and experience with young people, he has assisted many of the unwed mothers who have been in our home. As our goal is to assist and rehabilitate the unwed mother, we do not accept girls who plan to keep their babies.

The Home

The Home, located at 1250 W. Rosedale, Fort Worth, Texas, licensed by the City of Fort Worth, Texas, is a four-story, fireproof, brick structure, consisting of 75 rooms with ample space for 50 girls. The building was formerly occupied by Harris Hospital and more recently by Harris Nurses' Home and prior to our occupying the building in February 1963, it was completely remodeled. We have a private room for each girl; however, on occasion, we find it necessary to place a girl in a semi-private room. A large, private dining area permits us to serve approximately 50 girls at the time. We have a large kitchen area with modern facilities for cooking and preparing the food. The kitchen, dining room, and other facilities have been approved by the Health Department of the City of Fort Worth and are inspected frequently by the Health Department. We have a large sewing room with sewing machines for girls who decide to sew and a large recreation room for the use of the girls. In the recreation room, we have reading material, television sets, and other forms of recreation. It is our desire to make each girl comfortable and relaxed with a home-like atmosphere.

Medical Services

On arrival in Fort Worth, the girl is examined immediately by our obstetrician who is a Diplomat of the American Board and is seen at his office and thereafter is seen periodically at the obstetrician's office. We do not operate a private hospital in our Home as we belief that an unwed mother, as well as the child, will receive better care and attention at a reputable hospital. All deliveries are made at hospitals, which have the reputation as the outstanding hospitals for maternity cases in the Southwest. The mother remains in the hospital for 5 days after delivery or until released by our obstetrician. She then returns to our home where she remains until released by our obstetrician, Dr. Jack L. Turner, who has a private practice and an outstanding reputation. He is in complete charge of our girls from a medical standpoint. After a child is delivered, our pediatrician, who is a Diplomat of the American Board, is in charge of the child until placement. In addition to our obstetrician and pediatrician, we have unlimited psychiatric consultation available when indicated.

Adoptive Practices

On receipt of an inquiry from prospective adoptive parents, a short application form is mailed to the couple. In the event the couple meet our minimum requirements, an application to adopt a child, a form consisting of seven pages, is mailed to the couple, together with a request the form be completed and returned to us accompanied by the names of three character references, medical reports on the couple, snap shots of husband, wife, natural, or adopted children and the home. After the application has been thoroughly processed, reference letters received, and all requirements met, an individual interview is conducted in the office of the Supervisor of Social Work. If the interview proves successful, a home visit is arranged and after the home visit, the couple is approved for a child. The waiting period varies in each case as our Agency attempt to match the natural mother with the adoptive mother in nationality, height, coloring, etc., and the same for the alleged natural father and the adoptive father.

Example of a Letter Mailed by Homestead Social Worker to Prospective Adoptive Parents

March 29, 1962

Dear [Prospective Parents]:

Thank you for your letter regarding your interest in adoption.

Listed below are the minimum qualifications for adoptive applicants as established by this agency:

1. Couples must be less than forty years of age.
2. They must be in good health.
3. A couple must have income sufficient for adequate family living. Preference is given to couples with more than $5,000 annually.
4. Couples must present proof of recent sterility tests before an application can be approved.
5. Preference is given to couples who are members of the same church.
6. Reimbursement for the care of the natural mother and her baby is required for such period of time as both may be in need of the agency's services.
7. Couples must have been married for at least three years if this is the first marriage or five years if this is the second marriage for either partner.

In the event you meet the above requirements, we shall be glad to have you complete and return to us the enclosed application. Following receipt of the short form application, your application will be studied and processed according to the date it is received and the geographical locality in which you live. An office interview is required of all applicants and later a home visit is scheduled by an agency social worker. Prior to the office interview, we will send you a more comprehensive application form.

Should you have questions about the agency program that you think I might be able to help you clarify, I would be glad to have you write or telephone.

P.S. Women now working must cease working upon placement of an infant in the home.

Very truly yours,
Carol Lee Frank
Social Worker

Transcribed Example of a Letter from Homestead Attorney Mike E. Powell to Adoptive Parents

September 12, 1962
Dear [Adoptive Parents]:

Following is general information regarding the rules and requirements of this Agency prior to the final adoption of a child:

1. At the end of three months and also at the end of 6 months, we must be furnished with a medical report from your Pediatrician or General Practitioner as to the condition and progress of the child.
2. Our Social Worker will make a home visit during the ensuing 6 months to check the progress of the child.
3. A studio picture (3x5) of the child at the age of 6 months must be furnished the Agency.
4. On the expiration of 6 months from the date of placement, the adoption petition will be forwarded to you and you must sign the original and copy of the petition in the presence of a Notary Public and return the original and copy to my office and I shall file same with the Court.
5. The reimbursement which you have paid to the Agency covers all expenses with the exception of $16.00 Court costs. At the time you return the adoption petition to my office, you may make a check in the sum of $16.00 payable to the District Clerk of Tarrant County, Texas. The adoption petition must remain on file for a period of 40 days and on the expiration of 40 days, I shall contact you as to the date of the adoption hearing.
6. At the time the adoption is consummated, a new birth certificate will be prepared reflecting that you are the natural parents of the child; however, you have been advised that

the Agency requires that the child be told, at a reasonable age, that he is an adopted child.

7. Our Agency requires that the Mother of the child not work after placement of the child in the home.
8. In the event you move your residence during the ensuing 6 months, we require the adoptive parents to pay any additional travel expense for our Social Worker that may be incurred as a result of your moving after date of placement of the child in your home.
9. We require that the Agency be notified immediately of any change of address for our records and in order that we may know the whereabouts of the child at all times.
10. We must be notified of any changes in employment, or any other material changes made after the placement of the child.
11. Legal custody of the child remains in the hands of the Agency until the adoption is consummated and physical custody of the child remains with you. In the event our Agency feels that the child is not receiving proper care or attention or for any other reason, the child will be returned to the Agency upon request. In such event, the amount you have paid as reimbursement to the Agency will be returned to you.

Sincerely yours,
Mike E. Powell, Attorney at Law
General Counsel for Homestead Child Placement Agency

AGREEMENT WITH ADOPTIVE PARENTS

(Transcribed from an original document with names of Adoptive Parents omitted)

The adoptive parents agree to file an adoption petition at a time agreed on with the agency, such time to be not less than 6 months and not more than 18 months following placement of the child.

The adoptive parents agree to participate in supervision by the agency during this time.

The adoptive parents agree not to remove the child from the state without the agency's permission.

The adoptive parents and the agency agreed that the child may be removed at the discretion of either at any time before the filing of the petition.

In adoptions the placement agency remains responsible for the child until the adoption has been consummated. This responsibility involves at least the following:

1. A minimum of one (preferably two or more) visits to the child in the home by a qualified child placement worker. Office interviews may be used to supplement the home visits.
2. Awareness of changes in the adoptive family such as in health, financial condition, family composition, etc., which may affect the child.
3. Knowledge of the child's whereabouts at all time.
4. Removal of the child from adoptive home if the placement is unsatisfactory.
5. Should an agency place a child for adoption and upon petition, the court refuses to grant a decree, the placing agency shall remove the child from the petitioner's home unless the court decrees

> otherwise. A subsequent placement of another child, except in the case of a child related to the first child, shall not be made until after consummation of the preceding adoption.

Before a subsequent placement is made in an adoptive home, the study of the adoptive home shall be brought up to date, including current medical examinations, and shall include observation of the adjustment of the first adoptive child and his participation in the plan of the second adoption.

Signature: [Homestead]Signature: [Adoptive father]
[Date of Signature]Signature: [Adoptive mother]

Confidentiality and Access to Texas Adoption Records: A Historical Perspective, Diane M. Wanger, September – October 1997 Issue, Adoption Triad Forum

This article discusses the history of adoption laws in Texas as it relates to the controversial issue of access to adoption information by adoptees, birth parents, and others. One cannot consider free access by adoptees without hearing the battle cry: What about the confidentiality of the birth parents? I set out to find the statutory basis for birth parent confidentiality, as no cases exist.

This article does not discuss constitutional issues or social issues that relate to access to adoption records. These have been previously discussed in length by many other authors.

No Adoption at Common Law

Adoption is a statutory creation, its sources being found in the Roman and civil law systems. The first adoption law in Texas was in 1850 and allowed one to "adopt" a legal heir by filing a written affidavit with the county clerk's office in the same manner as a deed!

It was not until 1907 that the law recognized that biological parents might have an interest in the adoption. The law allowed them to execute an affidavit transferring parental authority and custody to the "adoptive" parents. In 1920, a provision was added in the law to allow adoption in the case of voluntary abandonment of a child by the parent. In the event the child was abandoned for a period of three years, the parents were then held to have transferred their parental authority and custody to the adopting party.

In the beginning, the status of being adopted was a matter of public record. Not only were the adoption "affidavits" publicly recorded, but birth certificates were stamped with a large "illegitimate" across the front. The life of a person branded illegitimate in the 1920s was not very promising. Adoptive parents wanted to be sure that their adopted children would be entitled to the same opportunities as natural children, and that they would not be ostracized by society. Also, remember that in the 1920s, unlike today, there were a shortage of adoptive parents, not children.

If one can believe Hollywood, the movie, *Blossoms in the Dust*, starring Greer Garson, portrayed Edna Gladney as the driving force behind adoption records becoming confidential. This confidentiality would secure the status of the adopted child as being the child of the adoptive parents for all purposes. No one would be able to trace illegitimacy.

Adoption Records Sealed in 1931

Gladney's efforts paid off in 1931 when the 42nd legislature enacted the following:

Section 10. The files and records of the court in adoption proceedings shall not be open to the inspection or copy by other persons than parties interested and their attorneys, (emphasis added) except upon order of the court especially permitting inspection of the records except that all judgments, orders, and decrees of the Court may be open to inspection by any person and certified copies may be made from the clerk of the court.

Interestingly, the underlying words were added as an amendment in the Senate. One has to wonder how confidential an adoption was if anyone had access to the judgment!

The law also required the consent of the living parents, except in the case of abandonment of a child for at least three years. This time was shortened to two years in 1937.

It is important to note that this statute and the others that followed, dealt with the closing of access to adoption records as opposed to termination records. This author could not document any legislative intent to protect birth parents from the children they bore until 1989.

In 1951, the law was modified to allow natural parents to confer on licensed child placing institutions the power to place children for adoption and the power to consent to the adoption without disclosing to the natural parents the names of the adoptive parents. Prior to this chance, blind placement was not permitted, at least in the law.

In 1965, the 59th legislature expanded on the confidentiality of the records of the adopted person by restricting access to information, (about the adoption, not the termination), held by state agencies and licensed child placing agencies. However, agencies could use or divulge information which they felt was in the interest of the child. No consideration was given to the "privacy" interests of birth parents from their children.

The same legislature also added Article 2332a-Confidentiality of Records, which provided that records relating to dependency hearings on children born out of wedlock are confidential and may not be disclosed to…a party to the dependency hearing or to his attorney…

Clearly, the legislature discerned a difference between the rights of a child to have information about their birth parents versus the right of the public to know the details of an undesired pregnancy. Sadly, this distinction is lost in most discussions on the matter today. The statute further went on to allow that the court could order disclosure, not on a showing of good cause, but if the court is satisfied that it would further the ends of justice. This author does not know what was meant by "the end of justice," but apparently this was the precursor to "good cause."

The cited legislative need for the modifications and additions to the existing law was that the law made no provision for protection of the confidential nature of adoption records filed with the State Department of Public

Welfare and licensed child placing agencies, although similar information held by the courts was protected.

Parties Lose Access in 1973

With the codification of the Family Code by the 63rd legislature in 1973, a significant change was made relating to confidentiality. The law established the Central Record File. Thereafter, all adoption decrees and records were transmitted to the State Department of Public Welfare and were held confidential.

For the first time, the law restricted access to adoption records to everyone, whether or not they were a party to the proceeding. No person is entitled to access to or information from these records except as provided by this section or on an order of a district court.....for good cause. But again, there was no similar confidentiality for the termination file.

This change did not affect adoptions consummated prior to its enactment, as it spoke only to adoptions granted after the effective date. A search for the legislative intent behind this significant change was provided in a phone interview on August 15, 1997, with Don Adams, the Senate sponsor for the 1973 Family Code. Adams related that at that time the State Bar legislative Council was not held in high regard by legislators, but the State Bar General Counsel, a friend of his, came to him with the Family Code draft. Due to his own interest in the subject, including adoption, Adams chose to sponsor the bill.

One must remember that this was the session that created no-fault divorces and allowed the state to remove abused children from parents, the two areas of the code causing heated debate.

Adams recalled the legislative code attempted to codify the adoption laws as they had grown up, particularly in relation to termination of parental rights. He remembers very clearly that they did not want the public or the birth parent to have access to adoption records, it was none of their business. He remembers that the court had the option to seal or not to seal the records, they desired to take away any discretion on the part of the court. This remark was interesting in that the law did not provide judges the discretion to seal the file until 1975.

When asked about the effect the law had relating to terminating access of information to adoptive parents and adoptees, Adams stated that he had not thought about that issue specifically. In his mind, adoptive parents already had access to the information and that closing the court records would not have a practical effect.

Explaining the "good cause" provision, Adams stated that he knew it would not be proper to close the records forever. "Good cause" was in the draft provided by the State Bar Legislative Council and seemed reasonable to him at the time. I was interested in Adams' definition of "good cause." He said essentially, it was whatever a good lawyer could convince a judge it was!

By 1975, adoption records were by outward appearances, closed to all. The 64th legislature required the district clerks' offices, as well as the Texas Department of Human Services, to keep adoption records, (not termination records), confidential. It deleted the requirements to transfer all adoption records to the Central File. Now, only the decree was to be sent. It also gave the court that granted the adoption the right to open the records in addition to any district court…..

One can argue that adoptions finalized prior to the effective date of Sept. 1, 1973, would still be subject to the law existing at that time. The new law was to govern all proceedings, orders, and judgments, brought after it takes effect….All things done properly under any previously existing rule or statue prior to taking effect of this act shall be treated as valid. The prior law, when "properly" followed, allowed access to records by a party.

Because this right existed without the need to bring a "proceeding" or acquire an order or "judgment," does the right not still exist?

Termination Files are Not Closed

The same legislature that closed access to the district clerks' adoption records also enacted a separate law that gave the court the right to seal the termination and adoption file on the motion of the court or any party. But if the determination file was not sealed by the judge, by implication there is still access to it. The Attorney General came to the same conclusion in 1976, when it issued the following opinion:

The records maintained by a district clerk pertaining to a suit seeking the termination of the parent-child relationship are not confidential unless the court orders the file in such cases sealed.

The 68th legislature (1983) deleted the right of a Travis County district court to open records and left the decision solely to the court that granted the adoption.

Birth Parent Identity Protected.....Sort-of

In 1989, the year in which the Health, Social, Educational, and Genetic History Report was created, the legislature granted to adoptive parents and adult adoptees the right to access to all of the information, working papers, reports and records relating to the social study on the child. This information was to be edited to protect the identity of the birth parent. Remember, however, termination files are still accessible unless there is a specific order sealing the particular file. And this provision did not relate in any way to court records.

The law, insofar as it relates to confidentiality, has essentially remained the same from 1989 to the present.

Trends on the Horizon

Many legislative bodies, nationally and internationally, are grappling with the issue of allowing access to adoption records to adoptees, birth parents, and other "interested parties" such as siblings. Kansas and Alaska have allowed access to records for decades. These states have significant higher adoption rates per capita and significantly lower abortion rights per capita than Texas.

Tennessee passed a law allowing access to adoption records in 1996 that passed federal constitutional muster at the court of appeals level. It is scheduled to be heard by the U.S. Supreme Court in 1997.

Montana passed a law in the past several months giving adoptees born before 1961 direct access to their records, adoptees born from 1961 through 1996 access through an intermediary, and adoptees born after 1996 access after reaching the age of 18.

Great Britain allowed access for adoptees in The Children Act in 1975. New Zealand allowed access for all triad members in 1987. New Zealand's law provided for the parties to file a contact veto which would allow access to the information, but a prohibition against using it. Contact vetoes expired in ten years. Only five percent of parties involved originally filed vetoes. Ninety percent of those vetoes have now been renewed. New South Wales allowed adoptees access to their birth certificates in 1991 under the New South Wales Adoption Information Act.

British Columbia passed an open records law in 1996 which has a disclosure veto provision. From November 1996 through July 1997, less than 3,000 people filed a disclosure veto out of 70,000 adoptions. A significant portion of these represent no contact vetoes under the old Acts which were converted to no disclosure under the new Act.

Additionally, Scotland opened records in 1930, Israel in 1960 (at age eighteen), Holland (at age fourteen), (then reduced to age 12 in 1979), Finland in 1925, and Australia/Victoria in 1984.

Two laws affecting access to adoption records were introduced in the Texas House of Representatives and the Senate in the 75th legislature. Neither provision passed for very different reasons. It is reasonable to expect that more bills allowing access to records will be filed in 1999. Requests have been made to the Speaker of the House and to the Lieutenant Governor to charge an interim committee to study the sole issue of access to information. At this writing, a tentative decision to charge a committee in the House has been made.

Summary

The following is clear from the statutory history of adoption law:

Terminations are not now, and have never been, closed to the adoptee.

Prior to 1973, all parties to adoptions had access to the information in court files.

In addition, the trend as represented by other jurisdictions is that access to records is a right whose time has come.

The author thanks Judith Wells, Judge of the 325th District Court, for her editing help.

Reprinted here with permission by the Texas Center for the Judiciary for whom the original paper was prepared.

Bibliography

Ancestry.com. *U.S. City Directories, 1822-1995* [database on-line]. Provo, UT, USA: Ancestry.com Operations, Inc., 2011.

________*1920 United States Federal Census* [database on-line]. Provo, UT, USA: Ancestry.com Operations, Inc., 2010. Images reproduced by FamilySearch. Original data: *Fourteenth Census of the United States, 1920.* (NARA microfilm publication.) Records of the Bureau of the Census, Record Group 29. National Archives, Washington, D.C.

________*1930 United States Federal Census* [database on-line]. Provo, UT, USA: Ancestry.com Operations Inc. 2002. Original data: United States of America, Bureau of the Census. *Fifteenth Census of the United States, 1930.* Washington, D.C.: National Archives and Records Administration, 1930.

________*1940 United States Federal Census* [database on-line]. Provo, UT, USA:

Ancestry.com Operations, Inc., 2012. Original data: United States of America, Bureau of the Census. *Sixteenth Census of the United States, 1940.* Washington, D.C.: National Archives and Records Administration, 1940. Bahrampour, Tara. *DNA's New 'Miracle'. The Washington Post*, October 12, 2016.

Benchmarks: Passing Sentence on Dallas Judges. Jim Atkinson and Rowland Stiteler, *D Magazine*, August 1979.

Bradley, Kathleen. Telephone interview and e-mail communication with the author, January 2016 –March 2017.

________*Texas State Journal of Medicine, Volume 60, Number 1, January 1964,* Austin, Texas. (texashistory.unt.edu/ark:/67531/metapth599863/: accessed September 22, 2016), University of North Texas Libraries, The Portal to Texas History.

Campbell, Paul, Family Service Coordinator, Greenwood Funeral Home, Fort Worth Texas. Email communication with the author.

Dalton Hoffman Fort Worth Collection, Tarrant County Archives, Fort Worth, Texas.

Davidson, Teri. Telephone interview with the author and e-mail communications, Milton, New Hampshire, May 2016 – March 2017.

Department of Professional & Vocation Standards, Board of Medical Examiners of the State of California; Directory accessed online on January 28, 2017.

Drabing, Patty Logsden, DNAAdoption. Telephone interview and e-mail communication with the author, French Lick, Indiana.

Fessler, Ann. *The Girls Who Went Away.* New York: The Penguin Press, 2006.

George, Juliet. Email communication with the author, Fort Worth, Texas.

George, Juliet. *Fort Worth's Arlington Heights.* Charleston, SC: Arcadia Publishing, 2010.

George, Juliet. *Camp Bowie Boulevard*. Charleston, SC: Arcadia Publishing, 2013.

Grand and Gone, Juliet George. *Fort Worth Weekly* magazine, October 24, 2012.

Gray, Connie. Telephone interview with the author, San Antonio, Texas.

Greer, Donna Staub. E-mail communication with the author.

Harry Hall Womack, Jr. Papers. Inclusive: 1940-1948, undated, Bulk: 1940-1946. SKCA – Cuadra STAR

http://nl.newsbank.com/Archives. Accessed on 01/16/2017 and 01/31/2017.

Knowledge Center for Archives. Baylor University. *The Texas Collection.* Accessed online on January 24, 2017.

Huckaby, Ronna Quimby. *Somewhere Out There*, Wild Horse Press, 2010.

Kennedy, Patrick, District Court Archives. Lubbock, Texas.

Knudsen, Mary Schwitters. Telephone and e-mail communication with the author, Saint Petersburg, Florida.

Louisiana State Board of Medical Examiners, directory accessed online on January 28, 2017.

Mangum, Antonio, Certified Copy Clerk, Tarrant County Records, Fort Worth, Texas.

Milian, Amanda, Archivist, Tarrant County Archives, Fort Worth, Texas.

Molina, Patricia. Telephone interview and email communication with the author, Austin, Texas.

Mooney, Christie, Open Records Administration. Texas Department of State Health Services, Austin, Texas.

NewspaperArchives.com. Various U.S. newspapers, Accessed online, February 2016 – January 2017.

Newspapers.com. Various U.S. newspapers. Accessed online, February 2016 – January 2017.

Richards, Dale, Assoc. Records Clerk, Tarrant County District Court Records. Fort Worth, Texas

Salazar, Nancy. Telephone interview with the author, Stone Mountain, Georgia.

Sanborn Fire Map Digital Collection. Fort Worth Library Central, Fort Worth, Texas.

The Pearl of Dorothy Lane, Juliet George. *Fort Worth Weekly* magazine, July 21, 2010.

University of Texas Digital Photograph Collection: *The Way We Were, Fort Worth Photos, C.L. Smith Collection.* Accessed online March 2016 – January 2017.

Valderas, Harold, Jr., Telephone interview with the author, Austin, Texas.

Wanger, Diane. *Confidentiality and Access to Texas Adoption Records: A Historical Perspective*, September – October 1997 Issue, *Adoption Triad Forum.*

Zeigler, Tricia. Texas Department of State Health Services, Vital Statistics Unit, Central Adoption Registry, Austin, Texas.

Index

Made in the USA
Coppell, TX
28 June 2021

58251285R00186